The Polyglot Project

YouTube Polyglots, Hyper-polyglots, Linguists, Language Learners and
Language Lovers, in their Own Words

as introduced and annotated by Claude Cartaginese
(YouTube: syzygycc)

The Polyglot Project

What is the Polyglot Project?

There are many language learning courses on the market today, some of them good, some not so good. All are designed to teach a specific language. It is extremely rare, however, to find a book which can give you the methodologies and techniques required *to learn multiple languages*. This is such a book. The authors contained herein are already either multilingual, or well on their way to becoming so. They are all passionate about languages, but most importantly, they are all willing to share their language-learning experiences with others.

If you want to *learn **how** to learn multiple languages*, i.e., become a polyglot, then you've come to the right place.

TABLE OF CONTENTS

Author	YouTube / Website	Page
Yuriy Nikshych	(yurithebest)	1
Shana Tan	(www.hangukdrama.wordpress.com)	4
Philip Price		7
Peter E. Browne	(alkantre)	19
Moses McCormick	(laoshu)	33
Amy Burr	(pinkpumkinn)	37
Ivan Kupka	(http://www.ivankupka.bloguje.cz/)	51
Dion Francavilla	(paholainen100)	66
Oscar	(OscarP282)	74
Nelson Mendez	(nelsonmendez.com)	79
Luka Skrbic	(www.youtube.com/LukaSkrbic)	86
Félix	(loki2504)	89
Graeme	(roedgroedudenfloede) http://www.hvadsigerdu.me	98
Paul Barbato	(Paulbarbato)	114
Anthony Lauder	(FluentCzech)	117

TABLE OF CONTENTS

Author	YouTube / Website	Page
Stephen Eustace		130
Skrik	(shriekshriek)	138
Raashid Kola	(sigendut1)	144
Anonymous		153
Christopher Sarda	(www.wordcollector.wordpress.com)	156
Vera	(LingQVera) (http://lingqvera.posterous.com)	163
Steve Kaufmann	(lingosteve) (www.LingQ.com	177
Stuart Jay Raj	(stujaystujay) (http://stujay.com)	184
Benny Lewis	(irishpolyglot) (www.fluentin3months.com)	218
skyblueteapot	(www.tracesofdodo@blogspot.com)	225
Lorenzo R. Curtis	(5Language) (http://5languages.wordpress.com/)	231
Dave Cius		237
Carlos Cajuste		240
Kristiaan		246

TABLE OF CONTENTS

Author	YouTube / Website	Page
SanneT		252
Jara		259
Aaron Posehn	(aaronposehn) (www.aaronposehn.net)	272
mick		278
Albert Subirats	(alsuvi)	290
Felipe Belizaire	(newstylles)	299
John Fotheringham	(www.LanguageMastery.com)	305
Fang	(http://creativityjapanese.wordpress.com)	318
Cody Dudgeon	(Codylanguagesblog)	321
Edward Chien	(propugnatorfidei)	376
Bart Vervaart	(Bartisation)	341
Kathleen Hearons	(katrudy7)	350
Mike Campbell	(Glossika)	361
David James	(usenetposts)	418

ACKNOWLEDGEMENTS

A special thanks to all who volunteered their time to make this book possible, especially John Perazzo and Robert N. at *World Studies Books,* for their skilful editing; Lorenzo Curtis for his tech support; Kathleen Hearons for proofreading certain passages; JolandaCaterina for her tireless work behind the scenes in promoting the book, Jane, Cassie and Nina for putting up with my long absences while occupied with the book's creation, and all of my "anonymous" friends for their helpful suggestions.

INTRODUCTION

I have always thought of myself as somewhat of an oddity regarding my interest in foreign languages. I like to study them, I like to read about them, and I especially enjoy accounts written by, and about, others who share this interest. The works of certain multilingual historical figures, such as Captain Sir Richard Francis Burton, Jean-François Champollion and Heinrich Schliemann, kept me enthralled. Any author who made any mention—even in passing—of how he or she was able to learn a language or two (or ten), excited me in the same way that others would get excited about a football game.

For many years I quietly collected books and articles about foreign language acquisition, and during that time I never really came across anyone else who shared this same level of interest in the subject. And then, one day, I discovered YouTube.

YouTube made me aware of others like me, who liked studying foreign languages *for their own sake*. Not only that, they were making videos about it! Soon, I was watching so many of those videos that I ran into a problem. Somebody would make a video, and give me an idea, but I often forgot who had said it. Or, I knew who had said it but I wasn't able to find that exact video again. That's when I had an idea.

What if I invited my favorite YouTube language enthusiasts to contribute a piece for a book? Such a book would be a valuable resource for others. And yet, as excited as I was about the idea, I did nothing with it for a few months. Would it work? What if I made a plea for submissions, and nobody responded?

Putting my ego aside, I made a video announcing the project. Within days, the submissions started coming in. The end result is now before you. If you want to learn how to learn foreign languages, read on to find out how it's done...

Within hours after announcing this project, I had my first submission. Yurithebest, hailing from Ukraine, was the first to rise to the challenge with this interesting piece...

The best way I can contribute is by revealing a tad about myself. I'm Yuriy Nikshych and I'm from Ukraine. To this day I'm fluent in Russian, Ukrainian and English, I used to be fluent in Greek but now I'm a bit rusty. At present I'm learning Japanese.

My polyglot training began almost from birth – I was blessed with a polyglot father. His job at the time as a diplomat required that he travel abroad a lot, and once I was born he started taking the entire family – my first experience happened when I was 3 years old – to Greece. Once there, apart from my first language (Russian), he started giving me daily lessons in Greek. Since I was immersed in the environment, watched Greek cartoons, etc., I soon started speaking Greek, much to his delight.

I attended Greek kindergarten, which solidified my knowledge. I was then lucky enough to get into an English language international school, where I became fluent in English – I am a deep supporter and an example of the theory that at a young age you can learn languages very easily.

Luckily, Ukraine is an unofficially bilingual country, and upon my return to Ukraine by 5th grade I had to learn Ukrainian, which I did and achieved fluency within a year. Ukrainian and Russian are similar languages (maybe you can understand 50% of what's said), and being immersed in the environment really helped.

The older I became, the more I lost faith in traditional language education, and the education system in general. I attended four years of French lessons in school. To this day, all I can remember is how to say a few token sentences in French. Total waste of time and effort.

After enrolling in tech school, I stopped learning new languages. All of this changed, however, once I got an mp3 player to avoid boredom on the bus. This was the best 40$ I ever spent. At first I listened to an awesome audio program called 'Verbal Advantage" – it was made in the 70's and designed to help Americans improve their active vocabulary. It starts off easy but you soon learn to use words like intransigent, tergiversator, defenestration, defray, etc.

After finishing that program I searched for something new, and decided on a whim that I'd study Japanese. The main reason is content. In my attempts to revive my knowledge of Greek I tried downloading Greek TV shows, but they were of a much lower production value than I was used to, and frankly, mostly boring and consisting mainly of soap operas. When faced with an alternative like House MD, 24 or the Big Bang Theory, guess who wins?

While it's possible to watch shows with Greek subtitles, the newer releases simply don't have them yet. Japan, on the other hand, has a much larger array of content--be it anime, or regular shows. I used be in an "anime phase," but that has past and now it mostly irritates me, due to the Japanese weirdness regarding sex (either total asexuality or total perversion, no in-between) and the social awkwardness of the main characters. Still, perhaps what triggered my wanting to learn Japanese was when Clair's dad in "Heroes" spoke Japanese – I simply thought to myself: "I wanna do that!".

I started learning Japanese by listening to the Pimsleur audio course – it was amazing and allowed me to have a rudimentary conversational knowledge of Japanese within months. Now I'm listening to JapanesePod101 and going through an awesome book to help remember the writing system, called " Heisig - Remembering The Kanji. " - Heisig splits the Kanji up and makes the parts of the symbols into separate different/weird stories,so when you look at them you instantly have this familiarity.

I'm also watching a Japanese language video series called "Let's Learn Japanese," which is quite awesome also and follows the life of the main character Yan in his diurnal activities.

One of my greatest inspirations though is Steve Kaufmann (if you haven't heard of him look him up on YouTube). By now I think he knows 11 languages, and it's always a pleasure listening to him ridicule the conventional language education system. He owns a language training site called LingQ.com, which is also worth checking out.

For me, one of the delightful aspects of this project is being the first to read these interesting submissions coming in from all over the world. Next up, Shanna Tan--a lover of all things Korean--artfully describes how her decision to embrace the Korean language and culture continues to alter her life...

The Polyglot Project
Shanna Tan, Singapore
Learning Korean

I used to think that foreign language learning is a 'personal and lonely journey' that you embark on. You go for language classes, learn the grammar, do your homework, practice in front of the mirror and slowly get better at the language. Hopefully in the distant future, you get to put your knowledge into real use. If not, it doesn't hurt to gain more knowledge.

How wrong I was! My Korean learning journey has brought me so many unexpected surprises and at the same time, introduced me to a brand new culture and worldview. I didn't expect to gain so many international friends. I didn't expect to gain so much more knowledge beyond the Korean language. I didn't expect to switch to Linguistics for my college major. Nor did I expect myself to persevere on after two and a half years since the day I signed up for Korean language classes!

Okay. Here's a short background. In Jan 2008, I wanted to spend my 8 month holiday fruitfully and decided to sign up for beginner Korean classes. I was interested in Korean dramas, and this lead to an interest in the Korean language. I took 2 beginner courses in the school and decided that I could self-study from then on. And so I did.

I started spending hours every day, poring over textbooks, guidebooks and other online resources that I could find. Although I am self studying, it is not a lonely journey. Throughout these 2.5 years, I have made so many like-minded friends from all over the world. Those who love the Korean pop culture, those who are learning the language and those who are learning other languages. I'm also deeply grateful to my Korean friends, most of them whom I have not met at all, who gave me so much support and help.

Self-studying can get a little frustrating at times though. There is so much more to language than grammar rules. I don't have much problem reading, but speaking wise, it's still a disaster. I am always afraid of using the wrong address term or wrong politeness level, and I get tongue-tied easily. I still remember the first time I met a Korean friend for dinner. That was in Aug 2008, and just 8 months into learning the language. I was so nervous and self conscious that I didn't dare to say anything in Korean.

After mumbling 'annyeong haseyo (hello)', I proceeded to switch to English! The friend kept probing me to say a few phrases in Korean, but I was so flustered. Thinking back, I simply lost an opportunity to practice.

There where periods of time when I was so caught up with school work that I didn't do much for Korean. I'm sure all the language learners out there have similar experiences. I was frustrated that I couldn't spend time on what I love most (which is Korean), but I made it a point to expose myself to some of the language every day. It can be something as simple as listening to Korean radio stations or even listening to some pop music.

After 2.5 years, I'm finally going, for the first time in my life, to Korea. I'll be attending the Yonsei International Summer School and taking formal Korean classes again. I'm looking forward to the people I will meet, and the new knowledge that I will gain. Of course, this is the time to put my language ability to the test. A new chapter in my Korean learning journey is just about to start. I don't know where my journey will take me, but I plan on enjoying every moment of it. ^^

(p.s. It's difficult to put the entire learning journey in words. For those who are interested, please visit my blog at www.hanukdrama.wordpress.com)

Everyone will be able to relate in some way to our next story. Here, Philip Price describes with great humor his fascinating journey through many languages and countries, while showing us how things don't always go as planned...

Philip Price

MY LANGUAGE-LEARNING STORY

I have studied eight languages in my 37 years with degrees of success that range from "laughable" to, at the risk of sounding arrogant, "pretty impressive". I hesitate to call myself a polyglot since I have always found it very difficult to switch between foreign languages quickly and, due to a combination of laziness and lack of opportunity, five of my eight languages now lie in varying states of disrepair. Nevertheless, language learning has been by far the biggest project of my life and has brought me love, a career, a home, and countless amazing experiences that I will treasure forever.

My first language was English. It is my native language. Everybody has one. Everyone learns it in much the same way. Pretty much everyone learns it to a greater level of proficiency than any other language they will ever attempt to learn; a sad fact, but one that I have learned to live with.

Having English as a native language has opened many doors for me, but it occasionally serves as an obstacle to my language learning since so many people all over the world speak it better than I speak their languages. I have used English as a default language in numerous cities with people of numerous nationalities. It is truly the world language of the twenty-first century. Linguists tend to be least interested in their own native language, though, and I am no exception, so enough of English, and on to the big, scary, foreign world.

I was just a few years old when I came to the realization that some people speak using words I did not understand. My realization came in that place of quietude and ultimate relaxation, the toilet. My father was an avid reader of the Russian classics, and the only place where he could find enough peace to enjoy his books was the smallest room in the house. So every day I would sit, looking at the big heavy books he had left in there with their thousands of tightly-packed words, and try to pronounce the unfathomably weird names on the front covers: "Tur-ge-n-ev", "Do-s-to-evsky".

I remember experiencing a particular sense of achievement when I managed to decode "So-l-zhe-nit-syn", a writer I would later come to love perhaps more than any other. My father also bought a book and some tapes to teach himself Russian, but family duties prevented him from ever getting beyond "Hello" and "Thank you". Other than that, no-one in my family had the slightest interest or ability in learning foreign languages, so I credit my father with planting the seed in my brain.

Jump a few years and I am 11, learning French at school. I liked it, but I didn't love it. I was good at it, but I wasn't great at it. I had obviously forgotten all about my younger self marveling at the names of the Russian writers. Due to the intricacies of the British school system at that time, I had two opportunities to drop French as a school subject, once at the age of 14 and again at 16. I didn't take either. At 14 I simply knew French was preferable to physics, and at 16 I was more or less the language fanatic that I am today.

My French endeavors finally ran their course at the age of 18. I knew I didn't love the language enough to study it at university, and by that time I was becoming more and more interested in languages that were less studied, driven by a teenage attraction for the obscure that has remained with me in my adulthood. As I type, however, I am a week away from a holiday in France, and I am curious to find out how much I remember of my seven years of study. I am not particularly hopeful…

A year after I began French, German was introduced as a second foreign language. This was quite normal in British schools of the 1980s, but is sadly becoming ever rarer in the English-speaking world. German piqued my interest considerably, not least because all the other kids appeared to despise it. I was good at German, top-of-the-class good, and I loved that this skill enabled me to stand out from the crowd. I chose to continue German at 14, when the size of my class dwindled to less than twenty as most people quit the subject with great relief, and again at 16, when only six diehards stayed the course. The greatly reduced class sizes led to quicker improvement, which led in turn to a greater sense of achievement, and, so on and so forth… I went on to study German at university, more of which later.

At the age of 16 I went to a so-called Sixth Form College,

which is a two year school where students study for "A levels" in just a few subjects in preparation for university. My three subjects were French, German, and English literature. My Sixth Form was nothing special, just a state-run, rundown college in the North East of England, but it had one great asset: the opportunity to learn Russian from an elderly Polish lady who had come to the UK via the Soviet Union (sadly I never found out how or why).

Funnily enough, I didn't jump at the chance. My French teacher persuaded me to take it up in my second year at the school, and I did so reluctantly, concerned that it would take away valuable time from my new teenage hobbies of listening to moody music and drinking beer in the park. Once I started, though, I was hooked immediately. There were only two of us in the class, we studied from a musty old textbook that proclaimed the glories of the Soviet system, and our teacher, Mrs. Starza, was the kindest lady you could ever hope to meet. I got an "A" grade in GCSE Russian (the level below A Level) in one year and decided without hesitation to continue Russian at university.

I was accepted to study German and Russian at Glasgow University. It was a five-year course, including a year spent in the country of one language and three months in the other. We had to choose another subject to study at a lower level for the first two years, and I selected Polish. The reason for my choice is one of the silliest episodes in my language learning history so please indulge me while I explain it.

In the summer before starting university I visited Glasgow

to talk to the professors about studying there. On my way to the Russian department I met a guy who was going to talk to the Czech professor about studying Czech. I told him I was also headed to the Slavonic Department so he asked me which Slavonic languages I was interested in. I said "Russian", and then, simply because I thought Russian was a bit too common and I wanted to sound impressive, I added "… and Polish".

It was a complete lie. Anyway, we went into the languages building together and eventually came to the office of the Polish professor. My new friend said "There's the Polish office", so I said "Oh yeah" and knocked on the door, figuring I'd better carry through my deception to the end. I went in, pretended I was interested in Polish to the professor, and came out an hour later *really* interested in Polish. And that's how Polish became my fifth language.

My first year at university was a joy for me. I studied only foreign languages, every class, every day. Before long I was good enough to read literature in the original and speak with a certain degree of fluency. My Russian progressed rapidly since I had chosen to join the post-A Level class rather than the beginners' class, and my Polish came along quickly as there were only four students in the entire university who had elected to study it.

I became fascinated by Eastern Europe and the Slavonic world, and my interest in German decreased accordingly. My Polish professor was a brilliant man who forced me not only to become more proficient at the language, but also a little braver. Just before the Easter break he pulled me aside and said "Go to Poland in the holidays. I'll set you up with some lessons and a place to stay". I agreed meekly, booked a flight to Warsaw, and found myself on my first trip abroad without my family, in a country that was only three years beyond the collapse of communism, with nothing but the address of a dormitory and a phone number of a teacher at Warsaw University.

Looking back, I don't think I was quite ready for such an adventure. I spent most of the two weeks in my room, reading English classics I'd bought for a small fortune at a foreign language bookshop, and longing for the whole trip to be over. I did, however, discover bigos and barszcz, and I suppose my Polish must have improved at least a little.

Just before the summer break my Polish professor pulled me aside again and said "Go to Poland again, for a month this time. The university will pay for everything except the flight". Again, I agreed meekly and found myself on another plane to Warsaw.

This time, though, I discovered I was participating in an international course for Polish learners, and I had a great time. I fell in love with Poland, shared a room with a Japanese guy, drank Polish beer on the steps of my dormitory with people from all over the world, and somehow managed to learn some more Polish, despite the default language being English yet again.

My second year at university was not quite so successful. My Russian went from strength to strength, but German was now for me nothing more than an obligation, and my Polish suffered a blow when my brilliant professor took an extended sabbatical and we received a replacement teacher whom I found it hard to like. At the end of the year I had to make two important decisions. I had to drop one of my three languages and decide where I was going to spend my year abroad. I regret both of my decisions.

Although I had lost all interest in German, I felt I just *couldn't* quit after so many years. This, plus the fact that I didn't like my new Polish teacher, led me to drop Polish. As to the year abroad, I still didn't feel confident enough to live in big old scary Russia for a year, despite my happy time in Warsaw, so I plumped for a German-speaking country, Austria.

It's difficult to say I regret going to Austria as I had such a good time. I shared a flat with three other Brits in the 16th Bezirk of Vienna, and we were stereotypical ex-pats, utterly indifferent to the mores and customs of our host country and only out to have fun, which mostly meant drinking too much. I must stop here and advise any young readers that this is absolutely not the best way to make the most of a year of immersion in the country of your target language! And yet I have so many amazing memories from that time. Even more surprisingly, my German somehow managed to improve quite considerably despite the fact that I failed to make a single Austrian friend throughout the entire year.

During my year in Vienna I took my first trip to Russia to visit my classmates, who were more mature than I and had selected to spend their year in Moscow. It was my first taste of Russia, and I loved it even more than I had hoped I would.

Back in Glasgow I had only two terms of lessons before setting off on my travels again, this time to Yaroslavl, a medium-sized city located between Moscow and St. Petersburg. My time in Yaroslavl was perhaps the happiest of my life. Once again my immaturity and shyness had led me to a poor decision: given the choice of a home stay or a dormitory, I chose the latter, figuring it would give me the freedom to do what I liked and relieve me of the stress of living with a family of strangers. However, in Russia I managed to become such close friends with some Russians that towards the end of the three months I, together with an English girl who was romantically involved with one of the Russian guys, spent almost all my time with them.

We were so sad to leave that we decided we would come straight back, and so we went home to England, borrowed some money, and returned to Russia for another three months. It turned out that our Russian friends were not very reliable and the apartment they had promised us didn't materialize. As a result, I spent the craziest three months of my life.

I slept rough in parks, borrowed beds in the homes of friends of friends of friends, read Izvestiya every morning while sitting on the banks of the Volga, stayed up all night drinking vodka in Sochi, gotmore tanned than I have ever been during a two-week stay at a children's camp on the Black Sea coast, obtained such a wide circle of friends in Yaroslavl that I couldn't walk down the street without stopping to shake at least three hands, and became more fluent in Russian than I had ever been in any language up to that point in my life. It was an incredible time, and even more precious since I know I could never do anything like it now.

After returning to Glasgow, my next task was to find a job. I knew I didn't want to work in the UK, and I knew I wanted to go back to Russia. Other than that, I had no burning ambitions and little motivation. I applied for two jobs in Russia, one coordinating foreign students in Moscow, which I knew would be given to someone far more dynamic and impressive than me, and another teaching English in Pskov, about which I was somewhat more confident. As a backup, I applied for a position on the JET Programme in Japan for no specific reason that I can remember. My heart was still in Russia and I barely even knew where Japan was. Sure enough, the Moscow position fell through and I was offered both the job in Pskov and a place on JET.

Late into the job-seeking process I heard about a position in Warsaw proofreading translated documents. The job had been originally created by my old Polish professor, who had never returned from his sabbatical, and included an apartment and free Polish lessons. I called him and asked about it, and he basically said it was mine if I wanted it and all I had to do was to telephone someone in Warsaw for a simple phone interview. And here is another huge "What if..?" moment for me. I was too shy to phone Warsaw and speak to a stranger with my by now very rusty Polish, and so I pretended to everyone that I hadn't been able to get through and let the job slip through my fingers.

Still now I ask myself why on Earth I did this. Perhaps I am simply fated never to study Polish. Or maybe I was just too young and stupid.

So I had to choose between Pskov, a pretty average job with bad pay and no future prospects, but in my beloved Russia, and JET, a highly regarded programme with excellent pay and, by all accounts, a major boost for anyone's resume. How I had been accepted onto the JET programme I do not know. During the interview my utter lack of knowledge about or interest in Japan had been painfully obvious. Throughout the entire application process for JET a large part of me had been hoping desperately that I would be rejected, just so I could have the decision made for me. But I was not rejected, and with regret, I decided to go to Japan, figuring I could always return to Russia with some money saved thereafter.

Being in Japan, it was utterly natural to me to begin studying Japanese. I couldn't understand those who did not. I had a lot of free time in my job, so I improved rapidly, even though I was for the most part living a similar expat lifestyle to that of my year in Austria. I enjoyed my first year enough to stay for a second, and at the beginning of my second year I fell in love with a native.

Gradually our language of communication switched from English to Japanese, and after a while I found I was quite fluent. I was also learning to read and write slowly but surely, and coming to love Japan more and more.
At the end of my second year I made probably the bravest decision of my life. I decided to move to Tokyo to be with my partner, even though our relationship was still quite new. Over the next couple of years I found a job and an

apartment, began a distance-learning MA course in Advanced Japanese, moved in with my partner, and eventually applied for, and was offered, a job as a translator.

And then I stopped learning languages for about seven years. Of course I was using Japanese every day in my job translating patents from Japanese to English, but I was not actively studying the language, and all my other languages had long ago fallen into disuse. I took up Thai very briefly but I soon became bored and quit after only six months.

And then, one day last year I was browsing the Internet and came across the website "How to Learn any Language". It came as quite a shock to me to remember that this is what I do. This is what I love. I had tried out various hobbies in the meantime – playing the piano, working out at the gym, tennis – but had not been able to muster much enthusiasm for any of them.

Thanks to the website, I realized that I could pick up any language I wanted, for any reason, or for no reason. So I chose Georgian. I have only been studying for six months, but I am loving it. My language learning fire has been well and truly relit.

I have lived in Japan for fourteen years now. I am very happy here, but it will never be the love of my life. That place is reserved for Russia, even though I doubt I will ever realize my dream of living there. I still consume vast amounts of Russian literature, history, and film. I collect Soviet propaganda and I love to cook Russian food.

I visited Moscow again last year and had the time of my life. My heart belongs to Russia.

As for my other languages, I have been using my German recently to study Georgian with a German textbook. I occasionally dip into a Polish textbook, and I love the films of Kieslowski and Wajda. French has become just a holiday language, as has Thai.

I don't love all of my languages equally, but they have all brought me to where I am today, which is a happy place, and so I am grateful to all of them.

Professor Peter Browne's submission is one that I really looked forward to receiving. He was one of my earliest friends on YouTube, and I have enjoyed corresponding with him for some time now. Here he outlines his foreign language learning methodology. Read it, and profit by what he says...

MY LANGUAGES

PETER E. BROWNE, Edinburg,Texas youtube channel: alcantre (or peter browne leyendo) alias OSO NEGRO, TECUANOTL ALKANTRE, MUSTAFA ABDULLAH, PETRO BRAUN

RATING OF MY LANGUAGES (based on both comprehension and production, factors which rarely come close to the same level—for instance, there are languages I can understand at about 90%, but that I can barely speak)

HIGH ADVANCED: English, Spanish, Esperanto
MID ADVANCED: French
LOW ADVANCED: German, Portuguese
HIGH INTERMEDIATE: Latin, Italian, Ido, Catalan, Gallego
MID INTERMEDIATE: Arabic, Mandarin Chinese
LOW INTERMEDIATE: Russian, Volapuk, Rumanian, Indonesian, Interlingua, Persian
HIGH BEGINNING: Nahuatl, Swedish, Dutch, Finnish, Japanese, Hebrew, Swahili, Bliss Symbols, Turkish, Hungarian
MID BEGINNING: Greek (Ancient and Modern), Albanian, Macedonian,

Old Provencal, Serbocroatian, Polish, Czech, Bulgarian
LOW BEGINNING Thai, Cantonese, Mayan, Icelandic

I actively study about 70% of these languages (the only one I haven't looked at in many years is Old Provencal). Even on work days, I usually have 4 or 5 different languages going on. I do not consider myself a hyperpolyglot, since I only have six advanced languages. My level may also vary a bit from week to week, depending on what I've been concentrating on.

REASON FOR STUDYING LANGUAGES. It may surprise some people to learn that my basic motive for learning languages is something akin to Tolkienesque fun. For that reason I don't perceive much difference between studying Volapuk and Mandarin Chinese--they both have interesting structures and patterns, and give interesting shapes to the human spirit--so I don't care that much if the former has only a few hundred speakers in the world and the latter countless millions. Each language has its own aroma and flavor--but you won't get this unless you dedicate some time to it. Also, studying languages is like practicing sports. It may not matter that much whether you play tennis or baseball. It is of course more enriching to have a command of both.

And yet I rarely have just one reason for studying a language. Sometimes it's the sheer beauty of the language that impinges itself on my consciousness--this is definitely the case with Arabic, Russian and Latin--and so I find myself wanting more and more. Some languages like French are just nice to do much of my reading in. Spanish is a nice language for conversations and making money.

It's all about multiple languages with multiple uses to them. It's possible to get quite high just on studying languages.

MY ADVICE TO OTHERS

Always know what your getting into. Don't rush into a language like Arabic thinking it's like learning a Romance language--it's not. When I started studying Arabic I was well aware of what type of thing which lay ahead, and that's partially why I'm still at it five years later. Many rush into Arabic and just quit after a few weeks or months, never to return.

Never allow your study to become tedious, unless you have to study for an exam. Always look at it as a kind of sport. A "plateau" may simply mean you don't presently have the right text book or other materials to guide you to higher spots. Until you find this guidance, turn your attention to another language for a while. If you're at a "plateau" in Arabic, do some Indonesian.

BRINGING ABOUT THE LINGUISTIC SUPERMAN

I believe this is possible, perhaps even for low income people. I have identified three languages American children should be educated in besides English. These are Arabic, Mandarin Chinese, and Latin. Arabic will give you a footing in Turkish, Indonesian, Swahili, Persian, Hebrew, and Spanish; Mandarin in all languages using the Chinese characters (and maybe some that do not), and Latin in all the Romance languages and in English itself.

BEST MATERIALS FOR LEARNING LANGUAGES
Pimsleur, Linguaphone, and Assimil. Pimsleur is the best thing for starting from scratch. Linguaphone is excellent for intermediate level and Assimil can consolidate your knowledge on all levels.

WHAT REALLY WORKS FOR ME
Always having a pack of flash cards in my pocket.

MY POLYGLOT PROJECTS
Essentially I have three polyglot projects, albeit they are closely interlocking at many junctures.

A. The oldest is the study of foreign languages. This began at the age of 14 with the study of Latin as a high school subject. I have acquired true fluency in only a small number of languages. I do not find fluency easy to attain. I believe it will normally depend on a felicitous combination of will power, circumstance and time invested. Other factors are the intrinsic ease of the language being studied and its closeness to the one(s) already mastered.

On the other hand, becoming acquainted with and even somewhat conversant in a wide range of languages is within easy reach. Especially with the materials now out there, the Pimsleur courses in particular. When I first started using Pimsleur courses for several exotic languages c. 2006, I found that they did provide me with the skeleton of these languages, at least if I listened to them enough times. By such means even a very busy person can get the groundwork of a language in less than four months. With sufficient leisure, about 3 weeks should suffice.

During the last few years my goal has been to get the foundations down for as many languages as possible. I try to do this without stress and strain, and without it interfering with my professional tasks and creative writing.

B. I have been writing in three languages for some time. The translation of pieces of my creative writing into an array of languages started around 2008, when I published a call for translation of my work in an Esperanto cultural magazine, LA GAZETO. The result was quite favorable. I can now read versions of some of my writings in Chinese, Russian, Albanian, Catalan, Portuguese, Ido, Volapuk, Latin, German, Dutch, Icelandic, and Nahuatl. In turn this turned out to be a major stimulus for my further study of these languages, and indeed frequently reading and rereading these texts has been one of the best ways of practicing them.

C. Initially my interest in posting videos on YOUTUBE was to provide a showcase out of my own work of what different languages sound like—I wished to bring out the special musicality of each language through these readings. Although this goal remains prominent, I have recently been influenced by the more pragmatic discourses of polyglots like Laoshu, Loki, and Kaufmann. This explains why I do things like trying to speak extemporaneously even in challenging languages like Arabic.

Finally, I would like to issue another call, this time to all polyglots with a literary proclivity, for translation of my writings into different languages.

Concerning this project, please contact me at editoracampamocha@yahoo.com.

TWO IMPOSSIBLE DREAMS OF A LINGUISTIC NATURE. To be able to speak Arabic better than Spanish, and Latin better than English.

VIEW ON VOCABULARY LISTS. Actually a very good thing. Language is about words. But I memorize words through creative visualization and preferably while walking about (thus generating biorhythms) not in a tedious scholastic sort of way.

VIEW ON GRAMMAR. Without grammar, you generate sentences like the following: YO QUERER QUE TU SABER EL VERDAD. Any Spanish speaker could understand this, but it sounds terrible. With more complex sentences, the meaning may even be lost.

VIEW ON INPUT

STEVE KAUFMAN and others are essentially right here. To give an example from my own experience: when I first sat in an a first semester Chinese class, I felt that the language was continually beating me up. Then I came back to a second semester class, having spent about 2 years doing input and self-study. This time I felt a great deal of ease and understood what was going on.

However, input alone will rarely if ever lead to fluency. Fluency will usually only come with years of active interaction; it is essentially a motor and social skill resulting from tons of practice.

THE PRACTICALITY OF KNOWING FOREIGN LANGUAGES

The other guy may very well be able to read your newspapers and journals. He has direct access to your perspective and worldview, as well as great amounts of data which might not appear in his language. You are at a distinct disadvantage if you can't read his newspapers and journals.

HOW IT ALL GOT STARTED. It's hard to say. Most of my early gurus were not people I knew in person. Sir Richard Burton, Mario Pei, Miguel de Unamuno...the virus came from that direction. As mentioned in several of my videos, my father was a military linguist, a fact which certainly lend itself to my getting infected. Also, growing up around the university, I grew up around languages. In college I had classmates who spoke Persian, Swahili, etc.. I would tend to pick up bits and pieces of the languages from them. Than in graduate school, where I was a TA in Spanish for almost a decade, I constantly heard French and German spoken around the Department. There was a weekly Table Francaise and a Stamtisch as well as the Mesa Espanola; I would frequently show up for all three.

Language tables are the next best thing to actually being in the country, believe me. At least the type of Language tables which flourished in Lincoln Nebraska in the 1980s. Then I had to take two semesters of Latin for my PhD. D. program, a very good thing indeed.

LATER MOTIVATION.

In the 1990s I was more focused on Spanish. I spend a lot of time in Mexico and considered it my "segunda patria".

However, it is hard to spend a lot of time in Mexico without noticing the influence of Nahuatl; hence my current interest in that language. I studied some German during that decade and wrote quite a few travelogues and short stories in Esperanto, but my main focus was on fluency in Spanish.

The only really exotic language I was starting to pick up was Finnish, due to a summer in Finland (1995). Sometimes upon returning from places like Monterrey, I would even converse with the US border guards in Spanish. Monterrey is supposed to be a bilingual city, but in the 1990s hardly anyone there would try to practice their English on me, simply because of my great fluency level in Spanish.

So why a return to ongoing multilingualism with the coming of the 21st century? A number of things came together. Arabic was offered as a UTPA non graded night class in 2005. I signed up. The first teacher was from Saudi Arabia, but he seemed more creative, fun loving and even open minded than many American instructors. So I found myself actually learning this language. About the same time I came across Rice's biography of Burton--wow! again, I wanted to be like that guy as much as possible! Around the same time I discovered Pimsleur language courses, and found that they worked for me! Chinese was first offered at UTPA in 2006; I was sitting in the very first semester. The third exotic language I started working on was Russian. From there it kind of mushroomed. The most recent stimulus has been discovering Laoshu's videos on YouTube.

He is the first hyperpolyglot I actually corresponded with. Later I established contact with Loki, and others.

A BRIEF AUTOBIOGRAPHY. I was born on the border (El Paso, Texas). For this reason I always felt I was sort of Mexican. In recent years I have returned to El Paso and spoken a lot of Spanish there. I love being out there. The Chihuahuan desert is overwhelming. However, I actually grew up in other parts of the country, like Montana, Oregon, and Nebraska. It seems like from early childhood on my life was always centered around the university.

Because universities are usually far more cosmopolitan than local communities, I found I could fit in better on campus. Becoming a professor was a natural decision. Spanish has a rich literature, and was capable of holding my interest. I first started teaching Spanish at the University of Nebraska in 1982, when I wasn't much older than most of my students. In 1984 I was teaching English in Spain (Santiago de Compostela), and sitting in on university classes, some of which were taught in Gallego. It was there that I read the entire New Testament twice in Latin, while watching rain pour down unceasingly into the inner courtyard. I also read it in Gallego. I spend 1991 bumming around Connecticut and wrote two books in Esperanto. From 1992 to 1993 I was teaching in Chattanooga Tennessee. I came to the University of Texas--Pan Americana in 1993, and have been here since, spending many weekends and summers in Mexico.

MY TEN FAVORITE RESOURCES FOR STUDING LANGUAGES

1. RUSSIYA AL YAUM: Russian news broadcast in Arabic (online)
2. LINGUAPHONE ARABIC COURSE
3. BIBLIA SACRA (the Vulgate, or Latin Bible)
4. LOKI for talks in Italian, Chinese, and French
5. PIMSLEUR HUNGARIAN COURSE
6. OSCAR for talks in Catalan and Spanish idioms
7. AHUICYANI (266pages of poetry) for Nahuatl
8. BERKHARD for talks in German and Indonesian
9. B. Traven novels for reading in German
10. Magazine LA GAZETO (philosophical and literary) for Esperanto

PEAK POLYGLOT EXPERIENCES (some of this stuff might sound boastful...but my hope is that the reader will enjoy similar experiences, or even better ones)

1. Having a Belgium European interpreter visit my French class when I was an undergraduate and her telling me that I was "TRE DOUE POUR LES LANGUES" ("very gifted for languages") (c. 1979) Perhaps not true, but it fed my ego and self-confidence.
2. On my first day at the University of Nebraska, c. 1981, upon asking for directions the first time, I was asked what part of Germany I was from (this is because I had been studying German intensively the previous semester, and the accent stuck clung to my English).
3. On my first day in Santiago de Compostela, 1984, a German asked me in Spanish what part of Spain I was from.
4. Getting an A+ in Advanced Spanish Grammar, c. 1982
5. Getting As in my Latin classes, UNL, 1982-1985
6. Getting a Ph.D. in Spanish Literature, 1991

7. Getting a job teaching Spanish to mostly native speakers, 1993 (up to present)
8. Attending The Universala Kongreso de Esperanto in Tampere, Finland, in 1995, and finding no one could tell where I was from when I spoke in Esperanto--most people thought I was either a Swede or a Finn, but no one even suspected I was an American.
9. Learning of the death of Solzhenitsyn through an Arabic language newscast (RUSIYA AL YAUM) and finding I understood everything that was said (of course, it was not on account of his death that I rejoiced...) c. 2008
10. Finding I could understand and follow French, Portuguese, German and Italian newscasts through my computer (c. 2008)
11. Listening to the sound recording of LINGUA LATINA and finding I understood every word of it upon the first listening..without even having read the book at the time.
12. Having the Spanish poet Jorge Camacho ask me if Spanish was my native language, on the basis of my creative writing skills in the language (c. 2000)
13. Arriving at the Universala Kongreso de Esperanto in Tampere, Finland, 1995, and immediately having a Argentinian ask me if my mother was Spanish, because my Esperanto pronunciation seemed to have an Iberian substratum.
14. Finding I can read the Book of Genesis in Chinese, and exclusively in Chinese characters (2010).
15. Learning that I have a reading knowledge of some 700 or more   Chinese characters (2010)

 LANGUAGES AS I PERCEIVE THEM:

THE MOST BEAUTIFUL: Russian (Italian among the

Romance languages)

THE MOST BEAUTIFUL AND INTRIGUING SCRIPT: Chinese

THE MOST PRACTICAL: English, Spanish, Mandarin Chinese

THE MOST HOMELY SOUNDING: Dutch and Swiss German

THE MOST MYSTICAL: Arabic, Nahuatl

THE COOLEST SOUNDING: Catalan

THE MOST SMOOTH: French

THE MOST MAJESTIC: Latin

THE MOST DIFFICULT: Finnish

THE MOST TRANQUIL: Japanese

THE EASIEST: Esperanto, Ido, Interlingua, Bahasa Indonesia

THE MOST PHONOLOGICALLY CAPTIVATING: Thai, Persian

THE MOST FORCEFUL: German

THE MOST PHILOSOPHICAL: Greek, German, and Latin

LATINIST MANIFESTO, or 10 reasons why you may wish to make Latin the first language of choice for you and your children:

1. LATIN is the language that best represents EUROPEANNESS, and the best vehicle of PANEUROPEAN sentiment. This is because for some two thousand years Europeans of diverse nationalities were either educated in Latin, or learned it as a chief subject in school. Latin was the language of the Hungarian courts even into the 19th century, although Hungarian is not even an Indo-European language. The heritage is clearly not

limited to English and the Romance languages. Latin influence can be found in the Germanic group and even in the Slavic group.

2. During the Renaissance period, men like Erasmus not only became extremely fluent in Latin; they became masters of style. And yet it was not their native language, indeed, there were no more native speakers. Latin had survived its own funeral. And precisely because Latin was nobody's native language, all users were at least potentially equal. Among the learned at least, Latin was a language of equal linguistic rights. For this reason also it should be resurrected.

3. There is evidence that Latin stimulates mental agility. It is an excellent introduction to the way languages work. A Latin scholar confronted with the case system of the Slavic languages, should for instance have no trouble understanding what is going on.

4. The higher registers of the English language often have much Latin, Greek or French, Latin perhaps being the most important of the three. Logically, for this reason Latin will give you the cutting edge in English. And then there is all the scientific and legal terminology which you will already know, all because of your Latin.
5. Learn Latin and the doors of all the Romance languages will be open to you. That's why I think American schoolchildren should start out with Latin, not with Spanish. Spanish is simply one of many derivatives from the mother tongue. Now that I am studying Catalan, I am surprised and delighted to find many words derived directly from Latin, like GAUDIRE=to rejoice (the Spanish

equivalent GOZAR wouldn't even help here). Learn your Latin, and learn it well, and then go on and master ALL the Romance languages.

6. The idea that Latin is an old-fashioned language is now itself becoming quite old-fashioned!

7. In the Medieval and Renaissance periods, it would be truly exceptional for royalty not to be well versed in Latin. If a Medieval Catalan king would quote from the Bible in a speech, the quote would come in Latin, perhaps with a gloss in Catalan. Perhaps by mastering Latin, we can all become a little more regal.

8. Those of us who have communicated widely in artificial languages like Esperanto, Ido, and Interlingua, are well aware that we are using offspring of the Latin mother tongue. Parenthetically, Dr. Zamenhof, the inventor of Esperanto, was not a good prophet: he considered Hebrew far too dead to ever be revived. If only he could visit Israel today! Yet his own invention also became a living language.

9. With Latin you will get great literature in the original, not just from antiquity, but from the Medieval and Renaissance periods.
10. Latin is perhaps THE major language of Western philosophy, although Greek and German also are most important.

THIS IS WHERE I'LL CALL IT QUITS. peter

What can I say about this next polyglot that he hasn't said better himself in his videos? Moses McCormick, a/k/a "Laoshu" has made YouTube his classroom, taking on the role of both teacher and student. I defy anyone to read his submission and not be moved by it...

Moses McCormick
"Laoshu"

I'm not good at writing, but I would like to participate in this polyglot project to talk about my experiences with foreign languages and how they've enriched my life.

First of all, my name is Moses Monweal McCormick and I'm originally from Akron, Ohio. Although I was born in Akron, I lived in Erie, PA for about six to seven years of my life. I'm the oldest of four siblings.

Growing up for us wasn't that easy. We were raised in a broken home, by both our father and mother. It was sort of a take-turns thing. One year we would be living with our dad, and probably two years later living with our mom. I would say we were probably raised a bit longer by our mom than by our father.

My mom had me at a very early age. She was only 14. Not only that, she didn't get her High-school education. I believe she dropped out of school when she was in the 8th or 9th grade, I can't remember. My dad, however, graduated from high school. It was pretty rough on my mom raising 4 children alone; hence, there were times when we had to live in foster care.

I would say that we were put in foster care a total of two times. That was probably the most painful experience in my life because I was separated from my sisters. My brother and I were lucky to be able to live with the same foster family. Our foster parents were good people. When I was around 13-14 and still living in Erie, PA, we almost went back to foster care, but my dad drove from Akron, OH to Erie, PA to pick us up and take us back to Akron to live with him.

We lived with him for about two years, and then moved back with our mom. So, like I said, it was a back-and-forth thing. But while we didn't have the best circumstances growing up, we didn't turn out to be bad children. Around this time was the most significant part of my life because I met a group of friends who were very different from each other. When I say very different, I mean they were into different things that the average person in our neighborhood wouldn't be into. They liked learning new things and always had a positive mind about things in general. This wasn't normal for me – at least coming from the place I came from. I was used to negativity, abuse and stuff like that.

One thing I had in common with these guys was video games. I think if it weren't for my interest in video games, I probably wouldn't have clicked with them. I hung out with them endlessly, which helped me open up my mind to learning about different things and what not. They turned me on to some very positive music which helped me look at things differently as well. I will never forget these times, and to this day I still talk with them. They are like brothers to me.

After living with our mom for about three to four years, we got evicted out of our house and we were pretty much living on the streets. I think I was a junior in High school at the time. It was very hard, but somehow we got through it. I lived with my uncle for a year or two then eventually finished up high school. I almost joined the Marines, but my brother stopped me from going because he felt that we would go to war and he didn't want for me to be part of it. This was in the year 1999. That was around the time when I started learning languages.

I had a bad experience with a girl at my High school, and shortly after that, I decided that it was time for me to step out of the box and try something new that had never been done in our community/family. I started to learn Chinese as my first "serious" foreign language. I felt that it would be nice to try and learn a language like Chinese instead of a language like Spanish, French or German. I felt that I wanted to do things differently than others. I realized that I had a knack for foreign languages, so I started learning more. I gained confidence in my ability to learn because I picked Chinese up pretty fast. I also picked up languages such as Japanese, Korean, and Arabic, etc. I think I was at the age of 19-20 at the time. A year later, I decided to move to Columbus because I saw that there would be a lot more opportunities for me there, as far as foreign languages. I made one trip to Columbus with a friend and from there decided that it would be the place where I would start getting serious with things.

I then met my wife at a library. At that time, I wasn't looking to get into any relationships because I wasn't on my feet. I just went there with a friend to practice foreign languages.

I talked to her one time and we decided to become language exchange partners. Somehow I felt that I was the luckiest man in the world to have met a woman like her. After that, we talked for a while and eventually started a serious relationship. She was and still is very supportive of my decision to study multiple languages, and I think that's a great thing. Two years after we met, we married. I was 23 years old.

Because of my decision to learn languages, I'm not only able to expand my knowledge for learning new languages and what not, but I can also share that knowledge with others and help them to become great language learners as well. Just from the decision to learn Chinese, I was able to meet a wonderful Chinese woman (my wife) who supports me for having this "strange" passion for learning so many languages.

Another enriching factor in learning languages for me is the open mindedness I have gained towards other cultures and what not. Before getting into the different cultures, I, like other people, had bad preconceptions about them. Where I came from, I'd never heard anything very positive about other cultures. Instead, people would in fact always ask me, "As a black man, why would you want to do something like that?" I would just brush it off because I knew it was just ignorance.

In conclusion, I guess I would say that, having this experience of learning about different languages and cultures has broadened my horizons by leaps and bounds, and I will continue on this path of learning. This will be a lifetime process for me.

A chance encounter with a song she couldn't understand sends the author of this next piece on a linguistic journey she could not have predicted...

Amy Burr
YouTube Channel: Pinkpumpkinn

My name is Amy Burr, I am 19 years old and I am from California. I want to contribute to this project because I feel like my story is a good example of how learning languages can enrich one's life, and I think it can inspire people who are struggling to learn a language. I feel that learning languages is the most important thing I have ever done for myself.

My language learning has given me a new perspective on life, because learning a language really is like discovering a new world. There is an endless amount of things out there that you will never get to experience because your knowledge of languages is limited. For example, there is literature, music, movies, and poetry that you cannot fully enjoy if you do not understand the language they are produced in. Even more importantly, there are all kinds of people and cultures that you cannot connect with and appreciate without understanding their language.

I realized this fact only after I learned a new language, and I cannot believe how many wonderful things I was missing out on before I did so. It is incredible to think about how different and limited my life would be had I not learned a new language. I made friends in a new country, discovered new cultures and art, and even got an opportunity to travel and experience one of these new cultures firsthand. That is what I love about language learning: without it, I never would have gotten to do these things. What I love so much about the story I am going to share with you is that it shows how language learning can be easy and enjoyable, but still extremely beneficial and inspiring. I hope that it will inspire people to learn languages, or help people who want to learn languages but feel it is too difficult for them.

I have always been interested in languages since I was a young child. It has always fascinated me for some reason, but I really discovered my love for it when I was about thirteen years old. This was the time when I began studying Spanish at school. I immediately enjoyed learning the language and therefore I really excelled at it. Throughout the next five years, while I was studying both Spanish and French in high school, I was often told by teachers that I have a "talent" for languages. The first few times I heard it, I just took it as a nice compliment, but after a while something about it started to bother me. At first I didn't know why, but then I noticed that many students in my class would say they "hate French" or "hate Spanish," for example, because they are just "not good at it". This is when I realized I do not believe that having a talent for languages really matters much at all.

What bothered me was that the students who said these things seemed to believe they were incapable of learning a language and enjoying it because they lacked this supposed talent. After pondering this for a while, I realized that what really made me excel in languages more than other students was that I simply had a passion for it. I now know that the key to learning a language and liking it is to simply learn it in a way that is enjoyable to you. I don't believe you have to buy language books and study grammar and complicated things that bore and frustrate you. I believe you can learn a language and love every minute of it if you so choose. In fact, I don't just believe this is possible, I know it is, because I have done it myself.

When I was about 16 years old, I was browsing through some music on Youtube, and I discovered a singer from Israel that I really liked. I did not understand any Hebrew, but I didn't care because I enjoyed the music anyway. So for a while I just searched around for more of her videos in English, and did not care much that I could not understand the language.

However, after a while I began to see how much this limited me. I saw how many things were out there that I couldn't access because I could not speak Hebrew. There was a point where this began to frustrate me so much that I decided to learn how to read the script so I could search for the names of songs in Hebrew. I really enjoy learning how to sing songs in foreign languages, but finding transliterated lyrics was a very difficult thing to accomplish. However, I could find every song I wanted to learn in the original Hebrew script, so I decided to try and use my limited knowledge to read and learn the lyrics.

I do not remember how long it took me, but eventually I could read the script fairly efficiently. After that, I immediately felt as if a whole new world of opportunities was opened up to me. Before I felt so restricted because I had no knowledge of the language, but now that I did have knowledge, I kept learning more and more until I could even write and speak a bit. Once my writing skills became proficient enough, I began to make new friends by going on an Israeli website where people talk about my favorite singer.

At first I only read the website, but one day I read something I really felt I needed to respond to. So, I used my limited skills (and a lot of help from an online dictionary) to respond to the post. The administrator read what I said and took interest to the fact that I was American, and sent me a private message. Long story short, we became very close friends, and a few months later even met each other in real life. At the end of her visit to the U.S., she and her family invited me to stay at their house should I ever decide to come to Israel.

To my surprise, it has only been less than a year since this all started, and I have already booked a flight to Israel for this summer. For me, this experience is going to be not only a cultural experience, but an excellent opportunity to improve my language skills. Unfortunately, at the time when my friend was here, I had still never spoken Hebrew with anyone, except in writing of course, so I was too shy to speak it with her. So we just spoke English the entire time. However, during the last few months I have been extremely motivated to improve my language skills, since I am planning to speak with my friends in their native language when I visit them.

I feel like going to the country is the best way to learn a new language, so I feel so fortunate to have this incredible opportunity. I am now going to get to travel half way across the world and experience a whole new culture, and it is all because I learned a new language doing things I enjoy.

I would like to point out that I have not actually "studied" much Hebrew per se. I have sort of just picked it up. I learned mostly by listening to music, watching videos, reading fun books and articles, and chatting with my friends. Even though I initially didn't understand a word of the things I was listening to, they were things I enjoyed, so I gradually learned to understand them. Like I mentioned before, you do not need to have a talent to learn a language this way, you just have to like it. The key is enjoyment. Just do what I did: find music you like, or find something you like to read. In the beginning, you will not understand it, but I promise you will eventually. I admit that the inability to understand things you want to enjoy will frustrate you, but this kind of frustration is exactly what inspires me.

Whenever I feel frustrated because I am watching something that I know I would find funny or interesting in some way, but I cannot understand it, I just think to myself, "Someday I will understand this, and it will be so rewarding." And trust me, it will be rewarding. I know, because I have experienced it multiple times. All it takes is patience. Yes, not being able to understand something is very irritating, but you must always remember that someday, if you wait long enough, you will understand. There is nothing preventing you from learning the language up to a fluent or even almost native level. The only limit is time. You will have to wait a while in order to gain this much knowledge, but it is not so bad, because in the meantime you can continue learning in a way that is pleasant to you. After you wait enough and gain enough knowledge, it will be one of the most rewarding things you could ever do, because you will get to see all your past frustrations and limits lifted away.

Another topic I would like to talk about is how people feel about language learning as hobby. For some reason, many people seem to consider learning languages a useless hobby and a waste of time. I used to sort of agree with this, even though it was a hobby I enjoyed doing. However, the only reason I agreed was that I never really thought about whether it was useless or not. I just assumed it for some reason that I can no longer remember.

I honestly can't see why I ever thought it was useless, and I do not understand why other people feel that way either. Although, I suppose that people who are only focused on their career and who are not interested in anything that would not help them in that respect could find foreign languages useless, because they do not use them at work. But nobody cares about only their career and nothing else. Everyone has some kind of hobby. Basically my point is, whenever people say learning languages is a waste of time, what do they suppose you should do instead? What would be considered a productive use of leisure time? The answer is that it depends on the person and what they want in life. As I have just recounted to you, learning foreign languages can absolutely be beneficial. So I do not see how people can say it is useless in comparison to other hobbies.

Honestly, I used to feel embarrassed to tell people I learn languages in my free time, because they would always ask me, "Why? What's the point? It's a waste of time." For example, when I tell people that I am learning Hebrew, they usually find it odd because I am not Jewish and do not have any family members who speak it. Also, I do not need it for work or business, so they cannot figure why I would possibly want to learn.

Basically, people often find it pointless to learn a language if you do not need to or if you don't have any preexisting connection to the culture. However, I feel that if you learn a language, this alone gives you a connection to the culture. Sure, I decided to learn Hebrew even though I didn't know anyone who speaks it or have any connection to Israel or Israeli culture, but *now* I do. That is why I find it hard to see how this is useless. Therefore, when people ask me "Why?," I just tell them I like it. It is none of their business what I choose to do with my free time and I do not feel like explaining why it is indeed useful for me if they do not want to hear it. It's as simple as that. Don't ever let someone else tell you what is useful or useless for you. Personally, I think that if you simply enjoy it, that is a good enough reason to continue doing it.

So basically, language learning is a great way to spend time. It opens up so many new opportunities. Also, just think about how many different languages there are in the world. Now think about how many possibilities this opens up to you. It's seemingly endless. And remember, language learning does not have to be hard or unpleasant. Of course, if you are an impatient person it may be frustrating at times, but that is only temporary.

Once the frustrations are over, you will get to experience

the most pleasant part of the whole experience: being able to speak and understand the language with virtually no limits. You never know what could happen if you learn a language. For example, it is a guarantee that if you learn a new language you also learn a new culture. Also, it is pretty much guaranteed that you will make new friends. After all, you have to practice with someone eventually! In the end, maybe all of this will lead you to have an opportunity just like mine. Like I said, you never know. Additionally, just remember that even if you are very shy you can still learn a language. I would know because I am a pretty shy person, but I have made tons of new friends.

Throughout my language learning adventure, I have discovered that you should not be shy when learning a language, because you will discover so many more amazing things if you just go out and talk to new people. I call it an adventure because it really is one: when it's all over, you will have discovered a whole new world.

POSTSCRIPT

I am writing this new piece because I have had a very interesting experience since I wrote my first one, so I feel like I need to update it. In my last piece I talked about how my interest in Israeli music inspired me to learn Hebrew, and how this ultimately led me to an opportunity to visit Israel. Well when I wrote my last piece I hadn't gone on my trip yet, but now that I have, I have a lot of interesting new language experiences that I would like to share with you all.

I also feel like what I want to talk about is a perfect

continuation of where I left off in my first piece. I concluded my last one talking about shyness and why we must overcome it if we want to learn languages. So that is what I will focus on in this piece. Personally, I am generally a pretty shy person, so before I went to Israel I was a little nervous about speaking Hebrew. I had only had one spoken conversation in Hebrew before I left, and it was just so strange for me to hear the language coming out of my own mouth. I couldn't even imagine how I was going to speak it with other people if I could not even bear to speak it to myself! However, once I stepped on the plane to Israel something strange and incredible happened: my fear was completely gone.

The moment I entered the plane, the flight attendant directed me to my seat completely in Hebrew, with no English translation. Now, for some reason I was not expecting this at all, but that is not to say that it irritated me. In fact, it had quite the opposite effect. I immediately felt like I belonged, and that I was welcome to speak this language without anyone treating me like a foreigner or assuming that I don't understand a word of it. This made me ecstatic, because until then I had the opposite experience: people would always ask me why and how I know Hebrew, and why on earth would I want to learn this language, and they would automatically speak to me in English unless I specifically asked them to speak Hebrew so I could practice. From this point on I had no fear whatsoever. I loved speaking Hebrew, it felt like the funnest thing in the world to me. I even got excited when the stewardess asked me what I wanted to drink (in Hebrew, of course) and I got to say "mayim" (water). I know it sounds so silly, but I think the reason I got so excited is because this made me feel like I fit in, like I was one of them. It was really an amazing feeling, and it gave me confidence that did not wear off once during my entire trip.

Now, I would just like to address a common concern that many language learners have, and that I feel extremely lucky to have avoided for the most part: getting native speakers to talk to you in their language. First of all, even though I am not Jewish and do not have any family connection to Israel, you could never tell that from looking at me. Israel is a very diverse country that people from all over the world have immigrated to, much like the United States. They have every race and ethnicity that we have here in America in their tiny country. And since I am of European descent and have brown hair and brown eyes, so I do not stand out as a foreigner in Israel at all. As many travelers know, when you stick out like a sore thumb in a foreign country, people often speak to you in English automatically. So that is why I feel extremely lucky that I was going to a country where people could not immediately tell that Hebrew is not my native language. The fact that I avoided this problem boosted my confidence a great deal.

However, as I mentioned before, other people might not be so lucky. I know many language learners are afraid that they will go to a foreign country and have a hard time practicing the language because they will stand out as a tourist. Well, even though I have just said this was not much of a problem for me, I still understand how it feels. You see, what I meant before was that this was not an issue for me when I came across *strangers*. However, when I was with people who did know my nationality, it was a different situation altogether. For example, when I met my friends' friends, or relatives of my friends, the moment they heard I was American they assumed that I didn't speak Hebrew. For the most part I was lucky enough that when I told them I did speak their language, they gladly spoke it to me. However, some people (especially my close friends whom I normally speak English with) basically refused to speak to me in Hebrew. Even when I spoke it to them, they answered in English, as if they didn't even notice that I was trying to practice.

This is a very common problem language learners may have in a country like Israel where almost everyone speaks excellent English. However, you must understand that they may want to practice their English just like you want to practice their language. Even though I understood and accepted this, it still made me feel extremely uncomfortable and discouraged when people spoke to me in English. I understand that they were just trying to make me feel at home, but in actuality they were doing the opposite. This just made me feel more like a foreigner, like I was someone who needed to be treated differently because I did not fit in with their people. This made me upset and angry because it was the complete polar opposite of what I experienced on the plane. There, I really did feel at home, because people spoke Hebrew to me, no questions asked.

Now, I know you are waiting for me to tell you how to avoid this sort of situation, but unfortunately, I am not sure I have a decent answer. However, I can give you this simple piece of advice: don't let it get to you. I regret that I let this little obstacle make me so depressed and frustrated. Yes, it was awkward and annoying, but it's not worth letting it ruin your trip. Some people are just not going to speak their language to you unless you beg them or convince them somehow, but sometimes it's just not worth the effort. That is why I offer you this suggestion: get a friend ahead of time who will agree to speak their language with you. Luckily, I made a friend like this without even trying, and once I started staying at her house, I felt much more confident and comfortable. My confidence was back up to the level it was on my flight.

The reason I have just told you all this is because I think it can help you overcome your fear of speaking a foreign language. First off, I have to mention that this trip to Israel has taught me that speaking a foreign language in a new country was not at all what I expected. I thought I would feel self-conscious and uncomfortable speaking to native speakers in their language. However, I discovered that I actually felt worse speaking to them in my language. The reason for this is that I was in *their* country, so it felt only natural to speak their language as well. When I spoke to them in Hebrew, for some reason I felt confident and natural, and I didn't feel even a tiny bit embarrassed about making mistakes. Now, like I said before, I am a pretty shy and self-conscious person, and that is why I feel that if I did it, anyone can do it.

I admit that I do not fully understand why my fear immediately disappeared once I stepped on the plane. All I know is that it is not worth it to be afraid. I don't even want to think about how I might have felt if I was afraid to speak Hebrew during my trip. Being confident was the best thing

I accomplished during my adventure in Israel. That is why I urge you to do the same. Now, you should not necessarily expect to have no fear at all. Just do not let it control you. If you feel afraid, fight it. I *promise* you will not regret it. Also, you cannot be afraid to make mistakes. The only way to not make mistakes is to not try at all, and obviously it is impossible to learn if you do not try. Also, remember that nobody is judging you as much as you think they are. Think about it, when you hear someone speaking you native language with an accent or mistakes, do you think bad things about them?

Of course not.

You probably barely notice their mistakes most of the time. And if someone does judge you or laugh at you, who cares? Just ignore it. That person is not important to you if they are going to be rude to you just for trying to learn their language. In fact, something just like that happened to me right after I got off the plane. When I greeted my two friends in Hebrew at the airport, they just giggled and answered me in English. But I did not care. I just tried to forget about it and move on. And trust me, it's easier than you think.

Basically, just have fun! After all, that is the best way to learn a language. You will not learn if you do not try. Loosen up and do not worry so much about mistakes. People will understand that you are learning, and most of them will be happy to help you. In fact, I was extremely fortunate to have met a wonderful Israeli person in the airport right before my flight. She was one of the security people who escorted me to the plane (El Al has very strict security procedures…), and what she told me changed my life. When I told her I was scared, she said that she had just traveled alone herself, and that she learned a lot in the process. One thing she taught me was that traveling is not meant to be easy, and you shouldn't expect it to be.

I think the same thing applies to learning languages. Yes, it is a challenge, and yes, it can be scary. However, this is a gift, and I'll tell you why. The girl in the airport reminded me that you should face your fears and go out and experience the world, whether by traveling or learning a new language, because it makes you a stronger person. She told me that it "breaks you and rebuilds you." That is the quote that changed me forever. It made me realize that you should not try to avoid fear, but you should face it head on. That is the only thing that will get rid of it: fight it, don't hide from it. Think of it as an experience. And trust me, if you do this, it will be the most rewarding thing you can ever do for yourself. Now that I have done it, I feel like I am a much stronger person. In fact, I no longer feel that I am even a shy person. It's so simple, just fight your fear. Remember, it is better to do something and regret it than to wish that you had done it. But trust me, chances are, you will *never* regret it.

In this next piece, Ivan Kupka not only passes on some valuable language learning advice, but shows you how to cultivate the right belief system...

Language learning and NLP

My name is Ivan Kupka. I am a mathematician, living in Bratislava, Slovakia. Slovak is my mother tongue. I love reading books. I have written some books, too. My interest in language-learning dates back to 1985. At that time, I was already 27 years old. I spoke Slovak, Czech, Russian, and English. I decided to test effective methods of language-learning. I started learning French from scratch, at home. At that time they were selling only one French newspaper in the Communist Czechoslovakia. It was, of course, the communist newspaper L'Humanite. By 1987, I was able to read French books. So, I learned to read French books five times faster than I had learned to read English books.

After the Czechoslovak Velvet Revolution in 1989, we were able to travel abroad freely. In 1993, I taught mathematics at the Universite de Bretagne Occidentale, in France, The same year I completed courses in neurolinguistic programming (NLP) in France and Belgium. My French adventure lasted only one year, but I learned much in France.

Today I read books in Slovak, Czech, Polish, Russian, English, French, German, Spanish, Italian, and Esperanto. And, of course, I admire all these polyglots who speak really difficult languages. My heroes are Heinrich Schliemann, Emil Krebs, Kato Lomb, Barry Farber, Steve

Kaufmann, LaoShu, and—recently—many others. Thank you, YouTube, for showing them to us! For me, too, it is time to aim higher.

My next goal is to be able to read Japanese books. So far, I have gone through the Pimsleur Japanese series, and in a couple of weeks, I will be finishing Heisig's "Remembering the Kanji 1." I also enjoyed a couple of Japanese haiku. If you are a native speaker of one of the languages I mentioned above and if you wish to learn Slovak, Czech, or even French, just contact me. We can help each other. My address is: ivan.kupka@seznam.cz

For many years, I have been interested in various aspects of communication. My areas of interest include effective learning methods, motivation, creativity, and interpersonal communications. I have held seminars on neurolinguistic programming communications techniques and effective language learning. The question I am always asking is, "How can we use our resources in a better, more effective way?" In my book, "Jak úspěšně studovat cizí jazyky," or, "How to Successfully Study Foreign Languages," published in Prague in 2007, I show how neurolinguistic programming can help us to use our resources for language-learning.

Below, you will find some extracts from the book. My friend Melvyn Clarke translated the book into English, so maybe one day it will be published in an English version as well. Here are the extracts. I hope the text will be helpful to some of you.

Resources, bankbooks and hidden talents

'Resources' are what we call anything from which you can derive benefits. They can be anything at all that enables you to realize your intentions and satisfy your needs.

There are many unused resources around us all the time; some are waiting to be made visible, while others are already known to us. In either instance, we often underrate them, or we first need to get into the habit of making use of them.

Some people live in the belief that nobody gets anything for free in this world. Actually, if they really had to pay for every resource they used, they would be in the red fairly soon.

We could start, for example, by giving them the bill for the air they breathe. This air is all around us, and we breathe it in for free. Our sense organs, our abilities to communicate in a language, and to come to an understanding with others are also there for us free of charge, as is our reason and our ability to experience feelings, to work up enthusiasm, and to laugh. In this chapter, we are going to systematically seek out and identify such resources using Bateson's model. We will be particularly interested in those that can help us to achieve our language goals.

1. Environment

Starting at the environment level, we shall present a couple of examples and ask several questions. Questions written in *italics* should be taken as a prompt regarding your own activity. Answer them as an exercise that can tell you something useful, recording your answers in a notebook.

Better somewhere than everywhere

Imagine that you wake up in the morning to find that your laptop is in the entrance hall, your CD with German phrases is in the bedroom and your phrase notes are in the living room. You still have seven minutes until the time you usually get up. What are you going to do?

And what would you do if the CD were in the laptop mechanism, and the laptop and phrase notes were within arm's reach? Say both of these situations can happen sixty times a year. How many minutes of time lost or gained for learning does this represent?

How can you change the spatial arrangements and the distribution of the objects around you to help you to study and use your languages?

For a long time Dave could not remember what the German word Kuchen (cake) meant. He somehow kept confusing it with kitchen, Küche. Eventually, he wrote the word with its English equivalent on a piece of paper, which he taped onto his toothbrush, so that he had it in front of him every day. Now, he is more than familiar with the word.

Do you have a special place allocated for the language that you are studying? Do you have your books, notes, CDs and cassettes on hand?

Stick up pictures, postcards, maps, and favorite quotations in the language that you are studying on the wall at home. Create a little "German corner" at home, in the garden shed, or at work. Collect objects, brochures and materials associated with the language and country in question.

Walking around town

Where in my town can I come into contact with the language that I am studying? How can I otherwise make use of the options provided by my environment?

When Petr can choose which side of Main Street he is going to walk down, he goes for the side where the tourists sit out on the terrace in front of the hotel, so that he can occasionally pick up fragments of German phrases as he is passing. A little way further down the street there is a foreign-language bookshop display window. He always has a look at the titles of two or three German books and then repeats them to himself as he is walking.

2. Elementary activities

Some people need to get their sight sorted out, to ensure that their eyes do not hurt when they read for any extended period of time. Others would be helped by learning relaxation techniques to make studying more pleasant.

Which elementary activity needs to be enhanced to make the study and use of languages easier for you?
Let your hearing make full use of its potential to help in your language studies. Use high-quality recordings and, if

possible, sound card, radio receiver, player and loudspeakers that are of high-quality as well. Be aware that to study German it is enough to use a device with a sound range of up to 4000 Hz, but to hear English correctly we need a device that attains the higher frequencies, up to the 11,000-12,000 Hz band. Also, consider how spending long hours with headphones on at excessive volume can permanently damage your hearing.

Use high-standard textbooks and aids. If you are learning phrases from cards, design them so that you can read them comfortably, and even with pleasure. Train your vocal cords without overtaxing them.

3. Abilities and strategies
A human is a miraculous little learning machine. Learning begins long before we are born. Not a day goes by in our lives when we do not pick up some new knowledge, a new behavioral pattern, or a new way of doing things. In comparison with others, people who work efficiently have an extra rare ability: they can transfer the skills and habits that they have acquired in one field to other fields.

Use what has been learnt in new contexts *Consider the skills and knowledge that you have acquired in life. How could you make use of them for studying a language?*

For example, if you did karate in your youth, you could revive the old habit of regular training, with its associated disciplines, maintaining a correct "mental regimen" and alternating hard work with leisure and relaxed concentration. You can decide for yourself which level of language knowledge would match a yellow or a brown belt and at which level you would be perfectly satisfied and receive a black belt.

Kindergarten teachers surely know a lot about how to make use of melody, rhythm, and rhyme when teaching new material. They know how important it is to vary different types of activities to make teaching interesting. They notice how children imitate general grammatical patterns more closely than adults do (e.g., "think, thinked"). They also see how much practice is required for them to learn the exceptions to these rules and to acquire correct pronunciation.

Which skills and knowledge have you already acquired in life?

Write them down on a piece of paper. For each of them, try to come up with at least one way it could be put to good use during your studies.

A former chess player will learn the German word for "queen" more readily than others might. A natural scientist will apply her knowledge of Latin when studying Romance languages. A mathematician will very quickly understand logical grammatical rules. A painter would find it a waste not to take full advantage of her visual imagination during her studies.

Used and unused abilities

Catherine learned French at school and university using classic methods.

Most of her time was taken up working with a textbook. She learned the language to quite a decent level, but everybody could tell by her accent that she was not speaking in her native language. As an adult, she began to study German and decided to make full use of her hearing. From the start of her studies she worked mostly with recordings. She listened to them and tried to reproduce aloud not only the characteristic stress pattern of speech, but also its rhythm and melody. When repeating, she could then make use of her auditory memory, which is stronger than her visual memory.

When she speaks German now, she talks with an almost perfect accent. Only a native German can tell that she is a foreigner.

More will be said on methods and strategies in the next chapter on polyglots.

Using your foreign language wherever you can

We have already met some study techniques in the previous chapter. One of these methods was to use your foreign language wherever you can. For example, if you are watching an international football match, you can just as easily watch it on an Austrian or German channel as on a domestic one.

Say you have a family chore of washing the dishes and cleaning in the kitchen every evening. You can either do it at eight or at ten. There is a radio on the table in the kitchen. At nine, the news begins in your foreign language. What time should you plan to do your cleaning?

How can you plan your schedule in favor of even fleeting contact with your foreign language?

What knowledge can you bring to bear as a resource for studying and using your languages?

Paul learned Italian quite well and wanted to test out his knowledge in some way. He decided to show some Italian guests around who were visiting his friend. On the way to the rendezvous, he was suddenly overcome by fear: "what if I get into a situation where I forget some important word, or where I just can't get a word out for the life of me?" But then he sighed with relief as he realized that the foreign guests could speak French well, just like he could. So if need arose, he could get by with French.

Another case of transference

Robert had never learned any Greek in his life, yet he enthusiastically reported how, for all of two minutes, he understood what his Greek colleague was saying in his own native language. In English, Robert told him a problem that had been very much occupying him. His Greek friend then immediately described it to another Greek in their mother tongue.

"Because he repeated it sentence by sentence as I had said it, and because a lot of international words come from Greek, I knew what they were talking about in practically every single sentence."

Let's choose

The number of methods and strategies for studying languages is inexhaustible. Choose those methods that suit you best. Do not automatically choose the first method or course that comes your way.

There are even better options awaiting you. Take into account your goals, abilities, and favorite activities. Work in a way that accommodates them.

4. Beliefs and values

This is one of the little secrets that gifted people have:

A basic ingredient of talent is the strong desire to make progress in a particular field, combined with the conviction that this is achievable.
Gifted people do not say to themselves: "Mr X does it three times faster than me. He's just got a talent for it. I should give up." They say: "How does that Peter do it? If he can manage, it then I certainly can."

Experts have found that motivation to perform a specific activity is effective when two conditions have been met:

1. Performance of this activity is in keeping with your main values.
2. You are **convinced** that you are able to achieve the goal in question. How many people give up on their basic goals before they've even started? How many say every day that they are too old, that they are "not up to it," and that others are more talented? But sometimes, your value

or belief is so strong that it sweeps all obstacles aside. That was the case of a Russian pensioner who began to learn Spanish as her first foreign language at an advanced age. She needed to communicate with her granddaughter, who she was meant to be looking after, and so she learned to speak the language within a year.

Another instructive case is that of the schoolboy who was dozing as the maths homework was being given out. When he woke up he quickly copied down two problems that were on the blackboard. Because he had been sleeping for some time, he failed to hear the teacher say that nobody at the school had ever solved these problems. He thought it was ordinary homework. At home he really racked his brains over these problems but he eventually came up with the answers, the first and only one to do so in the entire school!

How to start believing in yourself

One good, simple way to start believing in yourself is to start regularly working and taking pleasure in the progress that you make. Can you remember everything you did not know or could not deal with two or three years ago? If you kept a diary at that time, go through it. You will be surprised!

Even the most difficult journey starts…simply with a first step

The conviction that you will not be "up to it" often comes from the feeling that the task you see in front of you is too big. To a beginner the task of reading a German novel may appear impossible. So, first choose an easier task.

For example, reading the texts of the first five lessons from your textbook fluently and with full understanding. Then, just have a glance at a German novel, or even better, the dialogue of a play. Can you find at least one sentence that you basically understand? The chances are that there is one.

Step back with pleasure and applaud yourself over this – you could even award yourself some small treat. You have taken your first step towards reading German novels. Twenty steps like that will not be so hard, and yet you will have achieved your goal.

Where do I believe in myself and where don't I?

When studying a language, it is good to be able to the answer these questions:

What is my image of myself?

To what extent do I believe in myself and to what extent do I believe in my abilities and my future? In which situations and in which contexts do I and don't I?

Which of my beliefs assist my foreign language studies and which hinder them?

You can work on your beliefs

Neatly list those beliefs and values of yours that most

closely relate to language study and use.

Now have a think about how you could turn a belief with a negative mark into a belief with a positive mark. What would you need to change to make these values and beliefs support your studies?

For example, take the idea, "I have always been a bad student". Even if this remains unchanged, we can still interpret it as: "I have always been a bad student, so I should use my foreign language as much as possible in a natural setting in real life. When I use it, I should free myself as soon as possible from any dry scholarly or academic approach."

Systematically change restrictive beliefs

Sometimes you need the help of an experienced psychological counselor to alter a deep-seated attitude. In many cases, however, it is enough to look at things simply from a slightly different angle and to comment on them using different words – words that nonetheless fully respect reality. Let us take a couple of examples of such internal retuning:

The belief, "I can't do irregular German verbs" could be usefully
replaced by the beliefs, "I need to learn basic irregular German verbs," and, "if I learn five irregular verbs every week and do the appropriate amount of practice on them, I will be an expert on verbs in a couple of months." It would be good to back up this new belief as soon as possible with a specific decision, such as, "This Saturday, I shall

learn the first ten most frequently used verbs – those dealt with first in the Teach Yourself book."

The belief, "I don't have time to go on a company German course, because I am very busy with work and I'm on the go all the time," can be replaced by, "because I have too much work to be able to go on a company German course, I shall get on an intensive holiday course." Likewise you can look at things this way: "it took the offer of this course to show me how much work I have. What can I do about that? Who could stand in for me for some things? Is there anything in my activities that is less valuable than this course that I could give up?"

"I'm old now," and "I don't want to make a fool of myself in front of the youngsters" can be replaced by, "mental work rejuvenates you,", "I'm learning for myself, not for others," and, "I have a right to my own time." "I have no talent at all for languages," can be replaced by a range of sentences and statements, such as:

"I understand English, so I can also understand hundreds, even thousands of French, Spanish, Latin, and German words."

"When I was learning to swim, I had difficulties at first, and I didn't say that I had no talent for swimming then."

"I don't need to learn every language; German is enough."

"I'll find out how much study time was needed by those whom I see as talented."

"I'll have to devote twice as much time to the language."

"Do I have no talent, or do I just not feel like exerting myself?"

"Maybe I *do* have the ability to go through the first five lessons in detail. Then, we shall see. I might even manage the sixth."

"Above all, I need to be able to understand spoken German, to recognize individual words and phrases. I shall work with recordings a lot more."

"I'll give my speech organs plenty of opportunity to practice this new pronunciation to which I'm simply not accustomed. I'll get myself tutored by somebody who can teach me correct pronunciation."

"I'll get my memory to retain material by repeating basic phrases every day."

"I need to get into the habit of studying regularly." And, in conclusion, one useful maxim with universal application: **Phantoms fear actions.**

Ivan Kupka's blog about languages in Czech:
http://www.ivankupka.bloguje.cz/

From the "land down under," comes the story of someone who nearly lost his linguistic heritage, but then found it again...

My Facebook Photo and Polyglot Essay:

Please excuse my terrible writing, I haven't written anything in English for quite some time.

Dion Francavilla (paholainen100 on YouTube). Haven't quite signed up yet but will do so ASAP.

My name is Dion Francavilla. I live in Melbourne, Australia. I was born into an Italian family who immigrated to Australia some time ago. I was fortunate to have some exposure to a foreign language in a predominately monolingual, yet strangely multicultural society. My first language was of course, Italian. My grandparents and parents both spoke to me in Italian when I was at a very young age, which is the best time to absorb a foreign tongue. Hence I learnt it naturally and easily and from what many relatives tell me I spoke it very well. By the age of 5 or 6 perhaps, the time when I first started attending school, I began learning English, since it is the language of Australia, and (whether consciously or by accident) I stopped speaking Italian, or lost the ability to do so. This must have happened at quite a fast pace. I had no idea the problems this would cause me later on in my life. Fortunately, however, I was always able to understand the language. I vaguely remember one of my uncles telling me when I commenced my schooling. "Don't forget your Italian, when you go to school speak English with all your friends, but when you come home and when you come and visit us, keep using your Italian" I don't know what happened exactly after this but I vaguely remember protesting this or not completely understanding what was going on. Luckily I was always able to understand conversations very well but I couldn't hold a conversation in Italian.. What had happened?

I mean, I knew a few words and phrases but--to their and my disappointment--I continued to struggle forming sentences and certainly couldn't hold a descent conversation with my relatives. No one understood why though. They seemed to think it was bad attitude and lack of interest on my part (which may have partly been true). Yet I think it was much more complicated than that.

I was still very young at the time and as time progressed my Italian suffered more and more. Part of me wanted to communicate effectively with my relatives, yet I just didn't believe I could do it. They kept nagging me. Unfortunately there was nothing I could do. In fact, since I couldn't speak, everybody assumed that I couldn't understand, but they didn't realise how wrong they were. I could indeed understand 95-98% of their conversations. Time went on and not much changed in my linguistic abilities. Perhaps that couldn't be helped at that stage of my life.

Throughout my teens years I had to listen repeatedly to my relatives who missed that little boy could speak Italian so well. This didn't really help, in fact it made me feel worse and as though I could have achieved more, yet I couldn't really remember why I stopped speaking.

Throughout my teen years, I occasionally learnt a new Italian word or two to help me along (it demonstrated interest but was not quite enough to communicate), and my efforts were met with some enthusiasm.

I wasn't interested in improving Italian or any other foreign language for that matter, and it wasn't until I was about 16 years old when I found my interest. I was in high school, I had previously taken up Japanese, Italian, French and Latin, yet I lacked motivation with any of them. I just didn't enjoy the classes. I continued with Japanese up until the end of high school. Even though I was interested enough to scrape through the classes, I wasn't interested enough to really improve. During my studies, my friends and I stumbled across some German music which I took quite a liking to. Before long, I decided to take up German on my own in order to understand the lyrics. I soon became hooked and really wanted to get serious with the language. It started off as pure curiosity and grew into something much more powerful. This was the beginning!!

I studied German for the rest of my high school years and much after that. I wanted to go to University to study German, but I didn't get accepted due to poor results. As a result, I started a course I didn't like, I got a job that wasn't quite for me, yet I kept up my German as a hobby. I became a dental technician, and didn't earn much money, but for a guy living at home it was enough. I saved up as much as I could for a holiday. *"At the end of the year I am going to Germany"* I exclaimed. I told my parents, they were surprised yet happy and asked if any of my friends wanted to accompany me. No one was able to do so, so I left for Germany during the Christmas holidays. I had only three weeks and I wanted to make the most of it.

I was eager to practice the German that I had learnt. I arrived and practiced my rudimentary German with the locals and almost refused to speak English, since most Germans' English is impeccable anyway. They were surprised and my attempts were met with great enthusiasm. I also spent a few days in Finland, where I met a friend who offered me accommodation. I also had an exposure to the beautiful Finnish language, which of course I didn't get to use during my stay unfortunately. When I came back home, I decided I wanted to go again.

I dreaded my job, but I worked for another year and saved up some more money to go on another European adventure. In the meantime I kept up my German to an extent but I had other commitments so my time was somewhat limited. I departed again for the European winter which I loved. I visited some other countries as well during my short stay.

When I returned I enrolled in a travel-agency course which lasted six months. After that I commenced work again in the dental laboratory. I didn't go overseas that year. I kept applying for University and eventually got approved. I was very happy. I took up German and Italian. I did very well with German since I had previous knowledge, having taught myself before. I also did very well with my Italian since I had studied a more difficult language (German), and also because I already had an understanding of the Italian language.

I received good marks and understood everything the teacher was saying. All of a sudden things were making much more sense to me. I continued with my studies, my Italian improved and I quickly found myself conversing freely with my grandparents and also with my parents. I told my mother that I really wanted to use my Italian at home, and did so, and am still doing so. In my second year at university, I was disappointed that all my previous study of German didn't compare with students who had spent some time in Germany or Austria.

I could write, I understood the grammar rules, I didn't make many mistakes but I still couldn't speak fast enough or confidently enough without thinking beforehand. I became very depressed and decided to take up another language which aroused my curiosity, Finnish. I loved the sound of it and have always been attracted to less-studied and somewhat obscure languages. I quickly bought myself a *Teach-Yourself Finnish* CD and Book.

I have been working on it every since.

My knowledge remains limited since I spend most of my time writing the language and not speaking it. There is a lack of native speakers in Australia and not enough learning content for me to really improve and further my studies while in Australia.

My interest in Finnish stemmed from my interest in Scandinavian culture and music. Finnish is a unique language because it isn't actually Scandinavian (or even Indo-European for that matter). It's unique and belongs to the Uralic language family which isn't related to anything in Europe except Estonian and Hungarian (Hungarian being only a very distant relative of Finnish). I am currently studying the Uralic family and writing a book on the Uralic language family since it interests me so much.

I am also currently writing on how one should learn a foreign language. My Italian studies continue to improve even now, and I am fluent enough in an everyday context and can hold a conversation on most topics.

My German isn't so great, yet I can communicate with native speakers when I encounter them. Occasionally I keep a journal or listen to some audio material to refresh my memory, though this is less seldom these days.

I am still at university studying German and Italian, as these are currently my majors. I have nearly finished my studies. I am 24 years of age and do not know my career path, but I would love for it to be related in some way to foreign languages.

Foreign languages are part of my life and I am constantly

using them and thinking about them, especially at home with relatives or listening to music or keeping a journal in Finnish, Italian or German. I like to associate all my daily activities somehow with foreign languages.

I do not call myself a polyglot, though someday I would definitely like to be. I am an "amateur polyglot," or language enthusiast. I have been interested in languages for many years, and I imagine there will be many exciting times to come. I will continue with my studied of Italian, Finnish and German, and will possibly take up many more languages. I believe my next will be Hungarian.

Learning foreign languages is, in my opinion, an excellent self-improvement activity, and I would recommend it to ANYONE—that's right—anyone who is interested. I would encourage the learning of both common and also minor and overlooked languages, since they are usually very interesting.

There are some people I would like to Thank:

1. **Claude**, for this opportunity to write this short, rough essay of mine. I love watching his videos—they are very inspiring.

2. **Steve Kaufmann**. I discovered Steve's videos about a year ago and it completely changed my outlook on language learning. He is an example of a man who has learnt many languages on his own. I know I can do the same, and in a more natural way. I realized that learning

all these Grammar rules and doing grammar drills really do slow one down. Not just that, but they are slow and ineffective. I like his approach to Input and Output and how he emphasizes Input before output. I really believe he has the right idea to language learning. He has a practical approach that can be applied to anyone; get some learner content, then as soon as you can get yourself onto real content, content that native speakers would use.

Most importantly don't be afraid to open your mouth and make mistakes, words are far more important than grammar and don't waste your term and money at university studying languages.. You can achieve much more on your own, work at your own pace and learn much quicker and probably also save a lot of money.

3. **Moses Mccormick** – I watch his videos all the time and he continues to inspire me as a great polyglot. He learns many languages, many unrelated languages but above all his enthusiasm impresses me most.

Thanks everyone.

Oscar's easy, conversational style makes his YouTube videos a pleasure to watch. Reading his account of his false starts when learning English will motivate all of you to persevere...

THE BIGGEST CHALLENGE

First of all, I want to point out that I don't consider myself a polyglot. I can speak two languages as a native (Spanish and Catalan), and I am currently learning English, so my experience about learning languages is kind of humble.

However, what makes me want to share my experience with you is that I think it may be useful for people like me, who want to start learning languages.

So my story is not about how to learn a fifth foreign language, or to become an accomplished polyglot, but how to learn the first foreign language. And this is, my friends, the biggest challenge for a person interested on learning languages.

There is always a psychological wall for those who want to learn her/his first language. Each brick of this impressive wall represents a question like: "Is my brain able to learn a new language now that I am not a kid?", or "Is this the right approach for learning the language?" The list continues and it seems that there is no ending to such questions.

These type of questions have been on my mind for a long time. The problem that a newbie has in learning languages is that he/she has no references at all. When I started

English seriously, I wasn't sure at all what the best methodology was.

Here where I live, the public school teaching methodology is based on grammar, exercises and tests. Listening is infrequent. Speaking is also infrequent. Sometimes you have to read an easy adapted book (one per year and usually short), but that's it. Year after year, the same grammar (adding a bit more) is repeated. So, as you can guess, English classes are boring, non-compelling and ineffective. The result is that students who finish high school only get very basic knowledge of the language. This was exactly my case.

At university, I soon realized that my English skills were really poor. I had to tackle technical English –not very difficult– but, even if I knew many words, I wasn't able to understand the general meaning. Why? Because I had learnt by heart most of the words I knew, so it was odd for me to guess the meaning by putting them together. Besides this, I tried to haphazardly apply the grammar I had learnt.

Despite this, the situation made me consider the idea that the best way to learn a language wasn't by learning only grammar and lists of vocabulary. The best way is always to learn in context. This is the unplanned approach that kids use on daily basis while they learn their native language.

When I finished at the university, I was able to read technical English without too much difficulty. Technical English about computers and software is easy, because the vocabulary used is quite narrow.

At this moment of the story, I want to say that there is always a key moment for a person who is learning languages. This interesting, and important moment is when the person becomes independent. By independent I mean that he/she no longer needs a teacher, a language school, or whatever thing could be. At this glorious moment, the learner starts the real trip for learning a language.

This is when the learner becomes very receptive on the different approaches on learning languages. Often he/she tries to find other people in the same situation, and looks forward to share experiences and knowledge and learn strategies from others. Then is when the wall I mentioned before starts to fall brick by brick.

Continuing with my story, some time after I finished at the university, I wanted to improve my English, so I decided (silly me) to start very seriously to learn grammar, but this time on my own. It's not clear to me why I decided to learn grammar again. Maybe because I felt a little unsure. But fortunately, after a short and unproductive period of time (3 weeks or so) I gave up grammar. So I decided that what I needed was to use the language.

I hired a teacher, a native English speaker. My idea was to have conversations in English. I thought "Excellent idea Oscar! This has to be a very effective way for learning a language. Just talking!". The result was…a complete disaster. Why? Because I didn't have enough exposure to the language, and I got nervous and uneasy every time I had to speak. I felt I needed more vocabulary, structures and patterns! I felt really awkward when I started a sentence, and I didn't know how to finish. I felt horrible every time I had to ask to the teacher to repeat what she said because I didn't understand it the first time.

After a short time (one month or so) and some money wasted, I started to seek alternative approaches. I got rid of the idea of learning only with grammar, but there was still something missing from my plan (as illustrated in the previous paragraph).

Surfing the Internet (that wonderful tool), I came across people like Steve Kaufmann and Stephen Krashen, who stated that a highly effective way to learn a new language is the "input" approach. My intuition was already telling me that it was the right way, but finding out that other noted polyglots and researchers say the same made stronger that idea.

What is the input approach? In short, it's spending most of the time listening and reading, especially at the beginning. Is speaking forbidden? Not at all. You speak when you feel you want to speak. Some people like to speak from the beginning, and other people prefer to spend long silent periods of time without trying to speak--just listening and reading.

I am in the middle of both approaches. As I said before, starting to speak from the beginning wasn't working out well for me, but I think that after some period of time, it's good to put into practice what have you learnt, instead of waiting too long a period of time.

So I started to listen for about two hours every day to

comprehensible English. I also read a lot. After two months or so, I began to have conversations through Skype. At the beginning, it was a bit hard for me, but soon I was able to use what I had been learning. English became more natural. I had begun building up useful vocabulary and patterns of the language.

So I hadn't forced myself too much to speak. Of course, I wasn't fluent in many situations, but I was doing my best, and most importantly, I was enjoying the process of learning!

Currently, I am still learning English. I consider myself intermediate. I can have conversations about several topics. Sometimes I am not as fluent as I want, but I am improving little by little. Anyway, my current level of English is not important. What's important is that I became independent on learning languages. I know that I can depend on myself to learn a language. This knowledge is the best gift that the process of learning a language has given to me.

The bottom line is that by becoming an independent learner, I've overcome the biggest challenge--how to learn that first language.

Oscar

http://www.youtube.com/user/OscarP282

Next up is Nelson Mendez from Venezuela. His enthusiasm for language study comes out in the first paragraph of his aptly named entry, "An Endless Journey." Read it and just try not to get enthused yourself...

An Endless Journey
Nelson Mendez
nelsonmendez@nelsonmendez.com

My name is Nelson Mendez, a guy from Venezuela and starting his 30's. As can be inferred from my country of origin, my mother tongue is Spanish. However, I also can communicate in French, English, Italian and Portuguese. I have studied German but I do not consider that I have enough knowledge of it to claim that I know the language. How did I get to know all of these languages?

Answering that question is the aim of this essay. I will try and reflect on my language learning experience: **an endless journey**, as mentioned in the title of this paper.

First, learning a language is not a process that ends once you finish a course at the university or complete a book of exercises. Learning a language can take one's entire lifetime. Second, learning a language can create a desire to learn one more language, and then another…

My experience in this journey

I started seriously studying languages at the university – Universidad de Los Andes, Merida- Venezuela in 1998. Actually, I have studied all of my languages first of all in formal education settings.

In the case of English and French, I learned them by completing a bachelor in foreign languages. The program was focused on English and French, and for that reason, I had many courses in these two languages.
I had classes in phonetics, reading and writing, literature, culture and of course in grammar.

The courses at the University gave me a lot of information. Nevertheless, it didn't mean that I was totally fluent and I knew the languages perfectly. Even today I am still learning them, and every day I find a grammar point that I need to review or a new word that I must learn.

In 2004, I had my first real acid test with the languages I had been learning at the university. I went to the province of Quebec, Canada, in an exchange program. I arrived in Quebec City and I had to register in the university residences, but being exposed to Canadian French was very shocking! I could not understand the person that was talking to me. This experience was very frustrating, because I had the feeling that I had wasted my time at the University.

Over time I began to understand the people from Quebec very well, and today I am in love with Quebec French. This love for the language was one of the reasons I decided that I would move to the province of Quebec. Soon I will be moving to Gatineau, to be close to the language I enjoy the most.

Talking now in retrospective, I think that this shameful

experience in Quebec helped me a lot later on. Coming from a formal setting where you are corrected almost all of the time by the teachers, one grows up with a   sense of perfection. But, this idea of perfection collapsed in 2004. That's why I can say nowadays that a language is perfectible; however, you don't need to be perfect in the foreign language in order to communicate. It is more important to enjoy the world of possibilities that another language opens.

In regards to English, I learned it mainly at the University. In Venezuela we have English lessons from high school. Nonetheless, I didn't learn that much from my instructors there. As I mentioned before, I had many content courses in and about English in my university program. And here I learned a lot about the language.

Of course I spent many hours of hard work, doing a lot of exercises, writing papers, making presentations for my courses and reading all the information the professors gave me. English is the foreign language I use the most, and thanks to it I do business with people in the United States. I am able to communicate with my suppliers, my bank and even my cousin's husband, who does not speak Spanish yet.

English is also a language of joy. I enjoy watching videos in English on *YouTube*, listening to music and reading books. It is not an obligation that I have to follow in order to keep the language alive and kicking. I really love doing things in English, and thanks to that, my English gets better everyday. So, the investment I did in my university years is paying off well now.

I have been to the USA several times, and knowing the language of the country makes the trips more interesting, enjoyable and rewarding. I think it would have been a little bit boring to visit the USA without knowing the language. When you can communicate with locals, you can experience the country in a deeper way, even stealing a smile from someone when you ask for directions, ride the bus or go out to eat. And a smile gets "stuck in your mind."

These kinds of experiences help to create understanding between people and motivate you to keep on studying the language. Those good experiences that I have had have reinforced my desire to learn more languages in order to repeat such enjoyable situations.

That is why last year (2009) I started learning Italian, and reviewing my Portuguese. From this point, I will talk about my experience with these two languages.

In relation to Portuguese, I started studying it in Venezuela at the University. I took two levels of this language in 2003. I did these two levels and I achieved a good level of Portuguese. But, as I mentioned before, in 2004 I traveled to Canada and I forgot my Portuguese. I mean, I did not continue studying and as a consequence lost almost everything I had learned.

However, last year (2009) having more free time than usual I decided that I would recover my Portuguese. In that sense, I set a search for materials on the Internet. Watching the videos of some of the polyglots of *YouTube* I picked up information about resources. So, I got to know the *Pimsleur* method, *Teach Yourself* and others. I remember once Moses McCormick mentioned this page: www.uz-translations.net/

This was wonderful because this page gave me access to a lot of resources. Specifically for Portuguese, I found a book where the Spanish and Portuguese language systems are compared. This book helped me much at the formal level. However, for acquiring speaking skill my most important resource was the *Pimsleur* method. Nowadays, I also help my Portuguese by listening to the radio from Brazil through the Internet.

This has been important in two aspects. By listening to radio I have listened to real Portuguese, and have learned words that are in a certain way unique to Brazil. But also, I discovered a type of music that has caught my attention. I must confess that I don't like Bossa Nova or Samba. And there was not a connection to the language at the cultural or emotional level; something strong that encouraged me to love the language and motivated me to learn more and more.

However, by listening to the radio, I discovered *forró* and *sertão* music. And here I am, writing this paper and listening to Fernando e Sorocaba. Now, Portuguese accompanies me everyday thanks to this type of music.

Now, it is the time to describe a my experience with Italian. As with the other languages, I studied it at the university. In 2007, I was awarded a scholarship from the Organization of American States (OAS) to do a Master's degree in Mexico. So, I came to the city of Monterrey to do a program in Education.

Seeing that I had some free time, I thought it would be interesting to study a new language. So, in the second semester of 2008 I started attending an Italian language course at the university where I was doing the Master's. The course was the usual type. But I understood that I was there just to have grammar explanations and to receive some input from my teacher.

Once you have studied several languages, you know that the classroom is not enough, and that if you intend to really master the language, you have to be curious and look elsewhere, so I started my search for things that could help me. I discovered a radio station in Italian and began to listen to it every day. I also read the www.corriere.it, so that I was not only up-to-date with the news but I practiced my Italian at the same time.

As an exercise, I sometimes translated articles and pieces of news into Spanish and then published them in my blog at nelsonmendez.com. Theses activities boosted my Italian, and in a short time I was speaking Italian with relative ease.

At present I try to keep my Italian alive by watching RAI news on the Internet, by listening to music and by writing in Italian to a cousin who now lives in Italy. I still need to learn more in this language, and I think I will revisit my Italian with *Pimsleur's* audios.

To finish my reflection, I would like to mention that I am at this time studying German and Bahasa Indonesia. And

German deserves more of my attention—and here's why: I am in my third attempt at trying to learn this language.

In my previous attempts, I failed because I was not working hard enough with the language and I lacked the proper motivation. I now understand that German really deserves my devotion, and this devotion, or motivation, is something that we must have—not just for German, but for any language we may intend to learn.

Auf wiedersehen!

Luka Skrbic may only be 16, but he's already multilingual. Reading his piece will prove to you that it is possible to learn something new, if you really want to...

Luka Skrbic--Belgrade, Serbia

YouTube channel: www.youtube.com/LukaSkrbic . My email: lukaskrbic@live.com

I don't know where to start, but well... My name is Luka and I'm a 16 year old guy who's really interested in learning foreign languages. I was born—and I'm still living —in Serbia, near the Capital, Belgrade.

My learning of English has started when I was just a small kid in pre-school, and it has continued all through my elementary and high school years. But I can tell you that you can't learn a foreign language in school because teachers, first of all, focus on grammar—which is not a good place to start.

Well, I'm lucky to be living in this period when English can be learnt by watching television, using the internet... so most of my knowledge didn't came from learning at school. I was able to use so many other resources. Personally I don't think that my English is perfect, but I know that it would be much worse if I would only have relied on school as I had to do in the past.

But English is not a good example for this story because it has now become an international language (which nearly everyone should speak), and I'm proud that I have reached a level where I can use it. A much better example are my German studies. I started to learn this language when I was about 10 or 11 years old in school. We changed teachers a lot so it was impossible for such small kids to learn a foreign language in that environment.

First year passed like that and after that a professor came to our class who wasn't really interested in improving our knowledge and motivating us.

The years have passed like this in high school and while I studied German for so long my level is only equal to that of an absolute beginner. I'm really angry with this because I lost (we all lost) a opportunity to learn a language which can really help us in future.

I wanted to make up for all that I missed with German by studying another foreign language, but I didn't know which. At that time I was watching an amazing Spanish TV series named "Los Serrano." Watching it I became very familiar with the Spanish language so I decided to enroll some course in that language.

I heard on a TV commercial that Instituto Cervantes, a Spanish Government institution was working on the propagation of Spanish language and culture. I thought it would be great to study Spanish so I enrolled and I loved it. My first professor at Cervantes was Javier from Madrid. That is the greatest thing about Cervantes-the teachers are native speakers of Spanish (Spaniards or Latin Americans).

Javier has really helped me to immerse myself into the Spanish language and the culture of Spain. I had great time there; I learnt a lot and met many good friends. One couple I met moved to Chile soon afterwards. I'm in contact with them by Facebook and they're doing great.

After Javier, my next course professor was Manuel (Manu), who taught me a lot of grammar and helped me to further improve my skills.

Manu always insisted on writing things out and he thought that writing was the most important skill we could acquire in order to advance. A few days ago I finished my third course of Spanish at Cervantes. After Manu, Xavier, an Argentinian from Buenos Aires, became my professor.

He insisted on conversation. We talked a lot in classes, on breaks in bars... everywhere. He traveled a lot and he was teaching Spanish to people from Germany, France, Italy, Japan, US, Switzerland, Israel ... He is fluent in Spanish, German, English, Italian, French and Portuguese and he learnt many words of Serbian while he was living here.

It is very very interesting and useful to study the Spanish Language at Institute Cervantes. Spaniards and Latinos really want to teach us their language in the most exciting ways. It really helped me when I was traveling to Spain. I plan to continue to learn and practice English and Spanish, and I hope that soon I will start learning another language, maybe a more challenging one such as Chinese or Japanese.

I'm still in high school, but I really want to study abroad because it's a great experience when you're studying what you like in a different language and have the opportunity to make new friendships while at the same time exploring a new world.

Listen up guys, because our next Polyglot speaks 10 languages. Not only that, he's going to tell you how you can too! Félix—you know him as Loki—tells us his story....

Hello everyone, this is my contribution to the polyglot project launched by Claude.

First of all, let me introduce myself. My name is Félix. I was born in Brussels, the Capital of Belgium, but my parents are from Taiwan and Cambodia. I'm a polyglot on YouTube and I share my experiences about learning foreign languages. I can speak 10 languages so far, all at basic fluency-which means that I can have decent conversations with people without many problems.

For those who want to know which languages I speak, here is the list: French, Flemish,German (my weakest language), Italian, Spanish, English, Taiwanese, Mandarin Chinese, Teochew and Japanese.

Let me tell you the story of how I came to know so many languages:

At home we always speak 3 languages: Taiwanese (台語), trochee 潮州話, and Mandarin Chinese. I went to Flemish school so I learnt Flemish during those 5 years but then I changed schools to one where the primary language was French. I had a hard time adapting initially to the french language, but after a while it become natural, "second nature" let's say.

Afterward, I began to learn English at school. However, since foreign language learning was **focused on**

grammar, I didn't really learn how to communicate. So after a few years of English study I was not fluent at all. I think most Americans who take Spanish or French classes have the same problem--they know all the rules and can fill in the blanks, but can't have a simple conversation with a native speaker.

So I decided to try to learn it by watching movies and serials, like "Prison Break" and "Lost." I was very motivated, so I kept listening and I put on the English subtitles, so if I didn't understand something, I could look it up.

I also learnt a lot of English by watching YouTube videos of Americans who are speaking about their personal experiences about topics I like. The main thing is to get in touch with the language every day; it doesn't have to be very long, 30 minutes a day is enough.

That is the way I learned English- by watching tons of videos I got used to the American accent and the way Americans speak. **It was all due to watching videos, then copying and mimicking Americans.**

At this time, I already knew 6 languages without any effort —the environment I grew up in provided those languages to me. It was kind of normal to me to be able to speak many languages.

This is how how I taught myself the other 4 languages.

The first language after English that I taught myself was Spanish. My Dominican friend came to Belgium, and I was interested in learning about his country and language. I couldn't communicate with him because his native language was Spanish, so I decided to learn it on my own with his help.

I bought "Harrap's Espagnol Methode Bilinguale" book without the CD (which is why I don't have the Spanish accent from Spain). I always asked my friend to read some words I didn't know how to pronounce. That's how I learnt the Caribbean accent.

I worked hard on my own, and after covering the whole book I wasn't really able to use the language because I never spoke it. So after summer vacations I began to speak to my friend for at least 20 minutes every day in Spanish and I got to a conversational level within 3 months. I still have to learn more, but this is how I achieved basic fluency.

I also created a Spanish world for myself: I put everything in Spanish- mobile phone, PC, radio, TV, music etc. That helped me a lot by allowing me to stay in contact with the Spanish speaking world, even though I was not in Spain or Latin America.

If you really know how I learnt with the book, here is the answer to this question. I studied the first **chapter without paying attention to the grammar;** I would just have a glance at it but I never studied it. **I focused on the dialog and the texts, because it was clearer and at least your brain absorb the patterns.** You'll see that grammar doesn't make any sense at the beginning.

So my technique is to avoid learning grammar during the first year of study for a normal language (easy one), and two years for a hard one (Japanese, for example). Normally I would listen a lot to the dialogs, but since I never had the Cd's I couldn't do it for Spanish. So I followed this book chapter by chapter without wondering about the grammar. After 6 months I understood the grammar intuitively and I could use it without having studied it. My knowledge of French also helped because the structures of both languages are similar.

I practiced a lot with new South American friends, **I forced myself to only speak Spanish** with Spanish speaking people and avoid my native language (which is French). And when you don't know a word you use it in your native language.

Then I moved on to German, I have a very good German friend so I wanted to learn it as well. I bought the book: "Assimil Allemand" and began to learn with the CD's. You just follow the CD's and read the dialogs over and over until you know them very well. You'll get to a fluent level doing this after 6 months of work. Since I knew a very similar language (Dutch/Flemish) I was able to learn basic German in 2 months and I never continued… So I can get by in German and understand a lot but I'm not very good at German.

In 2008 I went to Taipei, where I met some Italians and Japanese. It was the first time I met people **with whom I couldn't communicate**. If you think English is completely international, you're sometimes wrong. So when I came back from Taipei I decided to learn Japanese. But be careful, **learning Japanese** has nothing to do with learning another romance language if your native language is English. It will be a very big challenge, because of 3 reasons:

1) The order of the words in a sentence is completely different;
2) You have to know 3 ways to write Japanese: hiragana, katakana and kanji. About 120 symbols to memorize and 2000 to 3000 Chinese pictograms to know; and
3) You have to learn two ways of reading each kanji: unyomi and kunyomi readings. One is the Japanese reading and the other is the Chinese influenced reading.

So why do a lot of people fail while learning Japanese?
Because they aren't patient enough, and they quit too early. Do you know how many hours you should learn Japanese in order to be able to have a pretty simple conversation? I would say *between 100 to 150 hours!* To be very good at Japanese, you should spend at least 700 hours of study.

I struggled with "Assimil Japonais Sans Peine" for 3 months and I didn't get fluent at all-so I lost my motivation and left Japanese. I wanted to try an easy language: Italian

Since Italian is very similar to French I was able to learn it very fast—four months. How did I learn it in 4 months?

Using the same technique, I took the Assimil book for Italian and began to listen to and read the same dialogs over and over. I wasn't trying to remember everything but my brain sucked every pattern it encountered from that course. I just listened and read Italian during that 4 month period every day for 30 minutes. I became fluent, and I became fluent **without having studied any grammar.**

After Italian, I went back to Japanese and I was now very serious about learning the Japanese language. I downloaded the Pimsleur course and I have to say that this is the best audio course I have ever found! It gives you a solid foundation in Japanese sentences, and since you have to speak right away you get use to its structure.

But Pimsleur alone wasn't enough to really get to the next higher level. I searched on **uz-translations.net** to see what I could find. And I found the **most useful book ever for intermediate Japanese learners: An introduction to intermediate Japanese by Nobuko Mizutani.**

This book has **a good layout: main text, dialogs about the text, vocabulary list+ translations of the main text and you also have recordings!** It was perfect! I was looking for a course like this without any grammar-just a lot of content.

I finished the book and since I wasn't able to find the second book of Mizutani Nobuko, I went to **the Japanese cultural embassy** here in Brussels and borrowed it from their library.

I went through the second book and I got a very good level. After the second book I could communicate with Japanese people. The main thing I need to do now is to enrich my vocabulary.

Once I got to an intermediate level I decided to **have some fun with Japanese**:

I began to study lyrics of songs I love, watch Japanese Dramas, speak to my Japanese friend, read Japanese novels and magazines. If you have an intermediate level and want to get better you can also use the "Hiragana Times Magazine" which is available on the internet.

How did **I stayed motivated** to learn such a difficult language? **Well, I watched a lot of videos of Canadians and Americans on youtube speaking Japanese** and it gave me a lot of motivation. I always though: "if they can do it, I can also do it. I just have to believe it and work hard"!

I also learnt a lot by speaking to native speakers who came from several regions in Japan. I had a lot of fun learning Japanese because it's a special language. Very challenging. You must be passionate about it in order to really learn it. If you invest enough time and energy, though, you will learn it. But if you stay in a classroom setting, you'll never be fluent!

Although I never learned a language while in a foreign country, I think people can do it. They just have to believe it's possible and never think: "it's too hard".

The best tools to use when learning languages on your own are:

Pimsleur, Assimil, Teach Yourself, and textbooks without too many grammar explanations.

Choosing your resources is also a very important part of language learning. Don't choose the book with too much grammar explanations and few dialogs and texts.

I don't recommend people use Rosetta Stone because it doesn't work. Have you ever seen someone speaking a language fluently after using Rosetta Stone? No!

The mp3 player is also a very important tool. After you put all your audio files in it you can listen to it when you're walking or commuting to work. When you cook or wash dishes, just listen to your Assimil recordings or to a podcast. Use dead moments!

If you're learning Korean, Japanese, English or Chinese please visit Hyonwoo Sun's site: **languagecast.net** and download awesome podcast from it!

Another great suggestion I can give you is **don't listen to what others tell you.** If you learn a rare language and someone is just jealous and says there's no need to learn this language, you don't have to believe him! You have to love what you learn and you'll succeed. If I had listened to my parents, I wouldn't be able to speak Italian, Spanish or Japanese!

A last thing I would like to add--learning languages can change your life. I met Colombian friends because I'm fluent in Spanish and I spend a lot of time with them. They invited me to their home and we ate delicious Colombian food: ajiaco and aburrajado. They were so kind to me!

You feel as you are Colombian because you can directly interact with them without the obstacle of the language. You really feel very good if you can take part in their jokes and discussions. If you just knew English, you would have a hard time in discovering their world! Believe me, you can be a tourist and just visit touristic places. If you know the local language, locals will treat you as a brother and not as a stranger or just a tourist!

For more information please visit my YouTube channel: loki2504.

Thanks for reading!

Graeme, one of my new frends from Scotland, talks about his experiences with a difficult language. His piece is full of useful advice for all language learners...

Don't forget to visit Graeme at: http://www.youtube.com/user/roedgroedudenfloede and his website at:

http://www.hvadsigerdu.me

My name is Graeme and I live in Scotland. Over the past five years or so, I have been learning just one language - Danish. So, I suppose I'm slightly different to most people contributing to this book, who are probably either polyglots or hyperpolyglots, but everyone has to start with a second language before moving onto their third, fourth, fifth…!

Anyway, how shall I start? Well, I should point out that I definitely do not class myself as someone who is "naturally gifted" at languages – far from it, as, despite the many hours, days and weeks I've spent with my head buried in textbooks and MP3 players, I still see myself as being a relative beginner in the Danish language – but I'd like to share my experiences, the approaches I feel have worked, and those I feel haven't.

Like most people in primarily English-speaking countries around the world, I was brought up in an English-only environment. Well, that's not quite true. We have a second language in Scotland - Gaelic - and, while I don't speak it (although I shall return to this later) we have a TV channel that broadcasts news, children's, and various other programmes in the language. We also have Scots, which, depending upon who you speak to, is either a dialect of English or a completely separate language altogether.

Having met with non-Scots, even people from other parts of the UK, who struggle to understand what people speaking Scots are trying to say, I'm on the side of the latter, but that's another story! Suffice to say that I generally understand both English and Scots (both written or spoken), but I haven't studied Scots at all. If you're interested in seeing the differences between Scots and English (and, in particular, if you think you might understand it), take a look at the Scots version of Wikipedia: http://sco.wikipedia.org/wiki/Main_Page

Anyway, back on topic. When I was growing up, I never felt any pressure to learn a second language and, while there was a twinkle of motivation at times, I never followed it up. My parents only speak English (although my dad speaks a little German having worked there for a couple of years), as do my most of my friends, relatives and native-English speak work colleagues. I'm lucky enough to work at a university, where many of my colleagues actually speak English as a second language.

In Scotland, as a society, we tend not to learn languages seriously until we are at high school, when we are about 12-13. Even then, we are generally only offered French, German or (at a pinch) Spanish. I took French for a few years at high school, and then as part of my undergraduate degree at university, but I really don't know enough of it to have even the most basic of conversations. Furthermore, apart from the Gaelic TV channel I mentioned earlier, we tend not to receive many TV programmes in languages other than English – those that are broadcast tend to be shoved onto some nondescript digital channel at 11:30pm on a Tuesday evening.

So, fast-forward to the year 2004. For reasons I won't go into, mainly because they are so silly rather than due to space restrictions, I appeared in an article in a Danish daily newspaper. I was interviewed in Copenhagen when I visited the country on holiday. I met up with some fantastic Danes, and I generally had a good time while I was across there.

Despite being in my mid twenties at that time, this was the first time I'd been to a country where the first language was not English (neither I am, nor my family when I was growing up were, particularly interested in Spanish/French holidays like my fellow Brits). For anyone in this situation, you sometimes feel as if you're on the moon.

The stores all stock strange items with funny names and even funnier letters. You hear people pass you in the street, speaking in some sort of secret symbolic code full of glottal stops and occasional short bursts of English (mainly swear words, it has to be said). You feel a mixture of excitement and fear – mainly because you are worried someone might speak to you in this strange language that you don't understand, and thus both parties will experience the embarrassment and awkwardness that will ensue.

Yet, despite all this, **everyone** in Scandinavia understands and speaks English. Sure, some are more confident than others (young people are especially good at it), but you can generally get by using English alone.

And that's where it all started.

When the article I appeared in was published in the paper it was, obviously, completely in Danish. I bought a copy of the newspaper, but I had no chance of being able to understand the text. I had a vague intention to pick up a dictionary at a local library and painstakingly translate it word for word, but that was never going to happen. However, when I got home, I checked my e-mail: three or four different people, none of whom I knew, had read the article, seen my e-mail address, and translated it in full for my benefit.

The natural liberal in me began to chastise my own country and its education system. Why was I, someone relatively well educated (and studying for a PhD at the time) unable to speak any other language apart from my own, and yet here were Danes who had never set foot in the UK or the US who, not only spoke, wrote and read English perfectly, but often spoke it in a mid-Atlantic accent?

Of course, the obvious answer to that is that the English language has permeated most of Scandinavia through television, film, music, the Internet and other media, to such an extent there almost isn't really much point in teaching English at school. Most kids will already be able to hold down intermediate conversations before they are out of short trousers.

Danes are, I assume, as bad as those from the UK or the US at, say, speaking French or Spanish, as neither of these languages is as embedded into their environment as English is. But I didn't think laterally – instead, I decided I would play them at their own game, and learn their language! Ha! I'll show them who's boss…

Before I went to Denmark, I popped into my local bookshop and bought the Colloquial Danish textbook/CD pack. And, for the next two years...it sat on my bookshelf. Sure, I picked it up once in a while, learnt the numbers from one to ten, and one or two other silly phrases I'd spotted in the book – *Jeg er meget glad for piger* (I am very fond of the ladies) being one of them! I found myself both excited and frustrated at trying to learn the language.

Unlike the more common Latin and Germanic languages, there are no language schools in my area teaching Danish, nor could I find any Danish language groups. Actually, I wasn't completely surprised by this, given that I can't imagine there's much demand for it. The closest place I could find was a university who did evening classes in Beginners' Danish every Wednesday evening, but it was a 4-5 hour train journey there and back, plus it would cost me around £600 ($1,000-ish) for ten lessons.

So, early on, I knew I was going to be on my own. This was a major problem - anyone who knows Danish, even the Danes themselves – admit that it is a **very** difficult language to speak. Having heard spoken Norwegian and Swedish, both very similar languages to Danish, I don't think I'm speaking out of turn when I say that Danish is the most difficult of all three.

The problem is that it is spoken "at the back of the throat", with consonants being left out altogether or pronounced completely differently from what a non-Dane would expect. Additionally, as I've experienced, Danes have a real hard time understanding foreigners trying to speak Danish. That's the advantage of English – there are so many different ways of speaking it, accents, local diphthongs, cultural differences etc. that a person from Malaysia speaking English can easily understand a person from Malta speaking English with very few difficulties.

Danish is not like that – Denmark is the only place in the world where Danish is the primary language and, until recently, it has been a homogenous society. Only recently has it experienced immigration from all the different corners of the world. Hence, due to the difficult pronunciation, it isn't all that surprising that they struggle to understand "new Danes" (as they call them) trying to speak a language that, until maybe thirty years ago, was their own private code.

I'll give you an example – only last month, I visited Copenhagen on a short break. There is a direct train that runs from the airport into the city centre, so I headed to the station and found myself standing next to an old Scottish couple on holiday, and who spoke with extremely strong Scottish accents. They were chatting away to a young Danish guy in his 20s, asking him which train they should get, and making general small talk.

Despite their accents, the guy seemed to have no problem at all understanding them. After they got on their train, I asked him, in my best Danish, if he understood what they were saying. In English, he responded – "Sorry, what did you say?". Major demotivator!

Despite this setback, I'm still motivated to learn the language as fluently as I can. I can't really pinpoint when the motivational turning point was, but from around 2006/2007 onwards, I began to spend more and more time embedding myself within the language. These days, I spend around half an hour to an hour every evening "doing Danish", and maybe two hours a day at the weekend. I'll now mention some of the usual, and perhaps lesser known, resources that I use, and which could be useful for others attempting to learn Danish on their own, or any other language for that matter.

Firstly, let's start with the most obvious – textbook courses combined with Cd's/tapes. Yes, these are old fashioned and very difficult to get into when it comes to motivating yourself, but you will eventually have to turn to these at some point in your language learning journey. As Danish is not a common language, there aren't that many courses, but I've tried to purchase as many as I could when I've come across them.

These include the standard Berlitz, Teach Yourself and Colloquial series of courses. The best is the Teach Yourself Danish course, which I still access regularly, despite having bought it 4-5 years ago. The Colloquial Danish course was, as I mentioned before, the first course I bought – it's a lot more lightweight than its Teach Yourself counterpart, but still useful, while the Berlitz is extremely basic.
I don't actually believe that there is such a thing as a "bad" course or a "good" course – if you're teaching yourself on

your own, you really have to accept you're going to need at least 2-3 coursebooks, as you will find that (for example) grammar discussions presented in one book might be missing in another. You should also make sure you get the course that contains a CD or DVD, particularly for Danish which, as I've mentioned previously, is not that easy to pick up at the start!

Also, make sure you have some sort of MP3 player – ideally something like an iPod Touch or iPhone – so that you can listen to the audio or watch the videos on the move. While I've seen numerous YouTubers show off the textbooks and courses that they use, the vast majority do not discuss what I feel are even more useful than the Teach Yourself series and their ilk, and that is courses aimed at new inhabitants to the country in which your target language is spoken. I've been to Denmark several times now, and every time I pick up a language course aimed at foreigners. The advantage of these courses is that they are almost entirely in the target language (as not all readers will understand English), so you are definitely in the deep end. As a result, I would suggest waiting until you have done at least one of the Teach Yourself courses before doing one of these.

Language books aimed at children can also be helpful for adults as well! Most of these can be purchased bookstores with a website – indeed, being able to complete a transaction online on a site with no English help should be part of your course! Some of the Danish stores I've used in the past include SAXO (http://www.saxo.com/en/) and Arnold Busck (http://www.arnoldbusck.dk/).

Note that both Danish books and Danish postage are extremely expensive!

Figure 1 - Some of the Danish textbooks/courses I use. The Teach Yourself book appears on the bottom left. The two courses top left and bottom right are aimed at immigrants to Denmark learning Danish. The red book on the top right is a "child's first dictionary" – very, very handy!

I also own a couple of dictionaries in the language – one small and one large – as well as a couple of "Grammar and Reader" books, which go into much more detail than the course books, which is really handy if your coursebook fails to describe a language point in enough detail or in a confusing manner.

Then there's the Internet – the WWW has provided us with a plethora of online courses, dictionaries, translation tools, you name it and it's there…some of them are fantastic, some of them are poor. The best online course I've come across is a course called "Speak Danish" (http://www.speakdanish.dk) which appears to have been developed as a labour of love by a South African guy living in Denmark. While it's quite expensive – around £100 ($160) – it's the best course I've found, either online or offline.

If you get the chance to visit somewhere where your target language is spoken, pick up a local newspaper, magazine, or a book to bring home with you. Not only will it be a good "souvenir" of your time there, it provides enough content for you to scan through for weeks, and even months, afterward. Indeed, a newspaper that costs you $1 contains more content than a course that costs you $60 – armed with a dictionary and a grammar reader, you have at least two months worth of study resources at your disposal!

Figure 2 - Some more useful resources: A Danish tabloid newspaper, a football (soccer) magazine, and a bilingual (Danish/English) book on Hans Christian Andersen.

Finally, before I mention the last resource I use, here's a little task for you. Go to your DVD shelf, and pick up any DVD. It doesn't need to be a foreign language film – in fact, it should preferably be a film from your own country (or a film in which the primary language is your own language). Stick it on your DVD player or your computer and press play. Normally, when the menu appears, you can select either to play the film, play individual chapters of the film, or a third option, sometimes called "Options" or "Extras". Select that option.

From the next menu, you might see an option "Subtitles for the hard of hearing". Select that, and play the film. You will notice that subtitles in your own language (sometimes called captions, depending on the part of the world you live in) will appear on the screen. Why am I telling you this?

Well, because films in your target language, when combined with the captions for those who already speak the language but are hard of hearing, are a wonderful resource. If you can, try to buy films and DVD box sets of TV programmes that are not aimed at an international audience – you will hear how the real natives speak, the local dialects and idioms that you don't get in language courses. You might also enjoy the film!

Then you can switch the captions on (preferably those in the language of the film rather than those translated into your language), you can make a bit more sense of what they are saying. I must admit that films are the most powerful resource of all – not only do you understand how "real" people speak your target language, you also get an idea of the local culture, accents and so on, that you don't get anywhere else. If you're geeky like me (with a PhD in computing) you might also be able to get both the English and Danish subtitles to show up on the screen at the same time – but that's a discussion for another day!

In terms of methods, I can only praise the Gold List method as suggested by a guy on YouTube who goes by the channel name of usenetposts (http://www.youtube.com/user/usenetposts). "Uncle Davey", as he calls himself, is an English guy living in Poland, who claims to speak around 20 languages. I won't go into the method itself – he has a couple of videos where he explains it in more detail, plus it's on his web site (http://huliganov.tv/2010/04/25/repost-of-the-article-thatused-to-be-on-www-goldlist-eu-now-extended/) – suffice to say that I was a bit suspicious of it at first. However, having used it now for 2-3 years, I would definitely advise following his approach, while at the same time listening to CD's etc.

The advantage of his approach is that you are "forced" to revisit anything you've learned every two weeks, so you don't "cram" your learning into a 2-3 day block and forget it all a month later.

So, even for a relatively "minor" language, there are a plethora of resources out there if you know what to look. But that's only half the battle. Lots of language-learning YouTubers talk about having time and motivation to learn a language. In my opinion, everyone has time – if you don't have even fifteen minutes a day to scan through a coursebook or listen to an MP3 recording, you are clearly overworked and should look for another job. Motivation is more important, but I'd go further than that – I'd actually use the word "obsession".

You have to be *obsessed* with learning the language, almost to the point that you feel you **have** to be able to speak it, even if it's never going to play a role in your daily life. You have to bore your friends and family with your thoughts on how great the language is – they might think you're weird, but that's their problem. That's not to say you won't always enjoy learning it or have time to do it – indeed, there have been times in my life recently where

I've had to put Danish to the side while I sort out a few other things in my life – but you should always return to it.

So, where am I now with Danish? I mentioned earlier that I feel I'm still a beginner and, to a certain extent, I think that's true. I don't believe in abstract terms such as "fluent" or "intermediate". I've heard some people say, "I think it takes 6 months to become fluent in a language". Sorry, but that's not true. Yes, you may be able to say and understand a few stock phrases (and even 1,000 phrases counts as "a few" in my book) but are you able to understand idiomatic or less common phrases? While you will always have an accent, will people understand what you're saying?

If someone asks you what you think of Barack Obama/David Cameron/the World Cup, will you be able to provide an equivalent answer in your target language as to one you would give in your own, rather than say (or indeed write), "Um…he's…fine. He's a good/bad president/prime minister"? Based on my experiences, I believe it takes at least a year to get to a "comfortable" stage, where you're at ease when people talk to you in a particular language, and two years to reach an advanced conversational stage, where you're able to hold a meaningful conversation that goes beyond the basics.

That sounds like a long time but, once you get into the process of language learning, it certainly doesn't feel that long. I suppose I am undermining my abilities to an extent – on my recent trip to Copenhagen, I generally understood all the street conversations I heard, as well as any questions I was asked in stores. I'm rather ashamed to say that, in most cases, I spoke English, as I am still not convinced my speaking abilities are up to the task. I know I have to do it one day (in fact, I'm heading back to Denmark next month, so I'll probably do it then), so I'm disappointed I didn't make the effort. That's why I'm critical of the terms "fluent", "advanced", "intermediate" and so on.

So, what of the future? I still see myself burying my head in books, DVDs, CDs, newspapers, magazines, etc. for a few years yet. I will shortly be setting up both a blog and a new YouTube channel devoted solely to language learning, where I will try to discuss some of the concepts I have presented here in more detail.

Anyway, I think I've droned on too much for now but, before I sign off, earlier on I mentioned Gaelic. Since studying Danish, I have attended an evening class on Beginners' German, and purchased Teach Yourself books on Gaelic and Mandarin.

Unfortunately, I haven't got far with any of these languages. I thoroughly enjoyed the German classes – I had a great teacher, and I received an A at the end of the year, but I'm afraid to say I haven't been as "obsessed" with any of these other languages. I can't quite put my finger on it. Maybe because they are more common languages than Danish – lots more people are learning them. On the other hand, I admit to having a "love affair" with Danish – those latter languages are but little "flings", bits on the side to enjoy when my Danish textbook isn't around. If I'd met German before Danish, I may have had a love affair with her first. You never know. So, while I'm not giving up on any of these languages, I don't think I'll be as competent as I am in Danish.

Right, I'll sign off. *Vi ses!*

Paul Barbato's YouTube Channel is one that I have enjoyed watching. Read his piece and wonder—as I did—how he was able to say so much with so few words...

Paul Barbato: *http://www.youtube.com/user/Paulbarbato*

Hey syzygycc!

I heard you were looking for people to write about their experiences with language as a passion so I decided I would jump in and help out! Here's my essay, enjoy!:

My name is Paul. I'm always on the run.

There are over 6 billion people in this world. Do you have any idea how many that is? It's a lot. As significant as you may assume your existence is, inevitably you'll have to realize you're just 1-six-billionth of the puzzle. Nonetheless I'm not saying you should sell yourself short, I'm just saying there's an entire PLANET out there. You're not alone.

-Go see it.

My heritage and upbringing plays a strong emphasis to my linguistic enthusiasm. My parents are both hapas (half asian mixed heritage individuals) and are fluent in Korean however they never taught my sister and me how to speak it growing up. They would converse to each other in Korean and only in English to us. Due to this reason half of my life I couldn't understand what they were saying and many conversational issues arose in our family.

Growing up in the north side of Chicago, nearly half of all my classmates were second generation Americans who were bilingual. My friends would greet their parents in a variety of tongues I had never been accustomed to. In a somewhat envious way, it intrigued me. Polish, Mandarin, Urdu. It was a plethora of verbal collaboration.

When I was 17, I moved out of my home and after graduating high school I went against my parent's wishes and ran away to Korea. I was given an offer to teach English to High school students in a church school. The funny thing is, I actually ended up learning more from the students then they did from me and hence was able to finally speak Korean. After living there for a year and a half, I decided it was time to crawl back to mom and dad. When I came back I noticed three things about my parents I never knew before.

1. Dad used a lot of slang
2. Mom had a Gyungsan-do accent
3. They both used LOTS of swear words

It was like I had just unlocked a secret door to the fortress of my parents. Language made me understand and connect to them in a way I never had before. Now I'm 23 and on a mission. I want to do exactly what I did when I was 18 all over again.

-But all over the world.

There's so much to see, hear, taste, feel, jump, run, climb, laugh at, meet, enjoy, appreciate, absorb, learn and experience in this world. Like I said before, you're not alone. You have over 6 billion teachers. My job is to meet as many of then as possible and become the student as many times as possible.

-최선을 다한다

-P

--
Paul

Anthony Lauder (a/k/a FluentCzech), has a YouTube Channel that all language learners should watch, even if they are not studying Czech. Like his videos, you will find his submission both entertaining and informative...

Fluent With What You Have

Anthony Lauder
FluentCzech on Youtube
Male, 45
British, but resident in Prague, Czech Republic

I Am Not a Polyglot

Let's get one thing straight: I am not a polyglot. I am not even a talented language learner. When I sat the German language examination at school, I understood so little of the paper that at one point I turned back to the cover page to check that it really was for German. It was, as they say, "all Greek to me".

To my dismay it takes forever for new words to finally get into my brain, but only a second for them to slip back out again. When it comes to grammar, things are even worse: I can read a grammar book for two hours straight, understand everything, then the moment I close the book I can't recall a darned thing. In short, I am a complete language dunce.

I have always envied polyglots and their linguistic abilities. I have always wished I could be just like them. Heck, to be honest, I often wished I could become fluent even in one foreign language! However, my complete failure with languages at school convinced me that my brain simply wasn't wired the right way. So, I gave up on languages early on and focused on the few things I actually was good at: throwing myself into mathematics, computer science, and other such "logical" pursuits.

Living in the Land of Polyglots

Around the age of 30, though, I found myself living in Luxembourg. This is an intimidating country for a language-dud such as me: every few years schools in Luxembourg switch the languages in which they teach, so that most children are fluent in at least four languages by the time they are 18.

Surrounded by a country full of polyglots, I decided to give languages another go. For a few months in Luxembourg I took a bunch of classes and bought a couple of books, and eventually picked up a tiny little bit of Luxembourgish. It was just enough to struggle along in very basic conversations with kind old grannies and accommodating shopkeepers.

Encouraged by this minor success, I then committed to learning French (a prevalent language in Luxembourg) by hitting the textbooks for an hour or two every day, listening to audio tapes on my way to the office, and talking in broken French during breaks at work. To be honest, the results were only a little better than at school. It was only ever "survival French". Still, I "upgraded" myself from being completely hopeless at languages to merely being very bad at them.

My Search for the Polyglot Secret

When my two years in Luxembourg were over, I looked back on my new-found language abilities and was dismayed at the amount of effort I had put in for even modest gains. All that hard work, and so little to show for it, confirmed my suspicions that polyglots were either genetically different from the rest of us, or they employed some secret trick to quick fluency.

Since there was nothing I could do about my genetic makeup, I clung to the hope that polyglots were indeed relying on a hidden secret. Once this idea was fixed in my mind, I lusted after finding out exactly what that secret was. I bought just about every language course I could find. I spend a fortune on books, audio tapes, and language classes. I committed to diving with all my energy into all of them, until I finally worked out just what made polyglots different.

Unfortunately, one of two things would invariably happen:

1. I would run out of steam part way through and decide this one book (or audio course, or teacher) didn't hold the "secret to fluency" after all.

2. On very rare occasions, I would actually reach the end of a book (or set of tapes, or classes) and think "well, I finished that, but I still don't feel fluent".

In either case, I would become discouraged for a few

weeks, then regain my enthusiasm and make another trip to the bookstore (or language school) in search of the one book (or tape, or class) that actually would reveal the secret to me. This search went on for years, and although I picked up bits of various languages along the way, none of those books, or tapes, or classes ever did tell me "the polyglot secret".

When the Hours Feel Like Minutes

When I had almost given up hope, I found what I was looking for. Perhaps surprisingly, the secret to successful language fluency came to me not from a polyglot but from a musician.

At the end of an exhilarating performance, the late great jazz pianist Michel Petrucciani was asked the secret of his incredible talent. This is what he said: "Whenever I spend an hour at the piano it feels like a minute, and whenever I spend a minute away from the piano it feels like an hour."

That is when it all "clicked" for me. Up until that very moment I had always seen language learning as hard work. Sure, there was usually an adrenalin filled flurry of excitement at the start, but a few weeks in the clock always seemed to move very slowly when I was studying languages, and I could hardly wait for each session to end. All the language lessons, the books, the tapes and in fact the whole process of language learning were all an unpleasant chore for me.

Quite simply, I didn't love language learning, and if I am honest with myself I didn't even love languages. I was merely in lust with the idea of being fluent. I realized right then and there that I was in a desperate rush to get to fluency as quickly as possible but I would never actually make it because I hated the journey that was necessary to get there.

I realized that the difference between people like me and polyglots is that polyglots don't just lust after results; they are in love with languages and the whole language learning process. I only had lust, and lust fades. Polyglots have love, and if nurtured, love grows. As with Michel Petrucciani, when polyglots are immersed in languages the hours feel like minutes, and when away from language the minutes feel like hours. For them, the hands on the clock don't crawl, they fly by.

How to Become an Overnight Success

To confirm this, I did something very simple: I started listening to what polyglots actually had to say about themselves. I watched videos, I read books, I joined forums, and I spoke to polyglots face to face. What I found was that are very few Daniel Tammets out there[1]. Many of the very polyglots we celebrate as "gifted" actually see themselves as moderate learners. Some have even remarked that describing their accomplishments as "a gift" actually undermines the tremendous amount of effort it took for them to get there.

From the outside looking in, then, we only see the polyglots' enviable achievements and not the many years

---

[1] Daniel Tammet is a high-functioning autistic savant, made famous by a documentary showing him achieving basic fluency in Icelandic in just one week.

of effort that went into them. One very well known polyglot recently told me that he has being obsessed with languages since the age of six. Since he is now in his thirties his outstanding polyglottery is due to more than twenty years of pure passion for languages, with continual and never ending improvement along the way.

His story reminds me of the comedian Eddie Cantor, who once said "It took me twenty years of hard work to become an overnight success". If we want the same "overnight success" we can have it too. It'll just take us ten or twenty years to get there.

If you can commit to full time immersion in a language you can probably speed that up a little, but most people have busy lives and can only devote an hour or two a day to language learning. Still, an hour and a half a day, every day, for twenty years should get you the results you seek.

A quick calculation shows this to be around 10,000 hours of dedicated effort to reach language mastery. Now, it turns out that the same 10,000 hours figure is pretty consistent for mastery of just about anything. The recent book "Outliers" by Malcolm Gladwell introduces us to decades of research searching for the elusive secret to what makes some people the top performers in music, science, medicine, chess, and so. Time and again, the researchers discovered that the only consistent theme was 10,000 of hard work, often starting from infancy right through to adulthood. In short, the most accomplished people worked harder and for longer, and never gave up, no matter what.

Language Bed-Hopping

This idea of never giving up, no matter what, is vital. Quitting when the initial excitement wears off has certainly always been my own stumbling block. Not just with languages either. I can't count the number of times I have started out giddy with excitement for playing some new musical instrument, participating in a new sport, exploring my well-hidden artistic side, mastering some foreign language, and (to be honest) even in romantic relationships.

Every time I would dive right in with all my passion and an expectation it would last forever. Then, invariably, within three months the heady excitement would vanish. Once the "chemistry" had gone, I would jump onto something new to rekindle the flame. Of course, three months later the magic of that faded too.

You see, the first three months of just about any kind of endeavor make for a very exciting time. The lust for results helps us keep up a tremendous pace. During this "beginner's stage", the brain is like a sponge, and we become giddy with our initial flurry of success. It seems like we are going from zero to hero, and there is no stopping us. "Wow, at this pace I will be fluent in another three months".

Then, without warning, progress comes grinding to a halt. The point where lust fades and reality hits is the beginning of the intermediate stage of learning a language.

People report that they feel "stuck", have "reached a plateau", and need help getting over the "intermediate hump". Unfortunately, the intermediate stage isn't a hump to get over, but rather a long term commitment to living with uncertainty and making progress that is often too subtle to motivate you on its own.

The kind of "no matter what" commitment that is needed here lacks the heady excitement that comes from the beginner's stage. It is no surprise, then, that the intermediate stage of language learning often becomes associated with pain, frustration, and boredom. As a result, plenty of people become serial monogamists: switching to a new language every few months to keep the excitement alive. Having following precisely this path of "language bed-hopping" in the past, I know very well that ultimately it is unfulfilling.

Falling in Love

I used to always apologize for my slow progress: "I am ashamed to say I have been learning Czech for six months already". Then I started to ask myself "Why be ashamed? Most people give up when the going gets tough. You should be proud of your commitment."

And with that, I learned to let go of the thirst for short-term excitement and go for contentment instead. This is where you allow yourself to slowly fall in love with languages and the whole process of language learning, and get a different kind of satisfaction that comes from long term commitment and slow and steady progress.

That commitment, I have found, is the secret to language fluency: you have to surrender to the language and allow yourself to slowly fall in love with it so that all the time you spend with it is a pleasure rather than a chore. Just as with Michel Petrucciani as his piano, it will feel like minutes rather than hours and even after thousands of hours of effort you will be able to look back and feel amazed at how much progress you have made and how much you enjoyed the experience.

I have now been learning Czech for quite a few years, and I have completely fallen in love with both the language, and the whole process of living with the language. Various people describe this as like being married to a language, where you stick at it, through good and bad, and allow the journey to become its own reward. Having said that, if it is like marriage, then I must admit to maintaining very close and long term friendships with other languages that in some cases are bordering on polygamy. Still, my love for Czech remains unwavering and the process of transformation into a language lover has without doubt rescued me from my lack of natural abilities. It has enabled me to gain a level of fluency that previously always eluded me.

Fluent With What You Have

Fluency is a slippery term, but my own definition of fluency is where a native speaker does not have to modify the way they talk in order to accommodate your own abilities. By this definition, I am pretty fluent in Czech in most everyday situations (at the bank, train station, in shops, and so on).

Despite this, I lack many of the tens of thousands of idiomatic phrases that a native Czech will have grown up with. Czech don't "cross their fingers", they "hold their thumbs". They don't "walk on egg shells", they "dance among eggs", and they are never "as happy as a clam" but "as happy as a flea".

I also lack the cultural background that Czechs have grown up with and take for granted. At parties, I am soon lost when Czech friends are swapping stories and jokes that reference TV shows or songs from their youth, or when they talk seriously about political or cultural figures that are unknown to me.

It is because of this idiomatic and cultural gap that I really appreciate the comment I once heard that you are are "forever intermediate". In other words, there is always more to learn. Accepting this allows you to let go of the certainty that comes from textbooks, and ultimately live comfortably, and even thrive, in an environment filled with uncertainty.

Here is some advice I gave on the HTLAL Forum[2] to somebody who felt stuck in their language learning, and wanted to know how to progress beyond their current textbooks:

> "It is time to put the textbooks away and start diving into authentic material. It is a big step, though, since you will no longer have the comfort of explanations that the textbooks provide. Instead, it really can feel like being thrown into a swimming pool and told to sink or swim. It can be quite scary at first, but after just a few months you will achieve one of the most important skills for

---

[2]   http://how-to-learn-any-language.com/forum/

language learning: getting used to living with uncertainty.

So, find a native text (such as a magazine or book) that is just a bit too advanced for you ... and just start reading. Take a highlighter pen and mark all the words and phrases you don't know - but don't bother looking them up. It helps if you have audio too for the same text, since you can then listen to it repeatedly and see which words and phrases really stick out as those you wish you knew.

Then do the same with another text, and another. After a couple of days you will notice that some of the highlighted things seem to bug you (maybe because they are repeated so much, or really blocked your comprehension) and others seem irrelevant after all. Look up only the ones that bug you, and put them on a list. When you have studied that list, read those same text again.

Then do it all over again with a whole new set of very slightly harder texts. Then again with another set of texts, and then again, and again, and again. For months, or years if need be, until one day you find you have reached the stage where you are reading the daily newspaper or novels with more than 95% comprehension. That day does come, trust me, it just doesn't feel like it is ever going too, because the improvements along the way are so gradual and almost at a subconscious level. There are two things going on here:

1: You are replacing short periods of intensive deliberate study, with much longer periods of slow acquisition. I have seen folks get very uncomfortable with this, since reading and highlighting doesn't seem like "real work". You just have to trust that you are absorbing things, and not be too tempted back to the textbooks (apart from a dictionary and occasional dips into a grammar to confirm things)

2: You are preparing your brain to live in the real world, where you really do have to be able to live with uncertainty. When the repairman comes around to replace the pump in your heating system you may only understand 70% of what he is talking about, but the immersion described here will have armed you for thriving in that kind of situation.

The other step relates to output. This is where you have to get used to looking foolish. The work with texts and audio mentioned above will have prepared you for the uncertainty you face in the real life conversations, now you have to build up the confidence - and that just comes through lots and lots of exposure. Practice a whole bunch of scenarios in your head, and then go out and live them in real life with a native speaker.

You will mess up more than you could have anticipated, and get embarrassed. I always say to people that each time you get embarrassed in this way you are one step closer to fearless conversation. So, you have to get back on the horse, and practice on your own, and then get out to the battlefield again. After a few months your confidence will have soared without you realising it, and it will feel perfectly natural to talk about just about anything in your target language - even if you are missing vocabulary, because you can always ask questions, explain things in other ways, and be fluent with what you have."

Perseverance and the right methodology yield the best results. Stephen Eustace explains what works for him...

Stephen Eustace, from Greenhills, Dublin, Ireland

Okay, I will try to keep out the "padding" and get straight to the point. My personal story!

I was born in Dublin in 1969 and grew up in a south western suburb called Greenhills. Anyone who has been to Ireland will soon realise that it is supposed to be bilingual with Irish as a first language. Ironically this was my first exposure to a "foreign language". From 1973 until 1981 I learned Irish alongside English, Maths and Geography and all the rest. Irish was used as the language of authority and some phrases are forever burned in my mind. We always had to ask to go to the toilet in Irish "An bhfuil cead agam dul go dtí an leithreas?" Besides counting, "what's my name," and "what bread and butter is," my Irish didn't really progress very much from 1981. This became evident at my first day at secondary school. There the new Irish teacher greeted us with pure disdain and disgust. He asked us what we could say in Irish, and was met with 24 mute, scared 12 year olds. He picked this one guy named Frank, and asked him to turn around and ask the boy behind to give him the book. At which, he turned around obediently and said "Gimme the book!" Now outraged the teacher yelled "NO!!! YOU MORON, IN IRISH!!! FOR GODS SAKE!!!" This phrase was then burned into my mind out of fear; "tabhair dom an leabhair!"

I, like the rest of my classmates was gripped in fear for the remaining five years of secondary school. Grammatical errors were always met with severe reprimands, and the teaching of the language was always the same—grammar and tables of verbs. My mother (who was born in 1944) went to an all Irish school in Dublin, and for the same reason (being terrified by the nuns and learning history in what was to her a useless language) did not pass on any love of Irish to me. I decided (in retrospect and erroneously) that I would never learn this language properly and left school for university in 1986 with basic conversational Irish which soon began to fade.

In contrast to Irish, on day one of French we were greeted with a pleasant "Bonjour mes enfants!!" and we had to answer "Bonjour Monsieur". I can still hear the sing-song answer of 24 pre-pubescent boys in my head. We did of course learn grammar and verbs, but this was interspersed with stories of France, French bread and Bordeaux wines. One school trip to Paris, and a chance friendship with a French exchange student called Nathalie (who stayed with our neighbours) and I quickly developed a love for French. I used to tune into LW and listen, desperately trying to understand what was being said. Another four years had passed, and being quite a loner at school, I would practice speaking French while washing the dishes. I continued writing to Nathalie and used to screech with Joy as the huge letters with French magazine cut outs, recipes with some of the ingredients included and even corrections for the mistakes in my previous letter arrived. I continued this for some time and even found another pen pal, a female Nurse from Paris who even complimented me on my good French. I last saw Nathalie in 1985, and still remember how heads would turn as we walked around together laughing and speaking in, French.

My love of French is a testament to my French teachers who brought this language to life for me. I started University, and even though my French was much better than my Irish, it too began to fade.

As part of my chemistry degree I had to study a "translation" course from technical German to English with the aid of a dictionary—fat lot of good! I got my degree in 1990, and started my PhD in Chemistry. Our University was a very international place with lots of students from France, the Netherlands, Germany, Italy. I have always been fascinated by travel, foreign places and foreign people.

Enter the Italians.

It happened that five exotic students, who were very well dressed and who presented themselves well (but had a very poor command of the English language) made their appearance at the school. Arrogantly, one of my colleagues at university disparaged their Italian and wondered how they could dare turn up not knowing English! As far as I was concerned, I secretly decided to go to Italy the following year, and I was not going to be singled out as a foreigner!

What gave me the real push was my interrail trip in 1991. I left Ireland, and travelled first to London, then over sea and rail to Saarbrucken, where a friend of mine was enrolled in a computer course. Again, my friends and acquaintances had informed me that "all Germans speak English," but to my surprise and dismay I hailed a cab and found that my taxi driver only spoke German! After a lot of hand gestures and strained communication, I arrived at my destination—the University of Saarbrucken. The rest of my journey brought me through Germany, Switzerland, Italy, Austria and France, where I ended my holiday while spending time with a French friend of mine.

My French, although rusty, was the only language that I could (badly) communicate in. Having been exposed to the beauty and variety of the cultures in these countries (while appreciating any English speakers I met), I realised my own inadequacy and the arrogance of many English speakers. Along the way, a German friend had taught me how to count in German and another friend taught me some rudimentary phrases in Italian. This was not good enough!

Back in Dublin, I received a gift voucher for Eason's, a famous bookshop there. I cashed it in for the BBC language course "Buongiorno Italia". While everybody was watching the usual rubbish on TV, I would work my way through the course booklet and the tapes; repeating, memorizing and practising. I still remember my first day sitting on my sisters bed, book in one hand and the remote control of the stereo in the other. I thought to myself that this was a monumental, if not impossible task for a 22 year old. I knew not ONE word of Italian, and my goal was full fluency in six months! Lesson 1, ordering a coffee, "Un cafè per favore!" …..

The book instructed never to progress to lesson 2 unless Lesson 1 had been mastered. The results were slow, with lots of repetition; and after I completed lesson 5, I had to return to lesson 1 as lesson 6 was too difficult.

I finally reached lesson 10, and even then had to return to lesson 1 again!! After arriving in Milan in January, 1992, I began at once to practice my rudimentary "shopping Italian." I had managed after those 10 lessons, however, to build up to a sufficient level to have a rudimentary conversation! Back in Dublin, lessons 10-20 seemed to go a little easier, even though I was forced once again to return to lesson 1 and work my way back up to 20 again. The format was the same 1) listen passively 2) listen actively 3) listen actively again, and 4) hide the book and try without the text.

The book also contained some listening comprehension, reading and grammar. I followed the lessons, and the practice conversations where they prompted a reply. The next book in the series was also from BBC, "L'Italia dal vivo" where conversations (including mistakes made by natives) were recorded along with some excercises. This book was also more or less the same format, repeat some words, listen to a conversation, then finally the conversation practice with prompts. The 20 lessons only took me 2 months to master, in contrast to the 4 months needed to achieve the basics.

On April the 27th I arrived in Padova Italy, and it was also 27°C (80.6°F)! I arrived with 2 fellow Irish students, and on day two we were sent off for free language courses. I was sent to the advanced class! My goal while there for all 3 months was NOT to speak English AT ALL. This meant speaking to some of my fellow Irishmen in Italian, and I must say the first 2 weeks were hard! People had to repeat things and constantly explain; and some even got angry as I stuck to my guns, but my rule was: NO

ENGLISH!! I explained to the natives that there were plenty of other people willing to speak English to them if they wanted to practice.

One day, two weeks into my trip, the fog of not understanding lifted, and   like the feeling of a hangover going away after a night of drinking, the need for people to speak S L O W L Y and to constantly repeat things became unnecessary. It was amazing. I could understand, I could speak, and I was now having conversations. On July 27th I left Italy, fully fluent in Italian! When I returned to Ireland, I began to dabble in learning other languages, and took a trip to the University Language Lab and started learning Dutch. Although I practiced with a Dutch student who was in our lab at the time, my Dutch never progressed beyond, "hello, how are you?" and such simple phrases.

My Italian got dusted off on a number of occasions, but I took it upon myself to ALWAYS learn a few phrases in the language spoken wherever I go. Most notably, in 2001 I went to Stockholm, Sweden, and between reading my phrasebooks, listening and observing, I actually earned free drinks for myself and a friend because of my "good Swedish". I then started to bring phrase books with me everywhere. To date, I can order a beer in English, French, Italian, Spanish, Portuguese, Swedish, Czech, siSiwati, Japanese, Hungarian, Finnish, Catalan, Greek, Dutch and German!

Rolling the clock forward a little to October, 2001, I moved to Den Haag in the Netherlands, again having a fresh opportunity to obtain fluency in another language.

I joined formal classes, which really did nothing except drill grammar, so I turned to my old method--the Cds, the books and repetitive practising. I always repeated any chapters I was unsure of, and starting all over again if necessary. Within 3 months, I had a job, and in a room full with 100 new employees, introduced myself in Dutch: "Hi my name is Stephen, I am living in Den Haag for 3 months but I am Irish." I got a round of applause on my excellent Dutch. Of course, 8 years later, I still get compliments, as I make less mistakes and my accent is more rounded. The learning rate decreases over time as we have less to learn, so during those first three months I had made astonishing progress—probable acquiring 60-70% of my current Dutch vocabulary!

In 2005, I went to Brussels for the weekend and fell in love with a Wallonian (French Speaker) who insisted I speak French. I had basically decided at this point that my French was more or less dead in the water, but faced with HAVING to speak it to him (and all his friends and family) meant that within four months I was able to fully revive my French and even advanced to a very high level!

Learning languages my way is by means of focusing on a few key phrases:

- Numbers, odd words, simple greetings
- Shopping language; simple ordering, using numbers, and learning from audio and visual cues; for example, seeing a sign "Uien" in front of the onions in the supermarket in Rotterdam would generally imply that Uien is Dutch for Onions! No classroom involved
- Simple conversation with English as a crutch

- Conversation broken by occasional "How do you say?" It is important to say "How do you say" in the language you are using; even better would be to point to the object and ask what it is.

Refinement, listening, reading and learning, using Dutch (or whatever language) subtitles to learn and expand vocabulary. This final phase improves fluency!

Our first submission from a native Hakka speaker! Next up is Skrik, a resident of Taiwan.

You can find him on YouTube at: www.youtube.com/shriekshriek

Hello, I am Skrik from Taiwan. Before I start, I'd like to mention a little about my lingual background. I was born and raised in a family speaking Hakka, Taiwanese and Mandarin Chinese. I am the 'Benjamin' (youngest boy) in my family. I have two sisters who are way older than me, so much so, that oftentimes I've felt like the only child with one dad and three mums since I was a child.

I couldn't speak until I was three (3) years old, that is, based on my mum's observation I did nothing but roll my eyeballs. Also, she said that I looked like I was constantly thinking about which language amongst those three spoken around me I wanted to speak.

For a long period of time, a very long time, I enjoyed playing alone. I enjoyed being that way for several years from school age to puberty. Perhaps this is one of the reasons why, even now as a grown-up, I experience awkward moments sometimes not knowing how to behave properly whilst spending time with others.

I didn't go to kindergarten; instead, I went directly to primary school. None of us three kids did, in order to save money, I suppose. When I decided to join in this Polyglot Project weeks ago, the first thing that came to my mind was, surprisingly, a coin! I still remember once I went to my uncle's house. There, I saw a collection of coins from my cousin's sister which seemed to show the world and how rich their life was, travelling around the world every year, et cetera.

My one and only foreign coin was a gift attached to a certain milk powder can from a grocery store. I treated it as my lucky charm ever since I got it around 12. It's now rusty, of course, due to oxidization for more than a decade. As I write this, I am holding it, the 5 dollars coin from Canada. One side, a maple icon, the very symbol of Canada and on the other side is the figure of Queen Elizabeth II.

Such a seemingly inherent personality has brought me into more collections. Such collections reach into a world that is either exotic or unknown. A plastic bottle of jelly that I ate, with Japanese words inscribed on it, a picture of the Thai word 'Welcome' written horizontally that I took from an inn on my journey one time, books I bought, films I saw, and even now the numbers of my buddy-buddy foreign friends categorized by nationality, Hahaha!

I haven't studied Linguistics or any degree related to languages yet. However, I have obtained a Bachelor of Computer Science degree. This opened a world of programming languages, where I got an unexpected harvest so as to look into human languages and into myself as well in a very scientific way - not a good-or-bad issue, just a plain fact.

Before University, my life seemed fine but there was chaos inside, so much so, that I had no clue what I wanted to do with my life. Later on, nearly six years of a painful spell with computers taught me a lesson that I will only do things I love in my life. And yes, I love Psychology, Human Languages that connect with real people rather than cold machines and without question their overlapped section, Psycholinguistics, Neurolinguistics and so on. So here I am.

How did you Learn your Languages?

After picking up several languages since 2006 or so, (not in a too serious way though) I learnt to learn a language by Language Families.

1) Word Order - (could VSO or VOS, even OVS or OSV, possibly be a heritage from the last human civilization before ours this time?),
2) Alphabet - (i.e. the writing system) I hand write by myself,
3) Pronunciation - Basically, the pronunciation of each letter and pronunciation rules in combination in all cases.
4) Expansive Immersion through sentences,

articles, songs and whatsoever to grow knowledge.

In my case, I tend to analyze them more than I speak them. Unfortunately, I stopped it before process 4) and then went on to another newer language and began another loop from 1) to 3) over and over again. I guess 'focus' surely needs to be a big lesson for me when it comes to 'learning' things. But anyways, I am no linguist yet but I am a language lover, undoubtedly.

How has the study of Foreign Languages enriched your life?

The thinking. Always the thinking. The thinking has changed.

I fell into an aphasia-like symptom roughly one or two months after I set about my polyglot self-learning in 2006. I was too obsessed with it that I started brand new languages, about 10 or so, at the same time and in a short time. Probably something went on in my brain that as certain things came to my mind, certain images or the sounds of corresponding names in two or three different languages all coming together before I uttered whichever unconsciously. Or most of the time, I simply stayed numb and thinking. It's hard to explain.

During that time, I even had some flashbacks. When I was a kid, for a time, I slept with my folks in the same room. Before getting ready to sleep, we always said to each other 'good night, father' 'good night, mother' 'good night, my dear son'(and yes, we said it in English). Such image together with the vivid greetings popped up right the moment I learnt this particular phrase 'good night' in certain new language. Very strange, but well at least in an optimistic way! I guess it's sort of like the old Czech proverb, 'you are as many times a person as many languages you speak.' Can this be microcosmic?

Although different races of different languages have their own different ways to express and some languages dying out whilst some new ones evolve, the main core behind all these remains the same. As human beings, we can fear, we can cheer, we feel angry at times and we feel cozy at times. We might want to be thought of highly by those we think highly of. We hate injustice coming upon us. We are exactly the same in this regard and the basic elements to maintain a healthy life are really few and simple: food, sleep, and taking care of each other (i.e. love). That's it.

How has the study of foreign languages enriched my life? I might say, by it I've become more comprehensive and less judgmental, or rephrasing it: I've become happier. No one is perfect, I know. I'm still learning though. Here, I would like to have that proverb in my version, "The more languages one speaks, a more pure person one is to be." A macroscopic is? Ha!

Who influenced you?

Always the traveler, Ian Wright, a funny British fellow. I don't know him personally but his character is somewhat my own and I want to develop fully. In one word, I want to be like him. Confident, curious, humorous, not stressing people but surprising them, overall a child-like man with non-stop positive power to explore this world the way everyone does in childhood. I fancy travelling all over the world some day as I believe every language lover does too but before that I feel an urge to learn several dominating world languages and learn them well at first today.

Raashid Kola weighs in with this fine contribution. An encounter with a hyperpolyglot at the age of 16 made a lasting impression on this native Gujarati speaker...

Raashid can be found on YouTube at: sigendut1

"Polyglottery in Progress"

Before I begin delineating my experience of language learning I would like to thank Claude for coming up with the ingenious idea of the "Polyglot Project", a wonderful opportunity for us to share our experiences and methods, in our endeavors to become consummate communicators in our chosen tongues.

I intend to be laconic and not subject readers to a prolix as brevity is the key to maintaining reader's interest. I will briefly provide a description of myself, not something which I find easy as I am self contained, unassuming and self effacing by nature.

I am a 37 year old male of Indian extraction born and brought up in the UK; my mother tongue is Gujarati which is spoken in the Western Indian state of Gujarat.

Being born into an immigrant family within the UK I was blessed with having a mother tongue other than English. However, as is common amongst children of immigrants we become overwhelmed and absorbed by the host culture and prefer to use the dominant language in this case, English. Through my experience I have found that people will avoid speaking their mother tongue as they feel they will be perceived as "inferior". I as a child was no different and only in my late teens appreciated the rich diversity which language learning can offer.

My first real exposure to a foreign language other than the spoken environment at home and the poorly presented French classes at school was when I was approximately 14. There was a Malaysian boy in my class, whose father was a student at the local higher education institute, he taught me some basic Malay words and a single sentence which laid the foundation for learning, this is something which continued and developed organically later into my twenties. I never really considered my mother tongue as anything "special" as I had become blasé to this whole experience.

When I was 16 I befriended a middle aged man who lived in our city temporarily with an Indian family that I often visited. He was a Caucasian English man and was highly cultured and refined, well-traveled and spoke in the region of 19 languages, which I found incredulous at the time. He could even speak my mother tongue Gujarati! I asked what motivated him to learn and master so many languages.

He replied that as a child he accompanied his auntie on numerous trips abroad and spent significant periods in various countries. He later spent a few years studying in Germany and North India; such periods of immersion helped him to assimilate such languages. He once explained to me that he had a strong inclination to understand what was going on around him and even had to understand the radio broadcasts being transmitted in the background. This guy subconsciously sowed a seed which gradually came into fruition. I later imagined being fluent and being able to switch effortlessly from one language to another.

I think it is now time to fast forward to the present and outline the benefits and my approach in learning a new language. Before I progress any further I would like dispel what I consider to be myths and fallacies about language learning. We often hear people say that a person is "gifted" and has the intrinsic ability or "talent" to learn and speak languages. I vehemently contest this notion and feel that it is really a question of "interest" and "application" and ideally regular exposure. How much interest do we have and how hard are we prepared to apply ourselves is the real key to success.

In my view those individuals that went onto become "heavyweight hyper polyglots" were fortunate enough to have been exposed to various languages at a very young age, and does not necessarily imply ability. For instance most of us would have heard of the Berlitz publishing house a trusted brand name for language learning materials. Charles Berlitz was a member of the last generation of this notable family which managed the Berlitz brand and reportedly spoke 30 languages before his death in 2002.

Charles grew up in a household in which he was spoken to in a different language by relatives and domestic servants on the instruction of his father. His father spoke to him in German, his grandfather Maximilian the founder of the Berlitz institute spoke to him in Russian and his nanny in Spanish; by the time he had reached adolescence he was fluent in 8 languages. He later recollected of his childhood delusion of everyone in the world having their own language and wondered why he did not have one of his own.

We all know the benefits of language learning and I don't wish to sound patronising. However, I would like to note some of the benefits for those who are considering studying a new language and the enriching experience it can bring.

The obvious benefit is access to a new culture, a new world an opportunity to interact and meet and learn from different people. You may even experience "fame" on a micro scale with native speakers. Whenever I visit Indonesia I am often met with intrigue and fascination by the locals.

It is an oft quoted fact that language learning helps to develop "grey matter" in our brains. Grammar in every language works differently, so if person speaks 4 different languages it is as if his or her brain has been rewired to think in 4 different ways, therefore, enhancing cognitive versatility.

Learning a language whether it is just to a basic conversational level, can be immensely rewarding and can enhance self esteem and confidence. I suggest that you don't forget to mention it on your résumé or curriculum vitae as we call it here in the UK, which shows that you are not one dimensional and cosmopolitan in outlook.

I will now discuss my methods for learning languages arguably the most interesting segment of this essay.

Whenever I study a language I attempt to deconstruct sentences, to understand the syntax and the linguistic typological structure, or quite simply the word order. English follows the subject-verb-object (SVO) pattern. For instance, in English we say "Adam is sitting on the chair". I am currently exploring Turkish and the pattern is subject-object-verb (SOV) therefore, in Turkish "Adam on chair is sitting". I find this particularly useful as at least I know that the structure of the sentence is correct and half the battle has been won, although I may have conjugated the verbs incorrectly or used an inappropriate noun.

Whenever I try to construct sentences I study the grammar and try to produce phrases. In some languages you will find verbs in the infinitive form, a verb in a "neutral state" and you will need to conjugate, or to modify the verbs to reflect the 1st, 2nd and 3rd persons etc. For instance, the Spanish verb to eat is "comer" this is in an infinitive state, and you will need to conjugate the verb to reflect the correct usage for the 1st person, the present tense being "como, I eat" the 2nd person informally would be "comes, you eat" and so on and so forth.

When studying grammar I suggest "snatching "moments throughout the course of the day as opposed to spending hours trying to crack a language. I sometimes only spend

15 minutes per day and reread on occasions to consolidate what I have already learnt.

I also try to gradually incorporate new words into my vocabulary. I try to create sentences including those new words, as the best way to understand the connotation of a word is to use it in its correct context. This leads me to a problem which very many of us face, that of retaining new words. The best way to remember new words is by associating them which something which is already deeply rooted in our brains, and to be creative in producing mental images, the more absurd the image the easier it is to recollect.

For instance this morning I came across the Turkish verb "eritmek" which means to melt or dissolve. I imagined myself being exposed to the scorching heat of the sun in Eritrea; hence the use of the first syllable of the verb which corresponds with the name of the country. .

I will provide another example through the Javanese language which is widely spoken in Indonesia. Javanese is a hierarchal language and recognises social class, age and status, the use of the language has to be tailored according to your audience. The term to sell in Javanese in the *Krama* high form is "sade" and in the *Ngoko* low form it is "adol". Readers who are familiar with 1980's music may recollect Sade a British smooth jazz, soul performer who topped the charts with numerous hits. To help me retain these words I image Sade selling dolls in a market stall, you can now see how I have correlated both linguistic forms in a single mental image.

Our brains are highly sophisticated and each of us has a "right" and "left" side which perform different functions. The right side of the brain is concerned with rhythm, imagination, daydreaming, spatial awareness, colour and dimension. The left side of our brains are utilised for processing words, producing lists, managing numbers, and understanding sequence and lines.

To help retain words, if we can engage both parts of our brains through creative mental imaging and association can help us achieve this objective. Many readers may have come across a neurological condition known as Synesthesia. Synesthesia is a condition were patients use more than one sense in their perception of the world, such as sight, touching which is then transformed into texture. Therefore, for the most of us a word is simply a word. For synesthetes a word may contain colour, texture--even taste-- which causes words to be deeply rooted in their memory.

I consider myself to be discursive and have been known to "hop" around topics and subjects in daily conversations. I will now deviate slightly from my main discussion to substantiate my position about nurturing a form of Synesthesia to help us remember new words.

Daniel Tammet is a well known British Autistic Savant, who as a child suffered an Epileptic seizure this consequently caused high levels of brain performance with respect to words and numbers. In 2004 he recited pi a mathematical number to over 22,500 places in 5 hours from memory. In an interview with David Letterman, he explains that he visualises numbers and experiences colour, texture, and shapes which help him retain and recall such numbers.

I try to nurture a form of Synesthesia to harness both sides of my brain in remembering words, using mental imaging and association. I must confess that I still do forget words, and on occasions when do I recollect them can't always associate them, but generally I find this method far more effective than rote learning.

The internet has created a new avenue for language learners which previous generations were deprived of; we can now watch clips on youtube of the languages which are of interest to us. I intermittently watch clips and I am not overly concerned if I don't understand as I am gradually becoming familiar with the sounds and subconsciously learning. My beloved 2 and ½ year daughter Sara likes to watch cartoons in Arabic which often has an audience of 2 people!

There are various language forums on the internet such as www.turkishclass.com , www.spanishdict.com where you can post questions or construct sentences and have them reviewed by advanced and native speakers.

Finally I would like to conclude that learning language is something to be enjoyed. I am not learning a language to be assessed or to make a point to anyone, but simply for my own development. I wouldn't worry too much if we are unable to remember what we have studied or can't produce an instant response to a question in our target language, the most important thing is that we are trying. I feel that language learners should be congratulated and applauded as we may have learnt a new phrase or a word, which we didn't know before, so this is definitely progress.

Before I allow you to go I wish to apologise for subjecting you to a monologue as my intention was genuinely to be laconic! I hope you have enjoyed reading this essay as much as I have enjoying scribing it! I will now leave you in peace and take the sign "Polyglottery in Progress" off my front door!

Raashid Kola.

Coventry,
England, UK.

This next author prefers to remain anonymous. I believe she has succeeded in dispelling the myth that foreign language acquisition needs to be expensive...

The Polyglot Project

For me, choosing a language to learn is often the most difficult step. There is only one reason for this: there are too many. All languages can be interesting and useful-- even dead and artificial languages. So, choosing one language to study, *just one*, is an entirely daunting task in of itself. All I can do is decide which is the most accessible to me, which one I am the most motivated to learn, and which will give me the most benefits.

Deciding what materials to use is not that difficult. I simply get a few books with dialogues/passages and audio to listen to and read. I never buy anything that costs more than $40. I like Teach Yourself, Assimil, Colloquial, and Spoken World Living Language, but that doesn't mean they are the best, I just think they have a lot to offer for the cost. I also get a grammar guide, a verb guide, a dual language book, and of course, a dictionary. You must remember that you do NOT need more than this. It's a mystery to me how people end up spending thousands of dollars on language material when you don't need more than about $100 worth per language. The only really important decision of those materials is a dictionary. I only get a target language-native language dictionary because I never use dictionaries the other way around. If I don't have a dictionary to explain and help me translate words, then I don't have a chance in the advanced stage. I also use the internet for various things like writing journals, chatting with native speakers, streaming live tv, etc.

As far as the method I must say that the best method is… are you ready…it's going to blow your mind…in 5,4,3,2,1: …every method. I like to study by *combining* various methods like listening, shadowing, writing, translating, creating mnemonics and so on. Try them all and see which ones work for you.

I wanted to talk about learning Hanzi and Kanji. There are many ways to go about this and I want to point out that it is ever so important not to get frustrated in this process. Staying relaxed and not making a big deal about it will help more than you can imagine. You can use repetition, you can use the Heisig method, you can use whatever method you want; just don't freak out. Don't try to learn too many at once, and definitely don't expect to remember them all. You will eventually remember about 95% of them but it does take lots of time, lots of reading, and lots of writing.

One last note. You must remember three main things when learning languages.

Don't get frustrated: You must not let the fact that you don't know something annoy you. When you don't know something, learn it!
Stay on Track: If you are studying, don't get distracted in any way. Language time is language time. Even if the Ice cream truck is calling your name, you must resist. And focus on the language you are studying right then. When I was studying French, I kept thinking about Mandarin, but it was French time. That's all there is to it.

Don't lie to yourself: If you lie to yourself and set unachievable goals, you will never be satisfied.

I know I am not a very good writer but I hope this made sense. Thank you for reading and I truly hope I was in some way helpful or motivating to you.

-

Anonymous

I love the title of this next submission by Christopher Sarda. Enjoy his story, which details his plans to feed this "hunger," and be sure to visit his website at:

www.wordcollector.wordpress.com.

A Hunger for Learning
An Essay on Language Learning by Christopher Sarda

My hunger for learning and knowing reaches far beyond the focus of this essay, but if someone has the heartfelt desire to understand the human condition, how can at least some interest in language learning not exist? I don't believe it can, and I have to believe that those people who seek to live with a higher understanding of this mammal, that somehow, someway evolved self-consciousness simply has not discovered the beauty and importance of communicating ideas in different structures and methods than they are used to.

Though not as accomplished as some learners that will be featured in this collection, I know one day I will be. I simply do not have a choice in the matter, I'm interested, and therefore I will not stop. I didn't always believe I **could** learn a language. I didn't always believe that I **should** put in the work either.

SPANISH AND THE BELIEF THAT I HAD NO "EAR" TO LEARN IT

Half of my family is Argentinean. My grandparents do not

speak any English, and in the earliest days of my life (or so I'm told), I was using more Spanish than English, due to the fact that I was being taken care of by my grandmother while my parents worked. At some point, my English only mother put an end to that, although she doesn't recall doing it, but my grandmother today claims that that is what happened. Those are the origins of my current fragmented Spanish.

Later, my parents divorcing and our moving away from the Hispanic side of my family didn't help the level of my Spanish. A number of other things after that also added toward my apathy to language learning. For one, although I've always had a hunger to learn, I was an undisciplined, bad student. When I took Spanish in school, I didn't learn anything because I hardly did any work. My step-sister (of the same age), on the other hand, who was also from a half-Spanish speaking family, took classes and did well in them. That, mixed with the fact that she may actually also have a better ear for languages, didn't help my apathy. With Spanish, and later Polish, I also helped myself to block any advancement because of the fact I couldn't express myself or my ideas in my target languages as well as I felt I could in English. This is something I still deal with now.

I spent my adolescence and the beginning of my adulthood believing that I simply didn't have an ear for language, or the time to study, or the money to pay for classes. I lived like this until shortly after I met a little Polish girl on a work and travel visa.

~~STARTING A NEW LANGUAGE~~
STARTING A NEW CULTURE

The short story of how I came to be married to Gosia is as follows: she came to the US, we fell in love, I fell asleep, and when I woke up I was in Poland.

Though I would eventually become enamored with the Polish language, it would be a good three or four months before I would start to work on it. I was so taken by being in a different country and culture; the food, the architecture, the people, whether good or bad never failed to *interest* me. The new weather (Northern Europe vs Las Vegas is certainly a strange jump), and meeting my wife's friends and family, all made an impression on me over time. Mixed in with everything was the idea always in the back of my mind the language learning "wasn't my thing."

One day though, after Gosia's mother noticed I hadn't even tried to learn any Polish, we took a little walk to the language learning bookstore (yes, a lot of Europe has entire bookstores devoted to language learning). We bought a little book called <u>Polish in 4 Weeks</u> and my journey began.

From the very start, the book advanced my consciousness. Polish, with its grammar of noun cases, is far more complicated than Spanish's verb conjugations and perfective and imperfective forms, and immediately helped me see conversation and communication in a new light--in a way that I had never imagined or conceived. I plan to have that feeling again once I start an Asian language in earnest. Getting deeper and deeper into the Polish language and, subsequently into Polish culture opened my eyes to a wonderful new way to get to know a culture and a people better, and eventually drove me to start toying with the idea of learning other languages.

THE LANGUAGE LOVING EXPLOSION

It wasn't long before I realized that for the remainder of my life I would always be studying a language. Starting a new language is a far better way to learn about another culture than it is to read a newspaper article, history book or even to travel to the country. Once I discovered that it was possible to learn, and to learn on your own, I became addicted.

Like most of the people bothering to read this, I eventually discovered the most vocal internet polyglots on YouTube; people like Moses McCormick, Prof Arguelles and Steve Kaufmann. Listening to their videos had both positive and negative effects. On the positive side, the three of them, along with the "How to learn any language forum" and Khatzumoto's "All Japanese All the Time" blog introduced me to many methods of learning.

Each learner's style had slight to large differences from the others, and I had to decide what worked best for me. That was somewhat of a negative. I wasted a lot of time watching videos and trying everything methodology proposed half-heartedly, while the whole time I should have spent actually studying my languages. Even today, though, I'm still learning how to learn. I still cannot, however, fire up the webcam and give my opinions based on *my* experience and achievements, and talk about what the best way is to learn a language. I think I have to come a little farther for that.

There are things that I do know. I know that I will always be studying a language. I know that I will find a method, or more precisely a combination of methods, that work best for me. I know what ideas will encompass that method. They are:

- Motivation and Discipline
- Massive Input
- Not allowing yourself, *for any reason*, not to use the language when you can (especially concerning speaking)

I mostly argue in favor of input, and getting as much vocabulary as possible in one's head. Passive vocabulary is an investment in the future of really knowing a language, as opposed to knowing how to just get by in one.

With all of that said, I do think you should try to speak as early and as often as possible. This is my biggest problem. I can speak authoritatively here-- being afraid to speak, worrying that I'll sound stupid or not intelligent enough, and switching back to English because it's easier, are the main reasons I have not learned the languages I've studied better and faster.

Let me reiterate though, that the gaining of input by listening and reading is most important as a future investment if you want to read, speak, listen and write well, but don't be afraid to use what you've learned if you have someone to practice with, even at the beginning. If you don't have someone to practice with, then just work on your input and understanding of what you read and listen to, and it will be more than enough.

MY GOALS, MY ATTITUDE AND THE ROAD AHEAD

My general goals for life are quite ambitious; in fact I keep a whole blog about them. My lofty language goals reflect that ambition. I mostly want to learn European languages; the few non-European languages I plan to tackle are mainly Hindi and Japanese. I hope that these languages offer me new and more difficult challenges when I am ready to start them. Hindi and Japanese are the two non European languages that I want at high levels for--enough to be able to speak about politics and culture, and to be able to read novels. I also have a desire to learn at least one African language (probably Swahili), but I don't plan to start that for awhile. Arabic is a language I would most want to use to listen to and read about current events, so I'd be happy to just practice input when I'm ready to start there.

Navajo is a language I will be content to only play with; I'd be happy to spend just a year on it to get to a low intermediate to intermediate level.

I think my future, along with my wife's, will be in Europe; a Europe that is becoming more and more unified (but, lucky for me, unified in everything except language!). I plan of course to be at a high level with the major European languages: French, Spanish, German, and Italian. Home base will probably be Poland, so a near native level of

Polish will be essential, and because it was the Polish language that made me so interested in the world of polyglottery, I've also become a bit of an aspiring Slavist. That means I plan to gain high levels in two other Slavic languages: Russian and Czech. With a decent level of knowledge in those three Slavic languages it will allow me to play with some other Slavic languages I do not plan to study intensely.

Last, but not least, are two small languages that stay in the back of my mind as languages I would love to have. One is Catalan, which shouldn't be too hard with a good base in the major romance languages. The second is Hungarian, which—I don't why—just has such a mystique to it. How could I not let it draw me in?

I know 'lofty' may be an understatement for my goals (14 languages were mentioned above!), but sometimes the road traveled is as good a reason to go as the destination. My abstract focus will be on my attitude and motivation. My worry-free demeanor will be my sword—who cares about my rate of progress, so long as there is progress? I recognize I have a long ways to go, but I look forward to seeing all the beautiful scenery on the way to wherever it is that my languages take me.

I am very happy to have gotten this submission from Vera. If you have any interest in learning German, visit her at: http://lingqvera.posterous.com, and at her YouTube Channel: http://www.youtube.com/profile?user=LingQVera. If you are interested in learning about an efficient way to learn any language, read on...

Who am I?

Hi, I'm Vera. I'm from Germany, and German is my native language. I'm not a polyglot, but I'm a learner of English and French. At first I was reluctant to participate in this project, but a friend asked me to reconsider. Also, there was a thread about this project in the forum of www.LingQ.com. The fact that Claude, who became a friend on YouTube, had extended the deadline finally persuaded me to take part. So, I decided to give this project a chance, and here is my submission. I'll tell you my story of language-learning. I don't know if it is interesting—that. I'll let reader decide.

Why English?

In January, 2008 my boyfriend told me that he wanted to learn English. We were planning a holiday in the United States of America for the Summer of 2010. Because of this, my boyfriend thought it would be a good idea to learn some English. He had never really learned English in school, because it wasn't offered there. English wasn't usually offered at this time in many German schools. Some years ago, he had taken a basic course in English at a school that's similar to an "Open University," something that is very common in Germany. So, having some basic knowledge of the language, he decided to seriously start learning English. When he checked the times of the English courses that were offered at the Open University, however, he found that they didn't fit his time schedule.

I thought his learning English was a good idea, and it couldn't hurt for me to brush up my English too. Thirty years ago I had studied English for eight years in school, but I never had the chance to use it, aside from two holidays. I have to admit that I disliked language-learning in school. I did what I was supposed to do, but I was never happy with the results. I was able to express very basic things; I was able to read technical instructions about computers and software, but I couldn't follow an English TV or radio program, or read more complex writings. I never really enjoyed language-learning at this time. It was not a problem with the teacher—I actually had a very nice teacher. It's just that I wasn't interested. I think one of the problems was that my exposure to the language was just not enough. We had the books, the teacher and the language lab as resources, but I hated the language lab because of the terrible quality of the tapes. We spent our time learning grammar, vocabulary, reading uninteresting things, and doing exercises.

How to start?

At the end of January, 2008 I read a note about our

British/German-Friendship association in the newspaper. They wanted to establish an English conversation group. So we decided to give this group a chance. Unfortunately, the group met only every second week, and the leader of the group organized it in a way that reminded me of my school days, and no wonder—he was a teacher!

I decided to buy a book that came with CDs in order to study on my own. At this time, the Hueber Verlag (a German publisher) had a special offer. There was a book offered with 3 CDs for only 12 Euros (about 16 US Dollars). I thought that this was a good offer, and I was willing to spend the money. I bought the book and put the CD's's on my MP3 player. I listened to the MP3's and read the text of the dialogues in the book. There was a translation of the dialogues, a list with important words, short explanations of grammar, some small exercises (but not too much), and some cultural notes. I enjoyed these CDs because the dialogues seemed to be authentic and natural. They had different voices from different countries, and I never got bored with this enjoyable learning material. I know that I learned a lot with this book.

The authors recommend listening to the dialogue once or twice, without reading the transcript in advance. That's what I always did. I then listened to the dialogue and I read it at the same time. Then I listened again for a few more times. I did some of the exercises, but not all of them. I liked the cultural notes that gave me background information about Britain. When I felt bored, I stopped doing the exercises and I continued listening to the dialogues. It was easy going because most of this was a repetition of what I had been learning at school.

First goal: Better listening abilities

When I came to the end of the book, I thought about how to continue. I knew at this time, that I liked listening a lot, and that I preferred to have a script of the audio because of my poor listening abilities. The script often helped me to get the meaning. I thought there must be some something like that on the internet and started to search for material. There are some podcast lists available on the Internet, and I found some podcasts. One of the first podcasts I enjoyed was the ESLPod. It is spoken very clearly and slowly, but not as other podcasts, such as "The Spotlight Podcast". The script is only available for paying members, but I could understand most of the podcast without a script. It was ideal for developing my listening abilities.

In the beginning, I tried to find podcasts with free transcripts. I checked a lot of podcasts, but most of them did not provide a transcript. Then I found the EnglishLingQ podcasts. The script was available for free, and all I had to do was to sign up for a free membership. Honestly, I dislike signing up for websites, but I was very keen to get podcasts with transcripts. So I signed up in May 2008, and Wow—there was so much content coming with audio and text. What a huge surprise for me! I was very excited—I cannot describe how I felt. Maybe the way the gold diggers did in the good old days when they found gold in California? I was fascinated by the number and variety of content in the LingQ English library.

My surprise was much bigger when I figured out how LingQ works. The integration of numerous dictionaries, and the possibility of saving words and phrases of text in a personal database that you can use for your flash carding are very helpful. What's even better is that you can import each text you want to study on your own! In new texts, all unknown and unlearned words are highlighted, and it is unbelievably helpful to see this in one view. I got addicted to LingQ and to language learning. It has become part of my life.

Second and main goal: Fluency

I began to think about my goals in language learning. My main goal was to be able to converse in English, to reach fluency. I did a lot of training for my listening ability when I listened to podcasts, but eventually there was a need to speak. You need passive vocabulary for listening and reading, but you need an active vocabulary for speaking. Passive vocabulary includes all of the words that you know. Active vocabulary includes all words that you can use actively, while speaking and writing. The passive vocabulary is bigger than the active vocabulary, and it is much bigger even in your native language.

After talking to myself for some time in order to train my brain to find the words that fit a given situation, and practising shadowing (speaking at nearly the same time as the speaker of podcast) in order to acquire the ability to pronounce the foreign language, I decided that it was now time to speak, in order to learn how to speak. At this time, I was a free member of LingQ for two months. I then decided to upgrade to a basic account. The basic membership allows you to save more words and phrases and, most importantly for me, it comes with a discount for buying points that I would need in order to sign up for a conversation with a tutor. I bought my first points and signed up for a conversation.

I can hear you asking, "why don't you use a free language exchange?" I never thought about free language exchange. I was keen to get a detailed report about the conversations, and in my opinion it is very convenient to look up the availability of the English tutors and decide instantly when I could sign up to get started. It did not require having a lot of correspondence with a language exchange partner, and I liked this business model. I pay for something, and I know exactly what I'm getting. I also like the fact that there is no further commitment. I like not having to think about how to pay back what someone has done for me, and always thinking about what I could do for them.

Helping with German

At this moment Steve Kaufmann, the founder of LingQ and a polyglot who speaks more than 10 languages, has asked me if I could tutor German at LingQ. LingQ has helped me a lot, and I was glad that I could now help members from all over the world to learn German. Now, I earn points for tutoring German and I can use these points either for my own studies, or I can get cash for them. Guess what I do! I think you guessed right: I always use my points for learning languages. I'm now at the point where it costs me no money because of the points I accumulate through my own learning sessions.

At the same time, I started creating material for LingQ's German library. I wrote and recorded articles, and I transcribed German podcasts (if the podcaster gives me permission) to be used on LingQ. The main problem is that it is difficult to find enough German podcasts that include a transcript along with the podcast (an exception being the "Deutsche Welle" podcasts). I strongly believe that LingQ and Deutsche Welle have the greatest collection of German audios that are accompanied by transcripts on the internet.

Third goal: Less mistakes

After a few months using LingQ I realized that I was speaking much better than before. I made some mistakes, but I was able to express most of my ideas. I reached near fluency. I reached my goal in being able to converse. Next, I changed my goal slightly: I wanted to be able to speak more correctly. Don't get me wrong. I don't want to speak flawlessly. But I saw some potential for improvement. There was no pressure behind this—I just started enjoying writing in English. I write things, and then I then submit my writings to a tutor. The detailed report that I get back helps me to correct my weaknesses. This helps me a lot to improve my grammar. I know I'm still not perfect, but I get more and more used to the language. I'm now more aware of the structure. When I'm now reading texts on LingQ, I concentrate more on those structures and phrases that show me how the language works. What I do very seldom, however, is to read explanations in a grammar book. I like to pick up the grammar and structure from examples.

Fourth goal: Enjoy reading

Reading an English book was never fun for me. It was a duty. I had to do it for school or for my job. I wanted to figure out if it would be possible to enjoy an English book, and that's why I decided begin reading English books some time ago. One of my English tutors recommended "Chick-lit" to me, because these kinds of books are about daily life and are written in daily conversational English.

I didn't want to read graded readers. I went to a book store and read the first page of a few books. After some minutes, I decided to take a funny criminal story written in daily English. The story was not too challenging, and the language seemed very authentic to me.

It was a good choice! I had a lot of fun reading the book. Now I'm reading the third book of this series and can read English at a good speed. I don't read English as fast as German, but I'm more than satisfied with my progress. What I'm not doing is looking up unknown words. As long as I can follow the story, there is no need to know each word. It is much more important for me to feel the "flow," and to enjoy the book. When I read a book, I don't want to be like a bookkeeper.

The state of affairs

At the moment, I'm at the level of a high-intermediate or low-advanced learner. My knowledge of English was proved on our holiday in the United States, as I had no problem in dealing with any situation. I was able to converse, complain about things, or ask questions about the environment or anything else. I'm still making errors, and my pronunciation has a German touch, but I'm understandable and can make my point. That's all that I really wanted to accomplish. I never thought about reaching perfection. I'm very satisfied with the result of my efforts.

How I study English

I study English the following way:

For a minimum of one hour, I listen to different English podcasts—for example, "EnglishLingQ," "Interesting thing of the day," "Listen to English," "ESLPod," "Business English Pod," or "6 Minute English." Some of them are easy for me, so I can concentrate on structures and phrases. Others are more challenging and I can train my listening abilities and grab some new vocabulary. I think it is fine to have a mixture. As you can see, I use American English and Canadian English, as well as British English. I love all the accents. I do my listening while doing other things such as driving my car.

I work on two or three texts a week with LingQ, then I save a lot of words and phrases to the LingQ database. Usually, I do this for 30 minutes a day. I love to save phrases because phrases, show how to use the words in a correct manner.

I review my words and phrases for about 10 to 15 minutes a day. I don't learn them—I do this very quickly. I only read the word and decide if I know it or not, and then read the translation. I made the following observation: if a word is important, I'll encounter it again in another podcast. It will then stick with me without the need for "learning" it. Our brain works in this way. If I don't encounter the word again, it couldn't be that important.

I read 10 to 30 minutes a day, either in a book or on English websites.

I speak three times a week for 30 minutes with one of my tutors. I have tutors from England, the States, and Canada.

I submit writings, if I'm in the mood to write an article. Some months, I submit about 1,000 words of English. In other months I don't submit any writings. However, I write a lot on the forum of LingQ in English.

Sometimes I watch TV programs in English, but this is difficult, because my boyfriend is not able to follow them and he dislikes that. Maybe I can change this if his English gets better!

Starting with French

Recently I started learning French. In French, I'm a beginner. I learned some French in school, but I forgot almost everything in the past 30 years. I like the sound of French, and France is not only our neighbour country, it is a very beautiful country too. That's why I think it is worth learning French. I bought five or six cheap books that came with CDs. I think I spent about 70 or 80 Euros, which is less than 100 US Dollars.

As a beginner, I learn in a totally different way. I started to listen to three different audio courses. The courses come with some short dialogues in French, as well as oral vocabulary lists, grammar explanations in my native language, and some oral tasks.

In a small textbook, there were transcripts of all the dialogues. I decided to type them into my computer. Typing a dialogue has two effects. The words stay better with me, and I learn how to spell words in French. It takes some time, but it is a good exercise. I think it is a good idea, if you start with a new language, to type some texts on your own. The main advantage of this was that I could import this text and audio into LingQ and save words and phrases, like I'm used to doing for English.

The other books that I bought are courses with a book and

CDs. There is a lot of redundancy in this material, but I like that—especially at the beginning. The repetition factor can be high without your getting bored. And, you can get used to different voices. I typed the text of these courses as well, and added them to LingQ so that I can work with them.

What I now do for French is listening to audio CDs, reading the text, and saving words and phrases to review. Next, I'll start to study with the material on LingQ. In the past year, a lot of new content was created by members and added to the library, and I'm keen to use it.

Before I'll start to speak French I'll do a lot of listening and reading. It is important, in my opinion, to acquire enough vocabulary to be confident and able to speak.

Language learning helped me

I wrote above that I want to help German learners. Therefore, I created a lot of material for learners of German. The funny thing is that learning languages has helped me to develop other abilities and to master totally different tasks. Language-learning for its own sake is great, but it has helped me in other ways too! For example,

I learned how to use Skype.
I learned how to write articles (looking how other people do it).

I learned how to download podcasts with a podcatcher.
I learned how to record articles with Audacity.
I learned how to tag the MP3 files.
I learned how to create a cover for a podcast with different paint programs.
I learned how to design podcast collections and share them on LingQ.
I learned how to write a blog (http://lingqvera.posterous.com).
I learned how to use Facebook, something I never thought about before.
I learned how to use Twitter (http://twitter.com/LingQVera). I never thought about it as well.
I brushed up my knowledge of HTML to individualize my Facebook account and my blog.
I learned how to record a video with my webcam.
I learned how to overwork a video with Camtasia studio.
I learned how to convert this video in a format for YouTube.
I overcome my shyness and shared videos in English and German on YouTube.
I learned how to use YouTube (http://www.youtube.com/profile?user=LingQVera).
I learned how to use Google documents (https://docs.google.com/View?id=dgpj8nz7_5dw7pkvgj).
I learned how to write a Wiki (http://lingq.pbworks.com/Deutsche-Startseite).
I learned how to record a screen cast with Jing.
I learned to use Pootle, a translation tool used for the translation of the interface of LingQ.
Isn't that great? I'm sure I forgot things …

Language learning has brought me a lot of nice contacts from all over the world: other language learners, tutors and a lot of podcasters. It has opened my mind.

My advice

What is my advice for language-learning? Be as much in contact with the language as possible. The more exposure you have to the language, the better. Do language learning in the way YOU like! That's why I like LingQ. It is so flexible, and everything I need is available on LingQ.

Have Fun! That is the best advice I can give. If you have fun, you stay motivated, and you'll learn a lot more. That's how our brain works.

Steve Kaufmann is the creator LingQ, an online language learning system, and I am honored to include his submission within these pages. Steve's name has come up again and again throughout this book, as he has influenced so many language learners out there (myself included). LingQ is a resource that should be utilized by every serious language learner. Check it out—you have everything to gain.

Steve Kaufmann is a former Canadian diplomat, who has had his own company in the international trade of forest products for over 20 years. Steve is the founder and CEO of LingQ.com an online language learning system and Web 2.0 community. Steve speaks eleven languages, having recently learned Russian and Portguese at LingQ. Steve maintains a <u>blog on language learning</u>,and has written a book on language learning called <u>The Linguist, A Language Learning Odyssey.</u>

This is my contribution to <u>thepolyglotproject@usa.com</u>, described by its originator, Claude, in this way; "I want to put a book together, available to all for free which is written by you language lovers for all language lovers."

Language lover - what a great term for someone who speaks more than one language, a better term than polyglot, which, to me, sounds harsh in English. I also use the term linguist to describe someone who speaks more then one language. Everyone speaks one language, but to speak more than one is special, not difficult necessarily, but special. It requires a deliberate decision to learn something, and a commitment to sustained activity and practice. In this sense linguists are like a violinists, pianists, or even dentists. I am a language lover, and do not hesitate to call myself a linguist, (which annoys those who have studied linguistics), because I have learned to speak 11 languages, and have no intention of stopping at my present age of 65.

The world is full of linguists, and always has been. In ancient times, when a different language was spoken in every valley, people had to have the ability to communicate across language barriers, in order to trade. The teen-aged street vendors of Tangiers, when I visited in 1964, all spoke 5 or 6 languages, as they pressed tourists to buy their wares. The courts and aristocracy of Europe spoke Latin, French and several vernacular languages, to communicate with each other and their subjects. Today in places as different as Sweden, Singapore and Ethiopia, it is just considered normal to speak more than one language. Being a linguist is not a big deal, or at least should not be.

Linguists are not born, they are made. They are made because of need, or interest, or a combination of the two. In my case, it was interest rather than need that got me going. Nevertheless, I was often able to use my languages, and benefit from them. In learning my languages, I was able to do what the French call "joindre l'utile à l'agréable", in other words combine usefulness and pleasure.

It was 1962, when a professor of French at McGill University, Prof. Maurice Rabotin, turned me on to learning French, by stimulating an interest in the world of French culture, something a series of anglophone French teachers had been totally unsuccessful at doing during elementary and high school in Montreal. I stopped classroom learning and sought out the real world of the language, in radio, newspapers, theatre, movies, and French speakers in Montreal. I even ended up going to France to complete my university education at the Institut d'Etudes Politiques in Paris. What I obtained was not only fluency in French, but the conviction that I could convert myself into a fluent speaker of another language. Many people never have that experience.

As a result, when my first permanent employer, the Canadian Diplomatic Service, announced that they would be looking for someone to learn Mandarin, in preparation for Canada's establishment of diplomatic relations with the Peoples' Republic of China, I knew I could do it. I started taking lessons on my own and then volunteered. My initiative was recognized by senior management and I was soon on my way to Hong Kong to learn Mandarin, full time, at the Canadian tax-payers expense. It was while learning Mandarin, in a wholly Cantonese speaking environment in Hong Kong, that I discovered many of the language learning truths that would guide me through my learning of other languages.

These include the following:

- You do not need to be surrounded by the language or live in the country to learn a language.
- You mostly need to learn the language on your own, through a lot of listening and reading.
- Most grammatical explanations are obtuse, hard to remember, harder to apply, and need not be learned.

- The milestones on the road to fluency are the number of words you know.
- You need to make an effort notice the patterns of the language as you read and listen, and this gradually becomes easier to do.
- You should start using these words and patterns, as soon as you feel like it, and even if you make many mistakes.
- The language will remain fuzzy for a long time. There is no need to despair over what you forget, do not understand, or are unable to say.
- Your brain learns, inevitably, but on its own schedule.

As I watched my fellow language learners struggle with Chinese, I came to realize that need or obligation or external pressure were not as strong motivators as interest. I loved my Chinese language learning. Most of my unsuccessful colleagues saw learning Chinese as a chore. I was to observe this phenomenon over and over, whether with immigrants to Canada, or corporate language learners in Japan, or unsuccessful language students in school or college. To learn a language, you cannot hold your nose, and just dip your toe in the water. You have to jump in. You have to like the language, even to love the language. You have to commit.

Just a few years ago a professor at an American university wisely told me that the secret to language learning comes down to three things, attitude, time on task, and attentiveness. It is worth looking at these in more detail.

Attitude: You not only have to like the language, and at

least some aspect of the culture of the language, you have to believe you can learn it. You also have to be willing to leave behind your own culture, and unquestioningly project yourself into the role of a speaker of another language, and therefore of a person carrying many of the behavioural traits of that culture. You should not worry about what you cannot do, and certainly should not expect to learn something just because you studied it. You have to enjoy the process.

I always laugh when I look at textbooks that tell you that in this chapter you will learn the subjunctive. You will not. You will exposed to some explanations and examples of the subjunctive. As to when you will learn the subjunctive, that will be decided by your brain, but it may not happen until six months later. So take it easy. Sit back and enjoy the journey, and wait for the fog to lift, slowly.

Time: For most people it takes quite a long time to learn a language. Therefore, you have to put in the time, regularly. In my own experience, the development of the MP3 player, iTunes and other similar technology has made it possible to immerse myself in the language, even while running my business. I have learned Russian and Portuguese, and dabbled in Korean, over the last 4 years, mostly using "dead time", while doing household chores, exercising or waiting in line, with a little investment of dedicated study time in front of the computer or with books. I did not attend any classes, and learned more than most students who did. Today I can listen to Russian radio stations, read Tolstoi, and enjoy Portuguese podcasts. But I have put in the time, probably around an hour a day on average, while working and carrying on my interests in sports, and other things, and working. Remember, also, that I am 65.

Attentiveness: We can do things to help our brain notice the patterns of the language we are learning. Different people use different tools, or combinations of tools, to make their brains more attentive. Reviewing grammar rules from time to time, without trying to nail anything down, can help. Flash cards can help. Being corrected when we write or speak can help. None of these are at the core of language learning. Listening and reading, and eventually, communicating are.

After studying Mandarin and living in Hong Kong from 1968-70 (I successfully passed the British Foreign Service Mandarin exam in 1969), I moved to Japan. Even though I lived surrounded by Japanese speakers, and took every opportunity to speak, most of my time was spent listening and reading, and building up my competence in the language. In this way, I became more and more confident in my interaction with Japanese people. I did not want to use the Japanese people I met, as teachers, but rather wanted them as friends or business associates. I did most of my learning on my own.

Back in Vancouver in the late 1980s, after starting my own lumber exporting company which involved business dealings in Europe, I again combined the useful with the agreeable, and at various times scoured book stores, especially second hand book stores, for German, Spanish, Italian and Swedish books and audio content. I also sought out similar material in order to maintain my Chinese. The problem was always that I was either limited to readers with glossaries, or would have to confront the time consuming and frustrating task of looking words up in a conventional dictionary. In my experience, I no sooner looked things up in a dictionary than I forgot them. It was in the 1990s that the world of language learning changed.

The Internet, online dictionaries and MP3 technology have created a new paradigm. I believe they will make the class room and conventional language labs largely irrelevant. The last 4-5 years have been the most intense sustained period of language learning in my life., and this is, of course tied up with my involvement in the LingQ project, and it is at LingQ that I have been learning my languages during this period.

On a final note, my languages have benefited me professionally, throughout my 43 year career as a diplomat and businessman. But these rewards are small compared to the personal, social and cultural enrichment my languages have brought me. In some ways, the greatest benefit of language learning is the process itself. As we gradually acquire confidence in another language, we sense a feeling of achievement and power or conquest. We make new friends, and discover aspects of humanity that were hidden from us. It is like being at a banquet and having more and more dishes to enjoy, without getting full. Of course if you are just a meat and potatoes man, you will never know what you missed.

Maybe that is the greatest role of a teacher, like my Prof. Rabotin over 40 years ago, not to teach the language, but to create an appetite for languages.

Stujay has more energy and enthusiasm than just about anyone else I can think of. Have a look at his fantastic submission, and feel the rush of adrenaline that is the natural by-product of reading his prose...

How to Become 'Gifted' at Learning Languages – You're Never too Old

by Stuart Jay Raj (http://stujay.com)

"That's O.K. for you – you're *gifted* when it comes to learning languages …. but what about us normal folk? How are we supposed to learn a new language when we don't have the ability to absorb them by osmosis like you?"

This would have to be the No.1 comment / question that I receive from my blog's readers, youtube channel fans and people who come to my workshops and seminars.

I personally don't believe that I am particularly 'gifted' at learning languages. What I am 'gifted' at is enjoying the journey of learning – no matter what it is that I'm learning. For me it's really simple. I'm a JUNKIE!

The Evolution of Stu the Junkie

- Stu can't do 'X' –>
- Stu wants to do 'X' –>
- Stu starts learning 'X' –>
- Stu has 'breakthrough moments' in learning 'X' –>
- 'Breakthrough moments' give Stu a 'high' and energize him to want to have more of them –>
- 'Stu gets addicted to the highs' –>
- The thresh-hold for the 'highs' gets higher and higher pushing Stu to NEED to learn more –>
- Language proficiency is a by-product of Stu's addiction!

I realised this 'Junkie' side of myself many years ago… probably around the age of 5 or 6. I suspect that it was because of my grandfather. Alcoholics shouldn't hang around bars if they're trying to give up drinking. By logic, that means the opposite is also true – if you want to get 'hooked' or 'addicted' to something, you physically and mentally put yourself in a place where the 'substance' that you're wanting to be addicted to is easily accessible and in abundance.

(Just for the record, my grandfather--God rest his soul-- was not an alcoholic nor did he abuse any substances … and likewise for yours truly)

Hit's on Demand

What my grandfather did for me was teach me how to get 'hits' on demand. He taught me systems and ways of managing my mind that meant that my capacity for getting hits was (in my mind at least) unlimited. Some of the systems that he taught me made it SO easy to memorize and learn new stuff that sometimes, just learning words or getting a 'WOW' reaction from native speakers of a language wasn't enough. I needed to go the extra mile – I needed to learn things that native speakers DIDN'T know. I needed to find out what people *thought* was difficult and find a way to make it easy for me.

Everything in this universe can be broken down into binary – 0's and 1's. I love to draw the curtain back and reveal the 0's and 1's… perhaps we could call this 'Wizard of Oz' syndrome – the Wizard is never as scary as he's made out to be. It's those 'Toto' moments that bring the biggest breakthroughs and in turn, the biggest highs.

Political Correctness and Semantic Dilution Kill Learning

The more graphic, vivid and non-politically-correct the images, emotions, sounds, actions and words that you use as memory pegs are, the more effective they will be.

The exercise that we're about to go through is going to change the way you think about everything.
I've done this exercise with groups all over the world and in many different languages and it works with everyone... mind you sometimes it has to be culturally and linguistically tweaked.

Just remember – the best systems are ones that are going to plant themselves into the deepest, darkest, most colourful and most fragrant depths of our soul. (You can almost taste that description can't you!?)
Doing this at an international level like in this blog then provides a bit of a rub, as for many reading this, English isn't your mother tongue. My cultural up-bringing is also probably different to yours. The key is to adapt what I'm doing here and link it into something in your own language and your own culture that sends those big barbed hooks sinking deep down into the flesh of your soul so that should what you learn ever go missing, it would physically hurt.
The more graphic, vivid and non-politically-correct the images, emotions, sounds, actions and words that you use as memory pegs are, the more effective they will be.

So here's a System for You!

This initial part was a rhyme I learned as a kid and was reinforced during my days as a Dale Carnegie trainer. Number '11' is a bit funny rhythm, but I think the imagery is very effective … you'll see what I mean. There are many other systems out there and many more that I use. Actually, the more languages and things you learn, the more structures you have in your tool-belt to reach for. The Major memory system is an oldie but a goodie. It's much more robust and can potentially cater for memorizing 10's of 1000's of items. For today's activity though, this one is very effective and easy to learn. Are you ready?

Part 1 – Erecting the Framework

Start clapping your hands at about 120 beats per minute (120 BPM). How fast is that? Look at the second-hand of a clock. You should be clapping or tapping your hand on the table at regular intervals twice a second.
Now read the following table out loud … yes OUT LOUD. Read it to the rhythm of your clapping / tapping – four beats per phrase.

1 (One)	Run
2 (Two)	Zoo
3 (Three)	Tree
4 (Four)	Door
5 (Five)	Hive
6 (Six)	Sick
7 (Seven)	Heaven
8 (Eight)	Gate
9 (Nine)	Wine
10 (Ten)	Den
11 (Eleven)	Ball Eleven
12 (Twelve)	Shelve

Please note – if the word's aren't rhyming, please check that you are speaking English ☺

If the '/' symbol represents one beat, it should be read like this:

/	/	/	/
One	Run	-	-
Two	Zoo	-	-
Etc…			

Now stand up from your computer, go and take a walk around the room and go through the rhymes for about 2 minutes. Take a nature break if you like. For the guys, if during your break you need to go and pee, remember – urinals make great white-boards! Try and pee in the shape of the numbers as you're saying the rhymes. If in a public bathroom, please be aware of your pee-radius limits… and it's probably not advisable to choose a urinal right next to someone else peeing. If you're doing this at home and you're married, please don't forget to put the seat down after you.

How was that?

Let me test you…
- What's ONE?
- What's FIVE?
- What's NINE?
- What number is HEAVEN?
- What number is GATE?
- What number is DOOR?

Ok – I think you've got it.

Now take a seat and let's start building!

Part 2 – Injecting a bit of Colour

One Run

Imagine Jerry the mouse (from Tom and Jerry) running across the Kalahari Desert. You're a camera man starting way up in the crisp blue sky, you see Jerry scurrying across the desert with his feet spinning around a million miles an hour kicking up dust as he runs. You then zoom right down on him and you can see him puffing and panting with his heart almost thumping outside of his body. Why? Because Tom's chasing him of course!

All of a sudden Jerry comes running up at you ... but wait, you're afraid of MICE!... now you start waving your hands about at Jerry saying 'Shoo Shoo! go away ... SHOO!'

Two Zoo

You're in what looks like a horrible, old smelly prison ... but it's NOT a prison. It's a ZOO! In the zoo, you would normally expect many different animals. This zoo is different though, there are hundreds upon hundreds of iron-bar zoo cells full of OXEN (plural of 'Ox'.. no bull!). The living conditions are horrible. The bars are pushing up against their heads, their horns are clashing together, there's stinky Ox poo all over the ground and all the Oxen keep saying is – "We want a NEWWWWW zoo ... we want a NEWWWWWWW zoo" – (Note the word 'New' is said in a deep questioning kind of way that starts pretty low and then goes up to a long extended 'OO' sound like in 'MOO')

Three Tree

There is a big, grand, glorious tree with a big fat trunk big enough for all the local fluffy animals to play in. You hear a rustling from the leaves at the top of the tree and then a long, scared quivering voice questions "WHO are you? WHOOOO are you?"

When you look at who it is up in the tree (still keeping in the spirit of the Wizard of Oz), you think at first it's the Cowardly

Lion!... But NO... Wait a minute... it's the Cowardly TIGER! Yes, a paranoid, manic depressive cowardly tiger and all he can say is "WHOOOOOOOOO?... are you?"

Ok... let's start to mix it up a bit here. Linear is so boring! Pick a number between 4 and 12 ....

...

Seven? Ok...

Seven Heaven

You're standing there looking at a big white, shiny set of escalators taking people up to the pearly gates of heaven. All of a sudden, a big white Pegasus like horse with wings like an eagle swoops up and you jump on-board as this giant white flying horse takes you up to HEAVEN. As you're flying up, you see an image of your mum floating out there smiling at you – you say 'Ma? Is that you?' ... 'Maaa? Is that really you?'

Ok – let's do a little bit of recap here.
- ONE – ??
- TWO – ??
- What were the Oxen saying?
- What animal was taking you up to heaven?
- THREE – ??
- What were the conditions of the zoo like?
- What were you saying to Jerry the mouse?
- What number was Jerry the mouse?
- Who is up in the Tree?
- What was he saying?

Ok – we're ready to continue ....

Ten Den

You are like Daniel... you've been thrown into the Lion's den. When you walk into the den however, you see that it's no normal den. These animals are sophisticated – sitting in big-armed chairs smoking pipes and wearing glasses. You hand

191

them a telephone and give them the home-delivery order for
KFC CHICKEN! They dial and order their CHICKEN and all
stand up, link arms and start singing in unison 'GEE we love
CHICKEN, GEE we love CHICKEN'.

What numbers haven't we done yet? Four? Ok –
Four Door

You're in Wonderland and the Rabbit is chasing you frantically
out of the rabbit hole into the real world. You manage to jump
through a door leading out and just as the rabbit jumps and
hurls himself both feet first through the doorway, you SLAM
the door shut on the rabbit's feet so hard that his feet are
severed and SNAP off of the rabbit's legs. With the door closed
and the footless rabbit on the other side, you pick up his TWO
bloody, twitching, fluffy white feet and put his TWO feet in
your pocket for good luck.

How many feet did the rabbit have?

Nine Wine

Haiya!... Hooooorrrrr ... HUAAAA! ... it's DRUNKEN MONKEY..
doing Bruce Lee impersonations with a big bottle of wine in
hand. This monkey isn't any ordinary drunken, Bruce Lee
impersonating monkey though!... He's dressed as SANTA CLAUS
and with every kick, kung-fu chop and back-flip, he's singing out
a jolly "HO HO HO! HO HO HO!"

NB. There were other images that came to mind that would enable our Drunken Monkey to cry out the words 'Ho Ho Ho' but…. but you see what I mean about Political Correctness? The less PC you are, the MORE you will learn!
Five Hive

Picture a giant hive, BUZZZING with activity. But wait!.. this is
no ordinary hive... and they're not bees flying out of it! They're
miniature DRAGONS flying out of the hive breathing little fire-

balls and all of them have LONNNNGGGG tails swooping upwards almost in the shape of the Nike 'Swish'. When you say the word LONNNNG tail, make the pitch of the word start low and follow the swish upward – DRAGONS have LONNNNNG Tails!

Ok – recap time again:
- What was coming out of the hive?
- What were you saying to Jerry the mouse?
- What number was Jerry?
- SEVEN – ?
- Who did you see going up to heaven?
- What were you riding on?
- Who is in the zoo?
- What were they saying?
- Who was impersonating Bruce Lee?
- What number was he?
- Who was the monkey dressed as?
- What was the monkey saying?
- Why did I choose the Santa Suit for the monkey?
- Who is up in the tree?
- What was he saying
- You're in the lion's den – what were they ordering?
- What did the lions all say after they ordered home delivery?

Twelve Shelve

You're in Israel minding your own business when all of a sudden you hear police sirens wailing in the street. You rush in to see what they're doing. There SWAT team busts down the door of a Jewish man and finds in his house shelves lining the walls with shelf upon shelf lined with PIGS. The police shocked look at the man and ask him 'What kind a JEW are YOU hmmm?'

Six Sick

You're sick in hospital lying in your hospital bed when your nurse comes in to give you an injection. This isn't any ordinary nurse though – and it's not any ordinary injection! The nurse is CHER (from Sonny and Cher ... If I Could Turn Back Time... you know the one), dressed in that black thing she was wearing as she was sitting on the cannon in the music clip for 'If I Could Turn Back Time'... but wearing a nurses hat of course. Instead of a syringe, CHER pulls out a long fanged SNAKE. It's fangs are protruding with green venom dripping from them and she plants the fangs – BAM! into you arm. (As you picture CHER placing the snakes fangs in your arm while you're sick in hospital, hold two fingers up, curl them around like snakes fangs and thrust them into the open side of your other arm. Let them sink in until you feel pain. As you think of that pain – of the venom running through your veins, think of CHER).

What numbers are left?
That's right – 8 and 11. Pick one? ... ok .. gottit.

Eleven – Ball Eleven

You're at an American football game (if you don't understand American football... or haven't ever watched it before, don't worry.... either have I!... but you've seen the movies right?... ok... just follow me on this one).
The number 11 footballer (Football 11) is throwing HOT DOGS up into the crowds just like they throw the football. These HOT DOGS have a twist though ... they're REAL DOGS inside! Little yapping chihuahuas are flying through the air between two buns covered in ketchup!
As the dogs are flying through the air, the crowds roar 'GO GO GO!'
Football 11 throwing hot DOGS saying GO GO GO!

and finally.......

Eight Gate

You're in a big green meadow / paddock in New Zealand. All of a sudden, you hear the railway crossing gate bells start to ring – DING DING DING DING DING … As the train comes closer, you can't believe your eyes! Instead of all the sheep normally stopping at the gate to let the train pass, this time, as the GATES go down, the train that's passing is being driven and also packed to the brim with SHEEP! Big sheep, little sheep, some with train engineer caps on, some with sun-glasses on, and some sporting some pretty impressive bling.

Just as this sheep-laden train goes past while the gates go down, a young New Zealand gentleman says to you quite matter-of-factly "My My... they're very YOUNG sheep now aren't they? YOUNG sheep indeed!
GATE comes down for a train full of YOUNG SHEEP.

What have we learned?

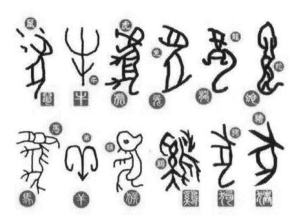

Aside from the fact that I have a frighteningly active imagination, we have indeed learned the animals of the Chinese Zodiac. Not only have we learned the animals, but we have learned the correct order and also the pronunciation of the characters. Well – we've learned a 'guide' to the pronunciation of the characters – enough to get our minds and our mouths in the right place. We can refine them down afterwards.

Why did I choose the Chinese zodiac (生肖 shēngxiào)?

In my Cracking Thai Fundamentals programme, I will often mention to students that if they feel that they are starting to become confident with their Thai, it's time to enter the 'shut up' stage. Many people jump into learning a language because they want to express 'themselves' in that language.

I remember a few years back, I was sitting with a bunch of friends who worked at an particular embassy in Bangkok that will remain nameless. Being an embassy, there are foreigners in there that speak fluent Thai – they've done their training both while back in their home country and then more language training on the ground once they were in the country. The complaint of the Thai embassy workers was that they said that they'd often be having a really fun conversation about some topic or other – maybe what soap-opera they were watching the night before on Channel 7, or about some member in their family who was going to become a monk, or what lucky number they saw on a car's license plate that ran into them on the way to work and in turn needed to urgently buy a lottery ticket with that number as the final 2 digits because it was already the 1st or 16th day of the month.. you know.. 'Thai' kinds of things.

They said that every time a particular foreigner (that spoke perfect Thai) came into the room, the happy raucous atmosphere that was going on just died. The foreigner would want be part of the conversation and join in the fun. He would come in and say something like 'Can you believe what they're doing in Iran at the moment?' , or 'What do you think about the UN's role in Thailand?'. These kinds of comments had the same effect as a fart in an elevator. Not just a normal fart – but one of those … you know … those silent, seepy ones that get past the firewall and glide out after eating Indian food for lunch. The ones that make all the people in the elevator start to contort their their face hoping that the contortions would close at least one nostril up and stop the pain.
Needless to say, the mood in the room died and the fun raucous conversation was but a memory of something that once was.

Ok, ok – I might be getting a little melodramatic at the moment, but I hope I've demonstrated my point. I don't like learning a language to express 'myself' in the language. I learn it so that I can learn about the people who use it, learn what they like and don't like and learn how to render myself in their language and culture in a way that won't come across like a fart in an elevator. Language is a social thing.

That's why the Chinese zodiac or '生肖 *shēngxiào*' is so cool. It's a fantastic ice-breaker and rapport builder.

The Language of Love

The intersection of language, mind-skills and dating opens up a whole new dimension of possibilities for Neil Strauss fans giving you an unfair advantage on most of your peers. I'll save that for my next book.

Supposing you were at Starbucks and you saw some cute Chinese girl sitting at the table next to you. (I'm saying this as though it would be me – you can choose the gender and sexual orientation of the imaginary Chinese Starbucks person to suit your own preferences ☺)

Let's superimpose all the 12 animals onto their corresponding numbers on a clock face. The animals 4 hours to your left and 4 hours to your right are the animals that best suit being your spouse. (These are called the 4 animal trines).

Now, you know that your own zodiac animal is the Horse. You think that she must be about 4 years younger than you – you're a Dog!. Dog = 11. Stand on 11 on the clock and walk clockwise 4 years. 11 to 12, 1, 2, 3. What's 3? RIGHT – She's the year of the Tiger! (Which just happens to be my year!).

Engaging the Mark

So now you introduce yourself to the cute Chinese girl and

say "You weren't born in the year of the tiger were you?" She says "No". Bummer! … All your plans and dreams are shattered … but not to worry, you can still salvage yourself. You say "Oh.. it just looked like you were the strong, leader type. I was convinced that you had to be a tiger". Now she's interested in hearing more about herself and intrigued that you know about her culture and probably more about the Chinese zodiac than she does. You sit, sip on your cappucino's and laugh on into the evening sharing anecdotes of paranoid tigers and young sheep.

A few dates went by, her clothes started appearing in your cupboards and drawers, she moves in officially, you end up marrying, you learn to speak fluent Mandarin as well as her family's own dialect, her mother hates you, she leaves you and takes the kids and you find yourself sitting in Starbucks one day commiserating your existence when suddenly… sitting at the table next to you is…..

Ok – you get the picture! Learning language is about learning 'people'. Learning what drives them – what makes them laugh … and what makes them wince their face up as though they've just been on the receiving end of a fart in an elevator. If you set this as your goal, the motivation to learn drives itself.

The Chinese Zodiac is a perfect social 'tool' to use to get into the people's hearts right across Asia. It allows you to peak their interest, get them speaking about themselves, what they like, how they perceive the world, who they like, who they hate, why they hate them and you might even get onto famous identities in their pop culture and history that are a particular zodiac sign. It can lead you down

many rabbit holes indeed.
(Side Note – what number was the rabbit? How many feet? – Good)

The zodiac animals and traits and words vary a little between different countries in Asia – Vietnam, Thailand, China, Japan are all slightly different. Again, the differences act as memory points – and knowing about them makes you a much more interesting person! Indeed the intersection of language, mind-skills and dating opens up a whole new dimension of possibilities for Neil Strauss fans giving you an unfair advantage on most of your peers. I'll save that for my next book.

Take a break!

This is a great time to go and take a break – go for a walk down the street… or better still, take a nap.   Find somewhere nice and quiet, close your eyes and take yourself into the scary fantasy land that we just painted with the numbers from one to twelve.

Notice how we didn't learn them in order? We didn't need to. Once the 'system' had been laid down properly in the beginning, we could learn in any order we like. The items just 'slot' into place. Plug and play vocab items.

If possible, try not to look at the following table first. Try and recall the vivid non-politically-correct images that we conjured up. Just in case though, here's a summary to help you:

1 (One)	Run	Mouse (Rat)	Shoo!
2 (Two)	Zoo	Ox	New (zoo)
3 (Three)	Tree	Tiger	Who?
4 (Four)	Door	Rabbit	Two! (feet)

5 (Five)	Hive	Dragon	Long (tails)
6 (Six)	Sick	Snake	Cher
7 (Seven)	Heaven	Horse	Ma (is that you?)
8 (Eight)	Gate	Sheep	Young (sheep)
9 (Nine)	Wine	Monkey	Ho!
10 (Ten)	Den	Chicken (Rooster)	Gee! (we love chicken)
11 (Eleven)	Ball Eleven	Dog	Go Go Go!
12 (Twelve)	Shelve	Pig	What kind of JEW are you?

Part 3 – Now Let's do some Magic

鼠	龍	猴
牛	蛇	雞
虎	馬	狗
兔	羊	豬

Now to get the most out of this activity in this textual format (normally I'd prefer to have a whiteboard / screen and write these up and drill at random), I would highly recommend downloading this PDF file CHINESE ZODIAC PLAIN - http://stujay.com/wp-content/uploads/public/chinese%20zodiac%20no%20subs.pdf and print it out.

Now because I'm not with you at the moment to point at

different characters, let's use a referencing system – like reading an Excel Spreadsheet:

A B C – Column Headings
1234 – Row Headings
So the order

1	5	9
2	6	10
3	7	11
4	8	12

will be referred to as

A1	B1	C1
A2	B2	C2
A3	B3	C3
A4	B4	C4

Mnid Yoga

No – I didn't make a typo. (Do a google search on 'Mnidcraft') Now it's time to stretch those synapses! This exercise works best if the chart of 12 characters that I've just given you takes up your full visual field. That's why I suggested printing out the PDF version of the chart and sit it on the table in front of you – or better still, stick it on a wall. Even better still, print out giant size versions of the characters and re-create the table on a white-board. Physically engaging yourself like that when learning vocab helps to embed the new words into 'you'.

Notice how I haven't placed numbers next to each one. You don't need them. The system 1-run, 2-zoo etc.. means that you don't need this anymore. The numbers are inherently there from the platform that we laid down first.

Now point at any character in the chart and just relax. Your mind will figure out what number it is. Just think of the rhyme. Think of the story. What is the animal associated with the story? What is the key 'sound word' to associate with that animal? – E.g. 3 – Tree – (paranoid) Tiger – Who?(are you).
Sit and do this for about 5 minutes. Just keep going over and over again at random.

As you're drilling yourself, change your mind's activity around. For example, after you've started to get a little more confident with the stories, animals etc, practice just thinking of the 'picture' of the animal only when you point at each character. That means when you point at location 'B1' the only thing that you are seeing in your mind is a picture of a fire-breathing dragon with a LONGG tail.

After about 2 minutes of just thinking of the 'animal pictures', do the same drill but this time round just think of the words associated with them. E.g. when you point at location B4 you are thinking 'YOUNG?'.
Spend the next five minutes drilling yourself.
Okay – Break time again!

A Healthy Diversion

Let me highlight a few points of interest about the characters we've just learned.

Look at the character 牛 for Ok – you can kind of see the ears, the horn sticking up and it's face … picture the bottom tip as the tip of the Ox's nose.

Similarly, look at 羊 the symbol for 'sheep' or 'ram'. You can see the little horns, hears running down again to the nose.

The character 馬 (ma) – 'horse' .. picture the 4 dots as it's mane flowing as it runs.. the top part is the head.

Look at these three characters 猴 (hou) , 狗(gou) , 猪 (zhu) – the component on the left represents a fuzzy or curly tail.

The character 蛇 (she) – pronounced like 'Cher' – rhymes with 'her' but no 'r' sound at the end. The component on the left 虫 represents 'creepy crawly' things.

I won't get into the whole tone system of Chinese too deeply hear. Just try and imagine the pictures and the emotions.. the tones will come from your emotional experience. Have a search around the internet after you get through this to read up on the tones and 'pin yin' which is the amazingly simple and accurate romanization system of the Mandarin sound system.

Part 4 – Mix and Match

Now let's look at these two tables. The first is the table that you've already learned. The second is a table of the same characters, but in random order.

See if you can work out which one is which by referencing the original table. You will find that soon enough you will start recognising the characters for what they are and your references to the original table will be minimal. Don't forget to (in your mind) always link the symbols to the numbers as you're recalling them. This is extremely helpful to have on call when you're in that Starbucks scenario we spoke about earlier!

Original Table

鼠	龍	猴
牛	蛇	雞
虎	馬	狗
兔	羊	豬

雞　　　　猴　　　　狗

龍　　　　虎　　　　馬

猴　　　　蛇　　　　豬

羊　　　　牛　　　　兔

Chinese currently uses two sets of characters depending on what country you're in. You have the Traditional Characters – 繁体字 'fan ti zi' (translated directly as complicated body characters) and Simplified Characters – 简体字 'jian ti zi' (translated directly as simple body characters). Mainland China, Singapore and Malaysia all use the simplified characters. Taiwan and Hong Kong still use the traditional characters. I personally prefer the aesthetics of the traditional characters, though for efficiency's sake, the Simplified Characters are in most cases faster to write. I recommend when learning Chinese that you learn both of them. Once again, the differences between the characters work to reinforce them in your memory.

Here is the original chart with the Simplified Characters next to the Traditional Character where one exists. As you can see, they are in most cases modifications of the original design.

鼠　　　龍 龙　　猴
牛　　　蛇　　　雞 鸡
虎　　　馬 马　　狗
兔　　　羊　　　豬

So What Have We Just Done?

How's your brain feeling? Excited?

Hopefully during the time you spent reading this article, you have at some point had an 'AHA' or an 'OH WOW!' moment. If we break it down, we have covered a LOT of ground and I have thrown many different disciplines / skill set training in there that you may not have even noticed.

Here are just a handful:

- Set up a memory filing system based on something we know
- Took away the scaffolding of what we knew and were left with a solid structure not based on language that we could file new words, meanings, pictures etc. in
- Used rhythm / music to help get our minds into state (120 bpm) to prepare it to be programmed
- Used rhyme, mnemonics and big, colourful, emotional and politically incorrect imagery to help us memorize stuff (no-one needs to know what actually goes on in your mind!… all they see is what's rendered in the end when it comes out of your mouth)
- Learned cultural points about Chinese Culture / Asia in General – Chinese Zodiac
- Picked up powerful 'pick up' techniques that can be instantly applied to your next trip to Starbucks
- Learned how to be a more interesting person
- Associated similar sounds in our language to help remember new words / sounds in a new language

- Once the new characters were in place, we could shuffle them up and revert to our original filing system as a reference. As the brain references back to the original table to look for similarities, we're learning more and more about the characters and they're being embedded into us
- Learned about the difference between Traditional Characters and Simplified Characters in Chinese
- Found out the scary things that go through Stuart Jay Raj's mind!

One important thing to note is that if you go over everything that I've just gone through, you might think that it's a convoluted way just to learn12 characters. When running this activity, I normally do it in around 30min – 45min … including all my commentary and the drills. The fact is though, that once you get the fundamental skill down of making pictures, word associations and inserting them into your mental filing system, all of the above processes happen internally within the space of a few seconds. Our brains can process things at lightening fast speeds. The trick is not to try to analyse it too much… and sometimes you just have to put your head down and plough into something and just have faith that your brain is going to make sense of it. Our brains can link two totally unrelated things quite easily – both a blessing and a curse. It only starts backfiring when our socially learned logic gets in the way and we start telling ourselves 'I can't do that' .. or 'that can't be done' … or 'I'm doing all this just to learn THAT!??' … In brain terms, the 'all this' isn't really all that much. It'll be over before you know it.

Finally, for your reference, here is an overall table of the

Zodiac animals taken from
http://www.orientaloutpost.com/chinese_zodiac.php. I
have tweaked the table a little.

Make sure you bookmark this article and / or print it out.
It's going to be something you will keep coming back to as
a reference and just know that you're going to want to
pass it on to your friends, employees and students to get
them inspired about learning again!
As for the full debriefing – let's leave that for the comments
section. I would like all of my readers out there to be part
of the discussion about what actually went on in this
article, the learnings that we can take from it and how it
can be adapted to learning other languages – and other
stuff in general.

Get as much input and inspiration as you can. Visit blogs
and sign-up for newsletters from people like Benny the
Irish Polyglot http://www.fluentin3months.com/ , Steve
Kaufman http://thelinguist.blogs.com/, Luca the Italian
Polyglot , Moses McCormick and other inspirational
polyglots out there. I think that many of these people are
like me – they love the buzz of learning and focus that on
learning languages.

If you've read through this far, you can probably tell that I
have a burning passion for communication, language and
people. I can't do it myself – I need your help too. It's only
through you sharing your learning experiences and ideas
with the rest of the community that we can spread the
passion for languages to the people around us – as well
as keep our own motivation up and move our learning up
to the next level.

211

All you need to do now, is drop by my Language and Mind Mastery website at http://stujay.com . In the 'JOIN NOW' section, drop me your name and email address, and I will give you free access to my Language and Mind Mastery bulletins, hints, tips and a tonne of great download resources. More importantly, you'll become part of an amazing community that is breaking new ground in learning and pushing the boundaries of what we can do with our minds. It's your opportunity to make a difference. Stay tuned for my podcasts on iTunes, and before the year is out, I should have my first batch of iPhone / iPad applications ready for downloading.

Special thanks to Brett from http://learnthaifromawhiteguy for preparing a cool set of Chinese Zodiac ANKI flashcards for this article that can be downloaded from here http://stujay.com/2010/08/15/chinese-zodiac-memory-technique-flashcards-on-anki/

Stu Jay Raj. ๒ जैय राज 王懷樂 http://stujay.com

Stuart Jay Raj

Appendices

Summary of Chinese Zodiac

Animal	Characters Simplified Traditional	Japanese Romaji (Romanized Japanese)	Various forms of Hanyu-Pinyin (Romanized Chinese)	
Rat	鼠 鼠	nezumi	shǔ shu	shu3 shu
Ox / Bull / Cow	牛 牛	ushi	niú niu	niu2 niu
Tiger	虎 虎	tora	hǔ hu	hu3 hu
Rabbit / Hare	兔 兔	usagi	tù tu	tu4 tu
Dragon	龙 龍	ryuu / tatsu ryuu/tatsu ryu / tatsu	lóng long	long2 long
Snake / Serpent	蛇 蛇	hebi	shé she	she2 she
Horse	马 馬	uma	mǎ ma	ma3 ma
Goat / Sheep	羊 羊	hitsuji	yáng yang	yang2 yang
Monkey	猴 猴	n/a	hóu hou	hou2 hou
Chicken / Rooster	鸡 or 鷄 鷄 or 雞	niwatori	jī ji	ji1 ji
Dog	狗 狗	inu / ku inu/ku	gǒu gou	gou3 gou
Boar / Pig	猪 豬	inoshishi	zhū zhu	zhu 1 zhu

Stuart Jay Raj in Brief

Background

Of mixed race, TV personality Stuart Jay Raj or 'Jay' has a fluent command in speaking, listening, reading and writing over 13 modern languages including Chinese dialects, Spanish, Indonesian, Thai, Danish and Sign Language. He has more than a passing familiarity in more than 15 other languages both modern and ancient and is proficient in several computer languages. From working with offshore Oil & Gas projects to Miss Universe, Stuart's ability to seamlessly communicate across cultures has become an invaluable asset for both multinational corporations and governments alike.

Entertainment

Stuart is a Television Host hosting programmes around the region in several languages including English, Thai, Bahasa Indonesia and Mandarin Chinese.

Stuart plays Jazz Piano with the Bangkok based ROL Jazz Trio and is also on the official interpreters team for Miss Universe.

From 2000 Stuart has been closely associated with the Foreign Correspondents Club of Thailand initially running his Cracking Thai Fundamentals programme to equip journalists to hit the ground running with Thai language and cultural skills. Most recently Stuart has been a board member of the FCCT and today continues to extend his network of key players that shape the happenings in SE Asia.

Facilitation, Training and Coaching

Stuart is an internationally accredited Trainer and Facilitator and under his company Kognisens, consults and trains for Governments and Corporations in several languages around the globe. Training programmes help participants develop both soft and hard skills covering areas including Leadership, Negotiations, Team Building, Simultaneous Interpreting, Key Account Management and Presentation Skills.

Through his experience with a diverse client base, Stuart has been trained in several disciplines in the Oil and Gas Industry, Modern Trade, Pharmaceutical Industry, Sustainable Development and HIV AIDS and works in conjunction with several agencies around the world as a buffer between western executives and local people in these fields.

More information on Stuart's activities, TV shows, learning techniques and video clips demonstrating them can be found in Stuart's popular Language and Mind Mastery blog at http://stujay.com and on his Youtube ™ Channel at http://youtube.com/stujaystujay .

TESTIMONIAL
"Stuart's background in teaching, marketing, translating and interpreting, music and computers are a testament to his multi-skilled versatility.

Learning with Stuart is not a chore – his methods build an indelible understanding of ways to apply fundamental principles that underpin the paths by which we actually learn. And his methods for learning apply equally to the learning of language, music and applied technologies. In short, Stuart Raj's methods reflect his sincere passion for the fulfilment of the human spirit"

Malcolm Smith
NALSAS Indonesian Project School of Languages and Linguistics
Griffith University – Brisbane, Australia

Benny the Irish Polyglot has a somewhat different approach than many of the other authors included in this book. As he told me, he wants to get people speaking right away, and minces no words in explaining why...

My name is Benny Lewis, an Irish lad that at 21 would never imagine speaking any language other than English to be possible for me. I took German in school and did quite poorly, and when I visited Munich I couldn't even order a train ticket – a frustrating place to be after five years of schooling in the language.

Now at 28 I can confidently say that I speak 8 languages fluently (European level C2 or better for several of them, and hopefully a 9th at conversational level by the time you read this), and have been told that I have an excellent almost-native accent in several of them. I am now at the stage where I only need about three months, starting from scratch, to reach a confident level in any given language.

I am absolutely 100% sure that anyone else could do this if they applied the right approach and mentality, no matter what their background is.

What changed for me is incredibly simple, and I don't need to go into details about how many words to learn, or grammar explanations, or precisely which courses or websites to use. All I did was speak.

That's it. I just started speaking my target language.

Speaking it wrong, making lots of mistakes, not having enough vocabulary to be "ready"... and doing it anyway.

Initially stumbling through a language may sound undesirable, but this is by far the quickest path to fluency. You will never speak a language quickly by avoiding speaking it. This is obvious for any task or goal – avoiding the actual goal itself will never get you anywhere.

Six months in Spain *studying* regularly gave me nothing more than a splattering of random words and a frustrated feeling about grammar. I needed a dramatic change, so I made the decision one day to try speaking no English *at all* for a month and that single month changed my entire life and converted me into someone who seemingly has a "talent" for languages. I don't have a natural-born talent for languages, I *created* and nurtured that talent, just like anyone else could. After that month *I was speaking Spanish*.

You don't have to move to the country to do this. I learned Portuguese while living in France and arrived in Brazil already at a confident conversational level, with almost no trace of using Spanish (or "portuñol") as my crutch. I made the same decision to put my self-doubts aside and to just *start speaking at every opportunity possible*. The pressure of a native in front of you and the need to communicate will force you to improve at an incredible rate. Paris and Toulouse being major cities, it was very easy to meet up with Brazilians.

Not being able to travel to the country yet is not a good excuse I'm afraid. If you live in any major city you have ample opportunities to meet with natives of any major (and some minor) language **in person**. Couchsurfing holds regular meetings (shown on the groups and events pages) and if you set up a profile you can host native speakers. This is how I have maintained my spoken level in any given language no matter where I live. In Berlin I hosted Brazilians and in Argentina I hosted French backpackers etc. Meetup.com also holds regular meetings and if you go into Facebook and search for your city name followed by your language name, you may find groups and events taking place that you should definitely check out!

Other than that, simply keeping your ear to the ground will reveal where all the opportunities that were previously flying by you for some real practise have been.

But surely you can't speak if you haven't enough vocabulary or studied enough grammar yet? Of course you can! If you know a single word, then use it! And no matter what language you are learning there is a vast amount you already know when you are starting. Focus on this positive rather than focusing on what you *don't* know as most courses are tailored to. The power of incrementing your speaking abilities by using what you have just learned is amazing and exponential.

Waiting until you are ready on the other hand is what will forever hold millions of learners back from ever trying. You will **never** have enough vocabulary. Not being ready is a state of mind that you can maintain until the day you die if you so choose. I choose to be ready after studying a travel phrasebook for just a few hours. It leads to lots of frustration of course, but it also leads to incredibly rapid progress.

This may not be as pleasant as studying books in comfort

and with no pressure for years, but if your goal is to speak – over-preparation will hold you back. Even if you knew the grammar and vocabulary of any given language inside and out, the cat would still have your tongue when the time came to speak if you are simply *not used to conversing in that language.*

While this advice may conflict with the advice of some other contributors above, who have a preference for input, there is a very important reason why I tell you that you simply **must** speak your target language as soon as possible: you need to do what your goal is. If your goal is to read excellently and understand foreign movies and streamed online radio, then you have to do that as the priority. To read excellently, read **a lot**. To understand spoken language, listen (attentively) a lot. To speak well, speak a lot. No waiting.

If speaking a language is not your priority, then my advice cannot help you and you would be better focusing your energy on input. Everyone *says* they'd love to speak a language, but I have found that some people really do have a preference for literature and just *hearing* native speakers. In that case speaking is a pleasant side-effect of their main goals and frustration involved in my suggestions to speak quickly and efficiently isn't worth their effort. For me and others it's the opposite. Focusing on speaking makes other aspects of a language improve themselves with time.

So what are you waiting for? No matter what excuse you have there is a way around it if you try hard enough. Because of making some tough decisions early in my language learning journey, I now go to a country and almost exclusively socialise with locals (or with natives of other languages I'd like to maintain). I have had incredible experiences getting to know cultures more than books can ever convey. My mission is to help as many people as possible to experience the same feeling, and to do that I have to pull people away from their books.

Of course, I study too – but with short-term goals. I study vocabulary to prepare for a meeting **this evening** rather than next year. This change in context changes your motivation and thus, your rate of progress. If you'd like to hear more about how I "hack" my way to fluency, <u>check out my blog</u> as I apply these tips on the field.

Reading through previous submissions in this document I saw some other polyglots that I hugely agree with and have had the pleasure to talk with directly, including Moses McCormick and Stu Jay Raj. I also see a huge preference for LingQ, which suggests to me that there was a big discussion about this polyglot project within that community. I think this is misleading as to how many successful language learners use that tool based on my experience in talking with many multilingual individuals.

Because of this, I have to give a word of warning that that system is commercial and there are free alternatives. I used LingQ myself for several weeks and wrote <u>an extremely detailed review of it</u>. My suggestion is to definitely use the parts of the system specifically for improving your reading and listening abilities. These parts are free and many aspects to this are unparalleled elsewhere.

But you should preferably get many hours of active written and spoken conversation practise through **completely free** alternatives rather than paying for it on LingQ. Paying for short sessions every once in a while is useful, but you can get similar advantages elsewhere.

If you are too shy to meet people in person as I had suggested above, you can still practise every day for several hours thanks to the amazing amount of online communities *in* and about other languages.

Although the courses offered at sites like busuu and Livemocha are dreadful, I highly recommend using these sites as tools to meet other native speakers, as the international communities there are huge. Get their Skype details and chat with them regularly for free. Natural conversations with a new friend (rather than a paid teacher) will help you in many ways, especially if your goal is to use the language in social situations. Depending on the language you are learning you can **easily** find native speakers through the Internet on the vast number of online communities and start chatting without ever leaving your home!

Other useful links I'd recommend (all completely free resources):
Rhinospike: Need to hear what a particular sentence sounds like? Submit it and a native will read it to you!
Forvo is a pre-made database of what particular words sound like.

Lang-8: Write short sentences and get them corrected by natives. Very useful to improve your written abilities.

To listen to content in your target language, after you have passed the elementary stage, don't get any more language learning material. Dive into how the language actually sounds by listening to real podcasts. These <u>can be downloaded easily</u> for free from iTunes. If you are used to hearing natives speaking very slowly and using simple language in sound-proof recording studios that may be all you are prepared to understand!

The benefits of speaking a foreign language deserve a book in themselves, but I will be frank to people to get them on that path. Listening to podcasts can be very beneficial and comfortable and fun, but with actual natives pushing you, you will progress at an amazing rate. Follow the advice of all of the amazing other language learners here to improve your understanding of a language, but please put the learning material down and step outside of your house and use your language to communicate with other human beings :)

That's what a language is about after all – it's a means of communication. It isn't a list of grammar rules of a competition for who knows the most words of vocabulary. It is your key to meeting fascinating new individuals. Use it!

This next piece comes to us from LingQ. "skyblueteapot" describes her journey from computer programmer to language enthusiast...

"My language learning journey; or: How I learned Russian despite the cultural handicap of being British"

by skyblueteapot, United Kingdom.

I went to school in England in the 1970s and 1980s and therefore have been handicapped with foreign language learning. It was taught very badly, you see. French, German and Latin were taught using the Classical Method, which mainly consists of writing irregular verbs up on the board and making everyone learn them for homework. I was startled, on visiting France at the age of eleven, to discover French children speaking French, easily and naturally and without even having to look words up in textbooks. The idea that it was anyone's mother tongue simply hadn't occurred to me.

The turning point for me was an exchange programme with a German school. I was shy and nerdy and therefore had no friends among the English kids who went over with me; I was, therefore, forced to hang out with the German kids. It was a revelation! I learned that for them, language learning was a much easier, natural and pleasant process than it had been for me. They listened to English pop music, watched English films and wore jeans with

English labels on them. I came home exhilarated and determined to learn to speak proper German, song lyrics, swear words and all.

I didn't have much time left. The unnecessarily restrictive English school system mean that, at the age of 16, I had to stop studying all languages to concentrate on physics, my university subject. And that was that. I was branded a scientist, an asocial computer-botherer, an art and culture-free zone. It was a life sentence. Or so I thought.

At the age of....erm...well, I was married and had two kids anyway.....I found myself suddenly out of a job. I had been a computer programmer, and as it turned out, a bad one. Why? I was hard working and I loved learning and using languages. It ought to have been the ideal job. Perhaps talking to computers in their language simply isn't as rewarding as talking to people in theirs. I resolved to restart my language learning, focussing on communicating with real people this time. Maybe failing as a technical person gave me a second chance to try out at being an arts person.

But where to start? The local adult education courses weren't much help. I was already overqualified for beginners' French and German classess, and nothing else was available. I tried local universities, libraries, and schools. None of them included helping mature learners to learn a foreign language within their remit. Even amazon.co.uk wasn't expecially forthcoming on language learning books and CDs beyond the very basics. Maybe I could find some learning materials on the internet?

After a lot of searching and frustration (and grumbling about it to penfriends in slowly-improving German), I found a site called www.lingq.com. It claimed to offer Russian, which caught my attention straight away. Russian had been on offer at my school, but sadly not to those studying science (Perhaps they were afraid we would defect to the Soviet Union and take the secrets of the Trident missile programme with us). Was this at last my chance to learn it? The danger of me defecting now and taking with me the secrets of really poor programming really shouldn't keep the Intelligence Services awake at nights.

I studied the so-called "natural language learning method" carefully. It looked too easy to be effective. You sign up for an account, help yourself to free lessons (mp3 + transcript), and study them. There is software to keep track of the words you have learned, the lessons you have studied, the time you have spent on listening, etc. You can learn new words using flashcards. Ah, but what happens when you have studied all the lessons in the library?

I studied the contents of the library. There were, as it turned out, a LOT of lessons, some of them really quite tricky. It didn't look as though I would run out of material any time soon.

I still suspected a catch. I lurked in the forum. It seemed to consist of a lot of clever, funny, people,

people who were well aware of the value of a dollar and very clear that they were getting value for money. Some of them were even learning Russian—including, it appeared, the founder of the site.

I decided to Skype him to find out what the catch was. We had a very pleasant conversation. It turned out that LingQ is the brainchild and baby of Steve Kaufmann, a former Canadian diplomat, who loves learning languages and is learning Russian as his tenth or eleventh one. Making money does not seem to be a major goal for him; spreading the word that learning languages can be fun does.

"But you DO want my money, don't you?" I asked. "You won't get much out of me. I'm unemployed!"

Steve shrugged. "I'm sure you can find a Russian who's keen to learn English," he said. "You can do a language exchange".

"What happens if I run out of lessons?" I asked.

"You use your own material," he answered. "Have you seen the size of the internet? Anything you can download in mp3 format you can put on your mp3 player and listen to; any text you can copy and paste you can import and use as a lesson."

"What about Dracula?" I asked. "I've got that as an e-book."

"Dracula's be fine," he answered. "You can write

pieces in Russian about vampires and have conversations with Russians about vampire-staking."

This was an intriguing idea.
"How about Hobbits?" I asked.

"If you must!" he answered.

"Heavy metal song lyrics?"

"Fine!" he said.

Well, this just had to be tried. Learning what you want, when you want, where and how you want, and asking for help only as and when you want to. That's flexible enough even for a stressed out housewife and mother of three to cope with.

Two years on I have to say, the "natural, input-based" learning method certainly works for me. I listen to audiobooks, podcasts and radio programmes in Russian. I read articles harvested from all corners of the web and, when I feel like it, I discuss my progress with native Russians. I keep a diary in Russian and get feedback on bits of it when I want it. In two years I have reached about "A" level standard. I have also found the time to learn a bit of Japanese and brush up on my French and German.

So encouraged have I been by my progress that I have signed my children up. The eldest is 12 and is learning French (without noticeable enthusiasm), at school. The youngest is 9 and has been taught to count up to ten in French. Once shown how to download lessons and play mp3s, operate the online dictionary and work the flashcard system, I set them a competition. Whoever learns the most in 3 weeks wins ten shiny new British pounds and the respect of all. The betting stands at evens: ten more days to go!

The sad fact is that English schools still make learning languages boring. Not only that, but the number of language teachers and the number of languages available in state schools has dropped since my day. Now it is only compulsory to learn 3 years of French, and impossible to learn any other language in my son's comprehensive school.
I am determined to show my children how to become independent language learners; to show them that, no matter how poor the language teaching provision in their schools is, no matter how restrictive the timetables or dismissive our society may be of the value of speaking a second language, the process of learning a second language can, nevertheless, be fun, rewarding and useful. Even for scientists! After all, Einstein could speak English well enough to work in America as a university professor. I bet no-one ever told him that scientists couldn't learn foreign languages!

--

more on my blog: www.tracesofdodo@blogspot.com

My friend Zo's serious language learning journey began with a $34 Dollar purchase at the local bookstore...

My Journey to Language Learning
Lorenzo R. Curtis

The Beginning

It brings me great pleasure to have the opportunity to participate in The Polyglot Project and to write about my experiences with Language Learning. Even though I am not a polyglot myself, I believe I possess a story that will be helpful to the average individual that is just starting out with learning a foreign language and needs that motivation to continue it. Certainly, if I can do it, anyone can. This endeavor has brought joy to my life untold and continues to enrich the course of my life.

I go by the name zocurtis on Youtube and the internet but my real name is Lorenzo Rico Curtis. Language Learning wasn't always a passion of mine. In fact, I grew up in a completely monolingual environment where no other language was spoken other than English. The type of environment I grew up in lent no room for interest in anything foreign. My mom was a single parent so my brother and I were brought up in a setting that taught us to be self reliant, always vigilant and street smart.

Nevertheless, I was always different. I would read books by Homer and Shakespeare and Ralph Waldo Emerson and write poetry. No one in my neighborhood wrote poetry. I was interested in art and coin collecting and soccer, all things that I don't know where I got the interest for from yet my passion and drive was to become more than my environment spawned me to be.

I began learning Spanish in the 7th grade. My then Spanish teachers name was Ms. Gelo; she was from Spain. Her name was pronounced 'Halo' but everyone just called her Ms. Gello because of how it was spelt. My impression of that class was not very memorable, except for the fact that the students would taunt the poor woman as she was a foreigner and had a funny accent. I wasn't particularly interested in the class either. I don't think any of us were. We just needed to pass and pass we did.

Ms. Gelo was a sweet woman but she didn't know how to control a room full of hormone charged pre-teens. She ended up leaving mid-semester of our 9th grade year. Someone stuck a bobby pin in her chair. I guess she never recovered from the insult. The administrators never heard back from her and didn't even know when she left. She did manage to teach me one thing that I think was very instrumental to my language learning journey. It was a simple song that went:

> *"Red is rojo, red is rojo, rojo is red, rojo is red.
> Learning all the colors is fun and colors are for
> everyone. I'd like to shout and let you know,
> red is rojo, red is rojo."*

We'd sing all the colors until we went through them all. As simple and as dorky as this song was, it stuck with me like an idea that had been planted in my mind. It began to grow into the realization that maybe, just maybe, I could learn to speak Spanish fluently. But I hadn't yet realized it back then.

Fast forward to age 17 and you'd find me in a bookstore buying a Living Language Spanish course. It cost me about $34.00 and came with 3 audio cd's, a course book and a dictionary. This was my first real attempt at truly pursuing my dreams of becoming fluent in that language. I had made the decision after I had written a list of goals I wanted to accomplish in my life. Thus, I had made my first step with this goal.

This was at a time when I had just graduated high school and was waking up each morning asking myself what exactly am I here for. To take a quote from my favorite movie, I had to, "Either get busy living or get busy dying." Figuratively speaking of course. Unfortunately, this jolt of motivation only lasted about a week. I chalked this up to the fact that another idea had started to grow beside the other one that told me, "I couldn't do it." I hadn't even really tried.

My Push over the Edge

The following year, I began to take courses at my college in Spanish. Finally, I would be motivated to continue with the language and with my dreams of becoming fluent in the language. So I thought. Though I'd learned quite a lot about how the language worked in the two (2) years that I studied it in college, I still could not speak. This was a common thread among all the other students that took these classes as well. But I sure as hell could conjugate a mean verb. All these classes did was further help to de-motivate me much more than I already was with all of the

233

grammar instruction that was given. It wasn't until I opted to take a class that traveled to Costa Rica for one month that I begin to see how easy it truly was to learn how to speak the language.

Costa Rica was a blast. I saw so much beauty in the place and fell so far in love with the culture that didn't want to come back home. It was truly a world beyond my own. The mountains, the trees, the rivers, the food and the people all inspired me and helped me to want to know more. The language was simply icing on the cake. We'd studied at Centro Panamericano de Idiomas and we traveled to different places all around the country. I'd finally found the motivation to continue with my language instruction in Spanish. However, this time, I opted to do it on my own.

When I began learning Spanish on my own, I had already had a basic knowledge of the grammar rules and the structure of the language. What I didn't know was how to speak. Speaking came as a difficultly, I realized, because I was not in constant contact with the language. Therefore, I tried to find every way possible that I could somehow get in tune with the language every day. I used a course book that is now out of print called 'Learn to Speak Spanish' by The Learning Company. It provided the bilingual text format that I loved and always provided simple grammar explanations and notes on the language. I also found people around me that I could speak the language with. One of my friends had just spent a year in Cuba and he was fluent in Spanish, so I used him as motivation and speaking and listening practice. After a while, I searched for authentic talk radio stations on the internet with which I could listen to the language. Even though I couldn't understand everything that was being said, I found joy in hearing the language spoken and thinking that one day I would understand it all.

This was about the time I started to watch videos on Youtube. Youtube was then only two (2) years old but it had already become a place that you could meet people with interests similar to yours and get in touch with them. Some of the first videos I'd watched were by renowned polyglots Steve Kaufman and Professor Arguelles. However, the very first video that helped me were by a guy on Youtube named JimmyR. He posted a video about the 'Top 5 Ways to Foreign Languages for Free.' This is how I found out that there were in fact places online that helped people with their personal language learning.

Professer Arguelles sold me on the Assimil method for learning languages and Steve Kaufman sold me on his imput method. There are many friends that I've found on Youtube that have had an impact on my language learning goals, probably too many to count but all in all, I began to improve in the language with varying methods being applied to my own. I can now speak Spanish, although not with total fluency but enough to be understood. I am proud of my accomplishments and am constantly improving.

On Language Learning

It is a sincere fact that anyone can learn a foreign language. They just need the tools that can get them over the hump of thinking that they cannot do it. This was the disease that I had suffered from but I had to get over it and thus, I used the stories of others and their achievements to help fuel my own motivation. I have since had aspirations of learning Italian, French, German, Haitian Creole and Indonesian and I know that with time and motivation, I will obtain this goal.

Language learning is like riding a bike. One sure thing that you know will happen when you first begin riding bikes is that you will fall. You will fall and get many cuts and bruises until one day, your determination will get you up and over the hurdle of failure. It is important too to have someone steering you along the way. That is what Youtube is all about.   There are guys there that have already done the falling for you and are willing to help show you the way if only you are willing to listen to their advice. I am continuing to learn and I know that one day, all I dream will become a reality. Dream big my friends.

See more of my views on foreign language learning at my Youtube channel: http://www.youtube.com/user/5Language and at my blog: http://5languages.wordpress.com/.

The next two submissions are courtesy of our previous author Zocurtus. Dave and Carlos tell their stories...

Journey to Language Learning
Dave Cius

My language learning experience was far more difficult than I hope it to be. Basically, in high school I wasn't really a fan of learning new languages. My thing or mindset at the time was if anyone wanted to communicate with me had to either know English or either learn it.

It's funny though how life works because back in high school I hated the idea that I had to take up a foreign language to go along with the course I was studying at the time, so I simply took advantage of the situation. One, I was already of Haitian decent so why not study French because it's real close to Haitian Creole (my native tongue which was easier for me) and two, I hated the Spanish language.

After high school, I was accepted to go off to school to study medicine. Apparently, the school or country that I would be studying in was Cuba and though I hated Spanish, I desired the education.

Learning Spanish was a very big step for me because I hadn't any prior studies of the language. So I was kind of indifferent about the idea. At first, I found it hard, basically because I hated the language. Due to this state of mind, it became more and more challenging for me but our Spanish teachers at the time were very patient with us and worked diligently with us braking down the language into two basic building blocks which are theory and speaking.

The professor really stressed the idea of attempting to speak the language even though we had very little experience of it. This technique allowed us to practice with the knowledge that we were making a bunch of mistakes but were corrected at the same time by the professors (as well as the school workers) which improved our listening skills as well as the speaking.

As we continued to improve in the language, we were introduced to the idea that our professor Marie use to say that, "There was more than one way to skin a cat" which goes to show that in Spanish there are many ways to get your point across rather than using a particular phrase over and over again. For example, "necesito ir al bano" which is Spanish for "I need to go to the bath room." Well it can also be said as, "tengo que ir al bano" or even "debo ir al bano." As we progress, we also learned the various tenses such as the present, the past, the future and as well as conditionally tenses.

As we progress in the various steps in the language, listening became vital and essential because everything we knew and grew to understand was or had to be translated into Spanish. Pretty soon we began thinking in Spanish which was where our professors wanted us to reach, the main thing that our professors tried to instill within us was that "yes it's possible."

"Si se puede" is a phrase well used in Cuba to encourage young people. Basically, our teachers placed us in position where we were compelled to learn the language in order to perfect our skills in speaking. Another important factor that we were taught and was practically preached to us was the importance of listening because the ability of interpretation would go hand in hand with the understanding of certain texts or any form of speech and as well as our ability to respond without the need to stop and think but to speak fluently.

My Language Learning Experience
Carlos Cajuste

When I heard the other day that a book was going to be written about experiences in language learning, I suddenly was elated to share my own experience with others out there who would think that learning a new language would be a hard and never ending challenge, however that's not so. With time and dedication anyone can learn a new language.

My name is Carlos Cajuste and I reside in The Bahamas. Language learning has always been a part of my life, per se. Come to think of it, I started learning languages from the moment I was born. In The Bahamas we speak English, however growing up in a Haitian household, I was forced to speak Haitian Creole. Whenever I spoke with my parents I wasn't allowed to speak English. They would get annoyed whenever I spoke English to them. Therefore, Creole became second nature to me. At this point, I didn't realize that I was bilingual; it was just something that came naturally.

For those of you who don't know, Haitian Creole is a debase form of French or rather broken French. It is spoken by 12 million people in a country called Haiti, located in the Caribbean. There are Haitians migrating to The Bahamas in search of a better life every year and are thus integrating into the Bahamian society. Therefore, I got the best of both worlds, both English and Creole.

In my opinion, Creole isn't a hard language to learn. As a matter of fact, it's actually one of the easiest languages on the planet because it is a phonetic language. The way a word is written is the way it is pronounced. Similarly, the grammar tenses aren't as difficult to remember because one word is used when introducing a tense as opposed to Spanish where every verb is conjugated to introduce a tense (past, present or future). Also it is not as difficult to pronounce as French is, even though it is derived from the French language.

It was in college that I got the opportunity to go to Cuba. It came as an opportunity of a lifetime for me because I was frustrated with the current academic program at the college at which I was studying. I heard about the opportunity to study in Cuba from my mentor who said that I should apply for the medical scholarship being offered by the Cuban Government. While applying for the scholarship, it hit me that I would have to learn Spanish in order to complete the program. Not knowing Spanish, I had doubts that I would learn the language to any acceptable level. However, I was encouraged by a previous student who had completed the program and was now completely fluent in the language and completing his specialization. To my surprise, I was accepted into the program.

It was the 11th of November, 2007 when I boarded an airplane to leave for the Republic of Cuba. I had travel to Cuba to study medicine, which would span a time of seven (7) years. We were told that within the first year we would be taught Spanish, and then afterwards we would enter our Medical programme. I had a sudden fear that came over me, not knowing a word in Spanish, because I never studied it in high school. This tremendous trepidation overtook my thinking, and followed me my entire journey. When I arrived at the school, the people greeted me in Spanish and I returned their greeting with a smile (not knowing what to say). From that day forward, my learning began.

My encounter with the other students that studied Spanish before coming to Cuba fueled my motivation to move forward because they were the ones that were having "small talk" with the cocineros (cooks) in the school's cafeteria. I started asking a lot of questions, which played a major role in my learning. Through asking questions about the language, I cleared a lot of doubts and misconceptions I had about the language. In addition to the asking questions, I made friends with those that studied the language prior to coming to Cuba, therefore whenever I made errors I was corrected, and taught the proper way which I noted on a piece of paper to revise on a later basis.

Classes began January of the following year, and I still had trouble articulating a proper sentence. However, I knew how to greet people, so that's what I did whenever I saw anyone (professors, classmates, workers etc.). There were about 15 students that were under the tutelage of a professor by the name of Mary Gonzalez. She was an awesome and patient teacher who would stress that "there is no English to be spoken in my classroom!" And so it began our vigorous training regime. For a period of six to nine months we were taught with a three part objective, listening, writing and speaking.

When it came to the listening aspect, we would listen to the news every night. The very first time, the only words I understood was "Buenas noches" (Good night). I felt depressed thinking that this guy spoke for about 30mins and I only understood one word. As the months passed I started to understand what the reporter was saying, it felt like a great achievement for me because I felt like I was advancing.

In my opinion listening skills plays a vital role in learning a new language, because through listening to the news every night, I began to understand the rhythm in which the reporter spoke, which was pretty fast. I started to understand how he pronounced certain words as well as learning new ones, so my vocabulary increased as a result. In my experience, I suddenly found out that assimilating yourself with the culture, no matter the language, plays an essential role, which includes: listening to music, reading the newspaper, watching a movie or the news in the language.

The second aspect we focused on was our writing skills. Writing was sort of hard to master at first, but with consistency and dedication I got it. Our professor was bent on us understanding this important aspect because all of our subject classes were in Spanish. For me, I needed plenty of work, so I started reading the newspaper daily. Through reading in Spanish, I began to understand how to construct a sentence, as well as increasing my small vocabulary by learning new words. Writing short stories as well helped my writing skills, because as my professor corrected the errors I made, I learnt the do's and don'ts when it comes to conjugating different verbs.

The third aspect we focused on was our speaking skills, which was vital to our survival in a classroom. In learning Spanish in a classroom setting, I noticed that there were a lot of my classmates that were afraid to communicate out loudly. Reason being was that they were afraid to make mistakes or being laughed at. However the professors encourage us to speak whenever we had the opportunity no matter where we are on the school compound. Being in a school that spoke predominantly English was hard to do (our school didn't have Cuban students).

To counterattack this disadvantage, we had to practice the language amongst ourselves. To achieve this we had to constantly remind each other that we must speak Spanish whenever we have the chance. I would like to say to anyone wanting to learn a new language that it is always good to practice with people who are knowledgeable about the language, because they can correct you whenever you make a mistake.

By this correction, you learn the proper way the word is pronounced or the tense it is used, so that later on you prevent this error from happening again. In learning a new language you can't be shy or passive. I spoke with anyone I came into contact with in the school; the cooks, the school gardener, and the professors on a constant basis. Through doing this, you expand your social circle.

Lastly, I would like to say that in learning a new language you need to have perseverance because hard work does pay off. With consistency, dedication and enthusiasm learning a language becomes effortless. This is what has helped me to become conversational in the Spanish language, almost to complete fluency. A little enthusiasm and motivation goes along way.

Kristiaan from Germany recounts his experiences with the Swedish language

How I picked up Swedish to a fluent level within a short time

Hello everybody, my name is Kristiaan, I am a student from Germany and I am currently 21 years old. I would like to tell you a little bit about my approach in learning Swedish and how I came up with the idea in the first place.

Everything began in summer 2009 when I was doing an internship at a large multinational corporation located in Düsseldorf, Germany. For the last three weeks of my stay, in July, a Swede, Oskar, moved into my shared flat, who was about to start his internship at the same company. He was participating in a program of the Swedish embassy, which connected an internship with an intensive German language course. In total, there were forty Swedes participating in this program. Through Oskar, I came in contact with this whole group of Swedes and thus also with the Swedish language. I asked them to teach me some Swedish phrases, just for fun. I started with basis things like "Jag heter Kristiaan, jag kommer från Tyskland" (My name is Kristiaan, I am from Germany). It was really fun to get started and I realized that Swedish is quite similar to German and Dutch (my second mother tongue). However, due to my studies, I had to unfortunately leave Düsseldorf three weeks after Oskar had moved in. I was now able to state the fundamental phrases about myself in Swedish (age, name, hobbies etc.)

Motivated by this positive language experience, I decided

to buy a Swedish language software in order to improve my knowledge. Due to the high stress level and work load at my university, I didn't find any time within the next semester to study any more Swedish. In the end of January, my semester abroad in the United Kingdom commenced and I had in advance made a resolution to really study Swedish within this time period.

On the first night of my arrival day, all the international students went out together to a pub, not knowing anyone. In the course of the evening, I was talking to one of the students, Ted, and we found out that we were staying in the same shared flat – *and that he was Swedish.* This was a real coincidence. The university had randomly put us together. The funny thing was that he wanted to improve his German in the same way as I wanted to improve my Swedish. So we decided to buy a large white board, just like the ones you know from class rooms in schools or universities, and put it into our living room. We started writing Swedish and German terms onto the board everyday. This was really effective, because the board was always there and thus one automatically read the stuff written on to it.

Additionally, we labeled all devices, kitchen equipment, and furniture in the whole flat with both German and the Swedish titles. This was very helpful since you use these things every day. In our group of international students, there were three Swedes in total: Two from Stockholm and one from Göteborg. I can tell from my experience that it is very good if you live together with native speakers while learning a language. They can help you with everything and correct you immediately. It's also funny that I was learning Swedish, not my native language, but in English, which has proven to be a very good and neutral starting point, especially for explaining grammar.

After the semester abroad had finally finished at the end of May 2010, I followed Ted back to Stockholm. While sitting in the plane, I was really nervous whether everything would work out with the language. Moreover, it was my first stay in Sweden.

After arriving and having had the first little conversations in Swedish, I was surprised how well it went: almost fluently. Sweden is a quite small country and the Swedes don't expect foreigners to speak Swedish. Therefore, they are even more impressed if a foreigner *is* able to speak their language. This appreciation gives you a very positive feeling and makes you feel welcomed at the same time. It also motivates you to go on and improve even more. I spent three wonderful weeks in Sweden which led me to my next aim: an internship in Sweden. Back home in Germany I actually managed to achieve this goal: I was accepted at a software company in Stockholm! ;-) So I could spend another four weeks in August 2010 in this amazing country before my studies in Germany continued again.

The next step I would like to take is a Swedish language certificate. There are currently (08.2010) existing two different ones:

- SWEDEX http://www.swedex.info/def_eng.asp
- Tisus
  http://www.nordiska.su.se/pub/jsp/polopoly.jsp?d=1538

The first one is currently available only at the levels A2 and B1. Level B2 has been announced for spring 2011. The second certificate is only available at level C1. This depicts a very high level and it also allows you to study any subject you want to at the Swedish universities and in Swedish language.

I would like to give you a short overview of some good advice which really helped my learning and improving the language.

1.)**MOTIVATION:** First of all, the motivation behind the wish to learn a language is essential for your success. It's important to set yourself an aim which you want to achieve. For instance: *By next year, I want to be able to study in Swedish.* My motivation was to be able to talk to Swedes in Swedish and be able to communicate with them concerning day-to-day issues. I actually reached this aim and even more. ;-) Moreover, it is very good if you put your money where your mouth is and book a flight to Sweden in order to stay there for a specific period of time. By this, you create a future event which pushes you to reach your goal – *learning Swedish.* Furthermore, this helps preventing procrastinating very effectively. ;-)

2.)**TALK TALK TALK:** This is the essential key in improving the language. It is, as I said before, very helpful if you have the possibility to talk to native speakers from the very beginning. This boosts your progress enormously.

3.)**LANGUAGE SOFTWARE:** Buy a language software and study with it, especially the vocabulary. The best way is to write them down onto record cards and learn them while walking through the park, the forest, or the city.

4.)**SWEDISH SONGS:** Listen to Swedish songs, translate your favorite ones then sing along with them next time you listen to them. ;-)

5.)**SWEDISH SUBTITLES:** Watch movies/series with Swedish subtitles. The good thing in Sweden is that films and series don't get dubbed. So the original language (most of the time: English) stays and subtitles are displayed in the bottom of the screen. This fact actually helps the Swedes to be very good in English since they get in contact with English very early and intensively. When learning Swedish, one can make use of this fact the other way around: You hear the English language and you can read what is said in Swedish at the same time. This function of course only works if you already have profound knowledge of the original language.☐

6.)**TIME:** Learning a language is very time-consuming, so make sure to take your time and the success will follow. ☐

7.)**READING:** By reading daily Swedish newspapers (also available online) you can easily expand your range of vocabularies. Some recommendations:

    a. http://www.dn.se/

b. http://www.aftonbladet.se/
c. http://www.expressen.se/

8.)**CULTURE:** Start loving the people and the culture. Be interested in the mentality and the Swedish way of life. Detect similarities and differences between the Swedish culture and your own.

9.)**COUNTRY:** Visit Sweden and suck in language and culture. The permanent confrontation will be a challenge in the beginning, but it will turn out to be a very effective training which improves your language skills step by step.

I hope you liked my little report about learning the Swedish language and found it interesting and helpful. In case you should have any questions or comments, feel free to contact me: deadmau5rox@googlemail.com

Good luck with learning Swedish and best regards!
Kristiaan

Reading SanneT's submission reinforces what many people tend to forget: *you are never too old to learn!...*

A Most Reluctant Learner
by SanneT

I may be one of your more mature contributors: I am in my mid-60s and still, or rather again, trying to learn various languages.

Ever since I remember I have been interested in foreign languages; as children in post-war Germany we had for a while exposure to Russian, English, French and "American". If we were careful and didn't let ourselves be shooed away, we could approach the requisitioned houses and spy on the allied soldiers. (Our town was well placed for spying activities and until 1948 or so Russians were still stationed there, within the British zone.)

My childhood was marked by lost languages: first there was Russian, which I heard as a baby before my family fled to the West. The sound of male Russian voices can still send me dreaming, although nobody in my family could ever speak it. Once in the West, we lived with my grandparents who spoke Plattdeutsch. It was lovely when my normally taciturn grandfather called me "Na, mien lütten Poch" or "mien lütte Uhl". My mother, however, would not allow us to use what she called a common dialect and so I have only a limited knowledge of the most loved of my childhood languages.

At grammar school we had English, French and Latin. My

trouble started with English: whatever I did, it did not make any sense, there was no connection. English remained one-dimensional, something on paper and destined to torture me for years to come. I was lucky in that my English teacher liked me. He didn't give me the worst grade (which I thoroughly deserved) and so I didn't have to repeat a year at school. French was somewhat easier, I liked the sound of it and some of it stuck. From my years of Latin all I remembered was that "agricola" was masculine.

By the way, I was ace at German and at German grammar (in the first year at this school we had a teacher who had us play grammar games and I was quite often a particle in our joint sentences) and thus am not too bothered about grammar in other languages. I also like buying and reading big fat dictionaries, although I never learn anything, I simply like reading the examples.

In my early twenties I decided to give English another go because a friend and I wanted to go to New York. Well, we never made it, but I married my Berlitz teacher! He wanted to practise his German and, because of my terror of speaking English, I was the only one who insisted on speaking German to him. He must have liked it; he very soon proposed and I must have said 'Ja' because a year later I found myself in the UK for the very first time. Horror!!! The food, the language (Bristolian is difficult to understand at the best of times, tinned peas would stain potatoes green), sheer and utter horror.

Well, as I was still not speaking English to my husband, I had to practise it elsewhere. I read the newspapers very carefully and made notes of words that I found interesting. BBC radio and children's television provided further input. I tried evening classes, didn't do it for me, we were all foreigners, so it seemed quite pointless. I went to work. I still pity the poor people of Bristol that Christmas: I was manning the "Trim a tree" counter and to this day don't know how many wrong Christmas decorations I sold or how often I gave the wrong change. The Brits were still using Pounds, Shillings and Pence and there were twelve of those in one of those and 20 of those in one of those or the other way round. It was traumatic. Count yourself lucky that you didn't have to count in that currency. I was so glad when it changed soon after my attempt at ruining the British economy.

So I decided to teach myself how to type. Office work had to be easier. I hired a typewriter and began my glorious career as a temporary. It led to great things and one of them was that after several years of marriage I had no qualms about speaking English to my husband. Curiously enough, he preferred to carry on in German.

Alright, so I had English under my belt. But what about French? I never quite gave up on it, had spent a wonderful holiday in St Tropez in 1967 and would buy the odd magazine or newspaper and spend months trying to decipher it. A visit to Paris revived my interest briefly and so it went for years: an on-off relationship. I just couldn't learn. I have well-stocked shelves of Beginners' French books. Evening classes were a total put-off, as I developed aphasia. No sounds would come out of my mouth: amazing.

Russian also reared its head from time to time and I bought (and still have) most of the Russian Beginners books in print, and many out of print. Same story, though: no progress being made. I decided I was just too stupid for words, or for languages.

When my husband became ill, I often sat with him as he watched his Spanish news, he was a gifted linguist and had continued with French and had started on Spanish a few years before. So, after his death, it seemed natural to take up Spanish, which I duly did at our local adult education college. Having to speak still threatened to lead to panic attacks. But because of the many similarities between English and Spanish reading and writing were easy. I still couldn't memorise vocab, though.

I then decided I wanted to learn Arabic. As with Russian, the script is easy and beautiful. I bought a shed load of Arabic books and started. Unfortunately, our teacher gave up after a year and so my career as an Arab speaker was cut short, for once not by me. Although since then I have hardly looked at my treasure trove.

Luckily, in 2009 I came across Steve Kaufmann's book and the amazing LingQ.com website.

It was such an eye opener to read that mistakes don't matter, that uncertainty is good for the brain, that language learning is like walking through fog. One day it will lift and there you are!

Thanks to the wonderful LingQ tutors and forum members I have now overcome my nearly pathological fear of speaking or of making mistakes and am happily working on my French and Spanish, am dipping into Russian, Italian and Swedish as I fancy. I have even started to learn a bit of Japanese. It seems that, for me, languages need a little rest from time to time in order to settle in the brain. They seem much stronger when I then return to them, the initial anxiety attached to them having gone. Absence makes the heart grow fonder? I am also using German much more than I used to do.

In this context I want to mention Vera F. Birkenbihl, a prolific German author who advocates decoding languages before one attempts to read or to speak. I used her approach to get an overview of Arabic. I didn't follow her method too closely as I didn't have any audio material and at the time was already attending evening classes. For my next language, I might follow her instructions but using LingQ material. I suggested to her she might want to contribute her story to this project and I hope she will do it. She has a good tale to tell.

The greatest pleasure I have gained from continuing and stepping up my learning is that I can now enjoy French and Spanish literature, practically without recourse to a dictionary. I think this even outweighs my delight in being able to speak ´foreign´.

Another welcome side-effect of being an ardent LingQer is that I don't buy as many "Beginners XYZ" anymore. Life has become less expensive. I have found that I can learn a language from scratch with the resources on offer, especially now that word for word translations are available for some beginners material.

As I am quite inquisitive I like to read as many threads of the LingQ forum as possible. I have noticed lately that I understand more and more of the Portuguese posts, a language I have never looked at. I feel a bonus language coming up!

I am writing this at a time when I have hit yet another wall in my quest for ease and fluency, but by now I have learnt to not think of myself as too stupid (well, just a little bit) and to live peacefully with temporary walls instead of trying to bash my head against them. I now look forward to finding out what's behind them. As a matter of fact, I have just signed up for two French conversations and I shall have to do a little bit of writing in order to spend my accumulated LingQ points.

My recipe for reluctant learners:

- Be curious.
- Surround yourself with the language, whether you are at home or abroad.
- The '3 Rs': read, read, read.
- Persevere, but allow yourself time off, as much as you want/need.
- Try different approaches and/or different languages if you seem stuck.
- Use the resources at hand: mp3, iphone, whatever technology you like.
- If you can afford it, spend some time in the country of your chosen language, this is not necessary, though. You can learn anything, anywhere.
- [Have goals: mine are not specific, but I know I'm there once I read with ease and pleasure.]

- Marry a well-educated native speaker of your target language (Warning: this could lead to problems if your aim is polyglottery!).
- Learn to live with and learn from your mistakes, they'll appear funny to you after a while.
- Remain curious.

Jara from the Czech Republic, who comes to us, like so many others, by way of LingQ...

MY LANGUAGE ADVENTURE

I would like to contribute this piece to the Polyglot Project.

Primary school

I experienced my first failure when I was in my second class and I should have decided if I wanted to go to the language school or not. I did not know, but my parents wanted me to study there. There was something like an interview and each pupil should have said what he or she knew in any foreign languages. I don't remember so much from the interview, but I do remember that I failed and that certainly influenced my life. Before that, I used to go to the class with a lot of friends and with my cousin; however they were successful in the interview so they went to study to the language school from a new school year. I have been told by my family members many times that my cousin studied at language school and I studied only in normal school - I was an average pupil. He was better than me in everything, not only with school. I was always the worse one.

My parents wanted me to have good results at school, so I really tried hard but it was difficult for me. I was always different from other pupils who seemed to enjoy their lives doing what they wanted much more than I did.

In my 4th class, I had to pick a language which I wanted to

study. I picked German, or maybe my parents did, but never mind. So I was studying German in my primary school from my 4th year there up to 9th year, so it was for 6 years. When I look back to evaluate my German knowledge in final year at primary school, it was not too bad. I was quite confident, because I had been studying hard. Unfortunately, I had too many teachers in such a short time – maybe four teachers for the six years, which was not so good, because we always started over again because each new teacher was not sure what we knew.

High School

After my primary school I wanted to study Management in machining industry in high school. I studied two languages there, German and English. German was my first foreign language and I used to have it three times a week. English was was only once a week (one lesson took 45 minutes). Fortunately, for both langauges we had the same teachers for the whole time, so there was not any problem with starting again and again as before. I started learning English there, and it was my first experience with that language. As a total beginner who did not know anything about English, we were issued a book printed at Cambridge University that was completely in English. It was quite a difficult subject, but for me no subject had ever been difficult enough that I would have given it up without trying my best. I mean, a lot of students did not make any affort while learning subjects in primary school and high school. Some of them were satisfied with their grades, even though they had bad grades (maybe their parents did not care so much). So that's why even languages were not such difficult subjects for me—I worked so hard on them.

In the beginning of the final year, I had to decide what subjects I wanted to do for my final exam at high school. I could have picked a language or maths. A lot of students picked a language – either German or English. For me, I picked maths. I really enjoyed maths at high school. To me it was playing with numbers and variables--it was a subject that I enjoyed most of all. I decided to go to a technical university and to have fun with the similar subjects based on that.

So that's why I focused on maths even more in my final year and I even picked maths as my final exam, and from that point on I did not care about languages at all, because learning languages was not really enjoyable for me. Why not? I was used to memorizing vocabulary for tests and preparing for conversations for a specific topic, but I must say that I did not listen to anything at home, I did not speak German with anyone, anywhere—it was only used in at high school. So, let's calculate: 5 minutes per each lesson, 3 lessons a week, four weeks a month, 10 months a year, for four years – so the result is 2400 minutes, which is 40 hours.

Forty hours speaking for four years with my Czech speaking schoolmates did make me fluent at all. How could it? When I randomly heard native German speakers on radio and television, I did not understand them. And that was after 6 years of studying at my primary school and 4 years at my high school! So after 10 years of studying German "properly," according to SCHOOL METHODS, I had made very little progress fro such a hard-working student. Thinking about it now, it's obvious that I did not really care about my results in German at the time.

University

Studying at university was quite difficult. All of a sudden, I
lived alone, in a different city, without my parents,and I had
to look after myself. It was an interesting experience.
There were some problems because of my attitude
towards to my studies. But in two years, I realised what I
wanted. I really wanted to get a master's degree, so I
overcame my distaste for studying and focused on it
properly. So I started studying as much as I used to at
primary school and high school. I did not care about how
difficult the exams were, or what everyone said about
each exam. I started studying hard, and even though I did
not enjoy it at all, I saw my future, and I saw myself with a
good job because of having earned a good degree. I hate
failure, and when I did not pass an exam, I always became
depressed. Getting my master's degree was very stressful
for me.

In the university, I had to have one language, so I picked
German, because It was most familiar to me—more so
than English, of which I had really only a basic knowledge.
I studied German for 1 year at the university, I passed my
exam with the best result I could have gotten and that was
the last time I was took any interest in it, because although
I did well I still was not able really understand anything or
to express myself properly. My good results were
meaningless.

I was more and more interested in English. I mean, when I
wanted to find something…anything about mechanical

engineering, I had to find an English article. Everything was in English. Next thing was that I always watched American television series and I really wanted to watch them in English and to understand them. Some of my friends were able to speak either German or English (or at least to understand) and I was always amazed that somebody could have been fluent in a different language. In my third year at university, I started thinking about my future. I knew that I would have to know a foreign language in order to get a good job, but I did not speak any other languages at that time. I was not interested in German-- I was into English, so I found native-speaking private English tutors.

It was really difficult to understand them and after spending many hours with the tutors, I improved only a little bit . I did not know what I had been doing incorrectly,or how I should have learnt a language. Nobody had taught me that before. I was always used to memorising grammar rules and vocabulary, which has not helped me at all. But I did not give up and went on paying teachers, because I still had a hope.

I must say that I am very very strong-minded person and for me it was a personal failure that I did not know any other language by the age of 26, and it was then that I decided to go to do a Ph. D. I knew that if you do a Ph. D you can go abroad and study there. It was a really great opportunity for me. I thought that it was my last chance to become fluent in English, and I really did not know what else to do.

I could have gone abroad in my second year in my Ph. D .,

so during the first year I chose an English program at my university in order to prepare myself for my second year in England. In the courses there were professors, docents and Ph. D. students from my faculty. The courses were divided according to levels and I was placed in the pre-intermediate level. I did not really enjoy the classes. I was stressed because I did not want to appear stupid in front of all clever people there. The methods were based on working with textbooks—the same principle as always before. At the end of the year, I did not pass the final test. If you pass the test, your English level is considered pre-intermediate and you can go on to the next level – the intermediate level. Since I did not pass the test, I was still considered an elementary student. Since most of the other people in the course passed the test, needless to say it was not good for my self-confidence.

Thinking about it, the language courses were not so good for me, because at primary school and high school, I only wanted to pass tests in order to continue advancing to the next level, but because of my test results (and the added stress of wanting to get into a good university) and my mediocre grades, I was now really stressed and did not enjoy it at all.

England

As I described before, I finished my language course with an elementary level and with that level I arrived in England in September 2009. It was very difficult for me, because I did not understand most of what I heard and I had difficulty expressing myself in most situations, even easy ones.

After a month of living in England, I improved my English only a little bit through speaking with people. At that time, I realised what it was that I wanted and that I would do my best in order to do it. I realised shortly after arriving in England that my goal had always been learning languages, especially English, and in achieving that goal *I had always been a failure*. Usually, when I had wanted to achieve a goal, I generally accomplished it. So why was I not able to master English?

I started to research articles in English on the Internet. I have read many articles about people around the world who struggle with learning languages just myself . I found a method called the "Effortless English" system which is based on deep listening. The founder of the method is American and I could understand him very clearly even with my low level of English. I became motivated. I bought his courses – the original "Effortless English" system and "Real English," and I listened to the recordings all the time, as he recommended--10 to 15 hours a day! My listening comprehension began getting better and better. I understood natives more and more and I got better at expressing myself. It was amazing. I kept going on listening to those courses over and over again.

One of the recordings was about a guy who can speak 11 languages who has his own system for learning languages--the "LingQ" system. I looked for the web page on the internet and registered there. This system was something completely new for me. I must mention that I have come across many language systems on the internet and that I haven't found one which comes close to being this good. At LingQ, I could do everything :

- I can pick a lesson which I want to listen to or read,
- I can have a conversation with a tutor I pick (American, British or Canadian),
- I can submit my writing for correction.

After a month of using the LingQ system I realised that a lot of things I had previously been taught about learning foreign languages was not at all suited to my style of learning. I have found, for example, that:

     a. I must learn languages independently, otherwise my mind tends to wander; and

     b. I can't be driven by anyone, and I can't work on a lesson which I don't like. I must always pick something that I enjoy.

At LingQ I could do that. I started reading and listening to podcasts about learning methods and about different approaches. I read a book, "The Linguist - A Personal Guide to Language Learning" written by the founder of the LingQ system, Steve Kaufmann. I did not think about learning for its own sake; I read and I really enjoyed it. It was interesting to read a language learning adventure by someone who was so successful at it in his own life. I have improved a lot by both reading and listening to that book.

I must mention that I had never liked reading--maybe because of school. I have read a lot of uninteresting books at school in order to pass my exams, and as a consequence I did not like reading. I always became tired after reading a couple of pages, or even paragraphs. At lingQ, there is a unique system which is very useful. I was always afraid of reading texts and books in English because there were so many words that I did not know. By using LingQ, in a few months I was able to read advanced articles , and now I can read almost everything in English. It is really an amazing and very powerful tool. I have become addicted to this system!

I have heard many times that language learning is about community, so I started reading forums at LingQ in order to get to know what was new and what type of members were on LingQ. I was amazed at finding out about people there who can speak many languages and who learn more than one language at once. The articles on forums are so interesting and have helped me a lot as I embarked on my own program of learning languages. I wanted to participate in these forums more and more when I realised the power of LingQ's language community. This has also helped me a lot to improve my English, since I really wanted to understand what people were talking about there. Personally, I think that it is beneficial when learning languages to participate in forums and read articles in and about your target language.

I was so influenced by members of LingQ that I started brushing up my German, which was not good at all when I took it up again. I had forgotten almost everything I had previously learned, but now, armed with LingQ, I know that I can master German. I don't care about making an effort in order to do it. I have always made an effort anyway so it is nothing new for me. But now, with the right method, *the method that works for me,* I know I can learn as many languages as I want.

I did not mention my previous experience with Spanish. It

happened a long time ago during my childhood, but it's a really nice story. I wanted to learn Spanish because of a singer/actress from Uruguay. I learnt her songs and sang them out loud. I was in love with her. I studied Spanish for three months back then but I remember it even more than German- which I later studied for 11 years!

A few weeks ago I listened to her songs again and I still really like them. I wanted to understand them properly, so I found the texts of her songs on the Internet, put them into LingQ and started learning it by using the unique lingQ method for linking each word. Then I picked a couple of Spanish lessons at LingQ , and it was not too bad. I was still able to understand a lot even though I learnt Spanish for only 3 months 15 years ago! I now have another goal of mastering Spanish. I have really a strong passion for it.

I have even tried to learn a bit Polish, since it is quite similar to Czech. I have read a couple of articles written by a Polish member and I understood them . It would not take a long time to learn it. Maybe when it will be added in LingQ in the future, I will learn it properly since I have now become a big language lover.

Conclusion:

Why was I not successful in learning languages before?

I did not really enjoy the process of learning before. I always had just a short-term goal (usually an exam)– so even though I made an effort in order to reach those goals, it was not enough to master the language. It was only just enough to fulfill the requirements in order to graduate. When I found how enjoyable the learning process itself could become, that's when I started to see the best results. I wanted to get to know people from all over the whole world and learn about different cultures. I finally learned to love the language learning process. I did not complain anymore about how difficult the language was or how it was different from my native language.

→ I did not enjoy learning languages at all.

When you don't enjoy doing something, you do it only when you have to (especially in my case). In the past I learnt languages for tests and so on, and I spent a minimum amount of time studying languages at home, as I always felt that there were better things to do. What little time I spent with leaning languages was occupied with memorising words taken from boring textbooks which held little interest for me.

→ I used to use methods which were not effective for me and texts which were not interesting for me.

As I mentioned before, when you don't enjoy doing something, you do it only when you have to and you do only what is necessary. I did not listen to the languages which I was studying at all. I did not have any podcasts like I do nowadays. I did not even know how powerful a tool they can be. I bought a couple of CD's which were together with textbooks, but they were really boring.

→ I did not listen to languages which I learnt.
I was thinking about the difficulty of the languages I

studied, and not how much fun learning them could be. I had this attitude for many years.

→ I had a bad attitude and a different belief than I do at the moment.

Everything I have experienced so far with learning languages has been very interesting, and I am glad that I finally found my own way to learn languages. There is not one universal method to learning languages.

Everyone must find their own way. I have met people who know many languages and who actually like learning grammar rules (why not…as long as it works for them!). But everyone can benefit from being an independent learner. An independent learner learning grammar rules is certainly much more successful than that learner would be just memorizing grammar rules at school.

RULES FOR SUCCESSFUL LEARNING:

- If you want to be a successful learner, be an independent learner
- As they say, "Practice makes perfect." Without practice, you won't be successful in learning languages.
- Listening is the key; you should listen to your target language as much as possible .
- In order to increase your vocabulary, you must read. Reading is so powerful.
- When you feel confident in listening and you know a lot of words, you should speak as much as possible.
- You should enjoy learning your target language; if you don't enjoy it it won't stick.

If you are successful in one language, you will want to learn more languages ;)

After being influenced by YouTube Polyglots, Aaron is off and running...

Aaron Posehn
Vancouver, Canada
www.aaronposehn.net
www.youtube.com/user/aaronposehn

Languages have been an area that I have been infatuated with for a great majority of my life. Though I'm not sure why I started to find them interesting, I do remember starting, and it's been an enriching experience ever since, not to mention just fun! There's just something about learning a language that is so appealing and interesting that makes all the initial hard work of starting to learn a new one worthwhile.

My first taste of foreign language learning started when I was about ten. As with many a resident in the predominately English-speaking parts of Canada, my initial encounter with a foreign language was when I was required to take classes to study our country's other official language: French. I had just started Grade 5 and so I wasn't either overly interested or disinterested at the time about having to learn another language; it was just one of those things a kid has to get through before he can go outside and play at recess. However, one day a few months into the fifth grade, I discovered that one of the bookshelves in my house was home to a curious (and massive) English dictionary, *The Reader's Digest Great Encyclopedic Dictionary*, newly published in 1975 (which would have made it about 20 years old at the time). At its back, I found several additional foreign language dictionaries, namely those of German, French, and Spanish. For some reason, the German entries so intrigued me that I started copying down words from this book and keeping lists for reference. I loved it! I even remember being at a parent-teacher interview at one point in which I brought my German lists with me and was asked by my teacher about my interest in the language (My victory was that I was able to tell him how to say *apple* in German – *Apfel*).

My initial interest in German may have been due to three of my four grandparents being native German speakers (though also born in Canada). Though they didn't habitually speak German (even amongst themselves as far as I could tell) by the time I came along to know them, they still had information they were willing to share with me if I asked them. I guess I was just a little boy who found a fascinating key to my family's past and was excited to take advantage of it.

Later that year, just before the fifth grade was over, I discovered another book, though this time it was in my elementary school's library. It was a picture book of sorts that explained one Chinese character per page, displaying about twenty or so in total. I found this book utterly fascinating, and once again, I can remember myself sitting out on the playground and crudely copying down these characters onto a piece of paper for later reference. My interest in German by this time had all but waned completely, so I was free to plunge myself fully into this newest interest – and plunge I did. By the time I was twelve, I had gotten my parents to enroll me in a local after-school Chinese course that was provided in my city.

The courses, and subsequently the school where the courses were held, were run by a large group of mostly Taiwanese women, therefore giving me a foundation in traditional Chinese characters (and therefore also Taiwanese culture) before I even really knew what simplified characters were; an advantage, I think, over the more usual way of learning the simplified characters first as it was easier to learn them after already having knowledge of the traditional versions.

My Chinese school had two streams one could enroll in: Chinese classes for students with no Chinese family background and Chinese classes for students who came from a Chinese family (the second stream was like the equivalent of high school students who already speak English taking English class; you're not learning so much how to speak English as you are the language's literature and writing). The first stream was on Wednesday afternoons and was similar to any other basic language course a person might take, and of course was filled with mostly Caucasian, Korean, and other non-Chinese speaking individuals mostly in the high-school age bracket. In the second stream, however, the language of instruction was solely in Mandarin, with the students ranging from age three to eighteen. Also, as I said, *all* of the students were Chinese, either born in a Chinese-speaking country or to a Chinese household here in Canada. This large amount of Chinese students would be expected, given the goals that the Friday lessons were trying to achieve, except that that wouldn't be the case for long.

After two years of attending the Wednesday, non-Chinese family background classes, my teacher suggested that I transfer to the Friday class. I did so, and found myself from then on, at age fourteen, in a classroom with mostly a whole bunch of nine and ten year old Chinese kids (what was even more interesting was that I was the only white person in this school of five hundred plus students!). Due to growing up in Chinese house-holds, the kids in my class obviously had better Chinese than me at that point, though their parents soon got to criticizing their children's bad attitudes towards going to class. The kids hated going, though the parents of these children soon were even telling their kids to work harder as I was showing such an interest in learning and they were not. That year, I also go to do a speech in front of the entire Chinese school, some five hundred students and their parents, about my experience and interest in Chinese. It was fun, and from what I can remember, most people seemed impressed, or else a little bit confused, to see some random white kid speaking Chinese in their school.

After graduating high school at 18, I stopped going to these Chinese courses (and also stopped the French courses I had been taking up until that point as well) and started taking a Chinese language course now at college. In retrospect, this course was designed rather poorly in that minimal Chinese was ever spoken during class time other than the occasional sentence when a student would have to read to the class from the textbook. By this point, though, I had a fairly decent grasp on conversational Mandarin (and my French was alright to an extent). However, after my first semester at college, I kind of drifted away from languages and, among other things, explored different areas of study for my degree. At one point or another, I touched on everything from business administration to psychology to computer science to political science to philosophy – you might say I had a very *liberal* education (I still find most of these fields interesting, so maybe it was good that I tried them all out!). I eventually transferred to the University of British Columbia where I majored in Asian Area Studies, focusing mostly on China and India. I realize now that most of my personal language learning at this point was focused much more on theoretical questions regarding language and second language acquisition, and not so much time was spent on actually learning new languages or improving upon the ones I had previously studied. This was fine for the time, however, as I was fascinated with the intricacies and grammar of many of the Indian languages as well as a lot of the Chinese languages, and my degree was a good place to get a lot of information about all of these things.

During my last semester or two at university, I started to discover the Youtube polyglot network due to my interest in second language acquisition (and just the sheer amazement that I got every time I watch some of these guys speak four, five, seven, eleven different languages. People like Moses McCormick and Steve Kaufmann (who I recently got to meet – fascinating guy!) were two of the first few polyglots I came across on Youtube, later finding many more who always impressed me. I found Stuart Jay Raj especially motivating in that the majority of the languages he seems to speak are mostly located in Asia, the subject of my degree, so I found that especially interesting since it was related to what I was studying. All in all, the Youtube polyglot network has caused me to become more focused once again on learning languages, not so much theoretically or linguistically (though I'm still interested in these fields), but in terms of speaking and communicating. I have since started once again to seriously study my Mandarin and French and have found myself greatly improving in a very short time. I've also started studying Japanese recently, though Arabic, Russian, and Spanish are on my list as well for future study.

Studying languages is a way of life for me now because it opens up so many doors and allows a person to learn things that wouldn't have been necessarily available to them otherwise. I've been able to make many interesting foreign friends, especially through avenues such as Facebook, and this has allowed us to help each other improve our language skills even more. It just feels so good when you know that you can be understood and can understand someone in a language that is not your mother tongue! Because of this, no matter what I end up doing in my life, I'm going to continue to make room for learning foreign languages until the day I die.

Mick uses a variety of techniques to help him acheive his goals. Here are some of the ones he has tried...

Maybe you know me through my occasional YouTube comments as mick1316591 or on the how-to-learn-any-language.com forum as mick33. I'm not a polyglot yet, and don't know whether or not I will become one someday. I am currently learning Afrikaans, Spanish, Finnish and Swedish. Maybe I will learn more languages and maybe I won't, I don't know for sure--but for now those 4 are enough. I believe I am still a beginner at learning languages because there always will be more to learn, so I don't have much advice to give. I will begin by introducing myself, then I will explain how I became interested in learning languages, and my experiences with learning languages.

A little bit about me
I want to remain semi-anonymous, so I'll use the name Mick. I live in Washington State in the USA. I am a college student working towards at least a masters degree in psychology. The focus of my studies is most likely going to be clinical psychology, however I am also extremely curious and passionate about learning foreign languages.

How I got started
I began learning Afrikaans in 2006, Finnish in the spring of 2009, and Swedish in summer 2009. It's difficult to say when I started learning Spanish, but Spanish is the first foreign language I was ever fascinated by, and may be the reason I'm writing this piece.

I began to be interested in Spanish when I was 5 years old. One day, my kindergarten class was taught to count from 1 to 10. I was very excited and came home to tell my mother that I could count and then did so. My mother decided this was the perfect time to teach me the little bit of Spanish she remembered from her class in high school, which included counting from 1 to 10, and how to pronounce the rolled 'r' sound. I still remember being excited that I could count to 10 in two languages, and I loved the how Spanish sounded. My grandfather on my father's side had learned some French when he had lived in Frnace in the 1960s, and not to be outdone, taught me to count from 1 to 10 in French as well. I didn't learn the French numbers as quickly, but my grandfather patiently repeated them until I could say them confidently, though I doubt my pronunciation was ever very good. Although I never learned any more French, and my mother could not have taught me more Spanish than she did, from then on I was fascinated by foreign languages.

Getting sidetracked as a teenager
I have never thought language classes are bad, they can be useful as an introduction to a language; but I now know that a class by itself will not get me reading, writing or speaking a language. I did not know what to take for the final class in 7th grade, so I registered for a Spanish class. The class was meant to be a brief introduction to Spanish culture with a little bit of vocabulary so I actually learned very little, although it did make me want to learn more. In high school, one of the graduation requirements was that every student must take two years of a foreign language. Again, I chose Spanish. The teacher I had the first year was a nice lady with a charming Mexican

accent and was an excellent teacher. Unfortunately, the school let her leave after that, which was a shame because I know I would have learned much more Spanish from her.

The second year I had a mediocre teacher whose sole qualifications for teaching languages seemed to be that she was originally from Switzerland, could speak 6 or 7 languages and worked as a translator at an embassy. She had a difficult personality, sometimes confused Spanish with other languages she knew, and her English and Spanish were both difficult for me to understand because she spoke with a very thick German accent. I learned almost nothing from her class. I learned just enough Spanish to barely pass the tests. I was so frustrated by the experience of not learning much Spanish that I ignored languages for the next 15 years, occasionally regretting not actually having learned any Spanish.

Rekindling my interest and learning Afrikaans
Regret does not motivate me to learn languages, or anything else,and I didn't really become genuinely interested in languages again until the summer of 2006. One day, I was reading about the history of South Africa and became very curious to learn more about the 19th century, which was a tumultuous time for South Africa. I wanted more than just the British perspective on South African history. I wanted to learn Zulu initially, but when I couldn't suitable resources for Zulu, I decided on Afrikaans after hearing it spoken on an internet broadcast of an obscure radio call-in show based in New York City. I don't recall the show's name or the web address

but the hosts were interviewing a South African woman from Bloemfontein and midway through the interview she was asked if she would like to say something in Afrikaans. She then spoke in Afrikaans for about 3 minutes. I was sitting at my computer in awe! I understood nothing, but I thought "What a beautiful language," and then knew I had to learn it. I did a web search and soon found http://openlanguages.net/afrikaans run by Dr. Jacques du Plessis, and started reading, listening and attempting to learn pronunciation.

I had no idea what I was doing and, after reading that Afrikaans is very closely related to Dutch, I decided I might try learning both languages simultaneously. My reasoning was: "I like both languages, they are fairly close to English, and besides many more people speak Dutch; this will be easy. I'll be fluent in both languages in a few months." I was mistaken. Instead of learning 2 languages, I became confused and decided I had to drop Dutch. This was an easy choice since I was more interested in Afrikaans anyway.

In the fall of 2006 I moved to Idaho and did not have a computer in the apartment I was living in, so I stopped learned Afrikaans until January 2007, when I moved back to Washington and had a computer again. I decided to start over using Dr du Plessis's site and the discussion group he started at http://groups.yahoo.com/group/learn-afrikaans/.

I like music, and after discovering that the *openlanguages* site had many mp3 files along with lyrics in both Afrikaans and English for many of its songs, I started trying to sing

along with the music. I also wrote a few messages for the discussion group and had my first embarrassing moment in a foreign language when I asked if "Ek het lemoensap gedrink" (I have drunk orange juice) could also
be expressed as "Ek het lemoensap verdrink" (I have orange juice drowned). I continued to learn Afrikaans slowly but surely, and just figured that doing so would satisfy my curiousity some innate curiosity about languages.

The last two years: Almost becoming obsessed with languages

Then, sometime in 2008, I found the HTLAL website. I began reading, and then contributing to, the discussions on the forum and decided it would be a great place to get advice on how to better learn Afrikaans, thinking maybe I would finally revive my Spanish as well. When I first joined, I thought that I couldn't possibly learn more languages by myself; that soon changed for a combination of reasons. It's difficult to say that one person's posts or experiences motivated me because there were many people who I read about that were in the process of learning many languages and I thought: 'If these people can do this, maybe I can too'. So, I started a personal log solely to write about learning Afrikaans. While writing messages there I began trying to figure out just how I wanted to go about learning languages, and that I definitely wanted to learn Spanish. I also read about something called the Total Annihilation Challenge (TAC), which is where one person keeps a log for a certain amount of time, a month, 6 weeks, or maybe a whole year describing one's language learning; with the focus being to improve whatever study habits are effective, and 'annihilating' those habits that are not.

I also read about other languages just because I was curious. I kept reading that Finnish had 14 or 15 cases, used more post-positions than prepositions and had other features that would make it very challenging to learn for someone who speaks an Indo-European language.

Surprisingly, reading these kinds of statements did not discourage me; rather, I was inspired and began listening to Finnish music on YouTube and finding books and websites to teach me the language. My progress is, admittedly slow (I'll explain this later), but I don't care—I'm enjoying it.

Around New Year's day 2009 I decided two things:

1. I was definitely going to learn Spanish.
2. I would begin a TAC log and attempt to keep it going for a whole year.

I was shocked to find that everyone and his dog seems to have a website or a book that claims it will teach me Spanish (for a price), and thinking that it might be easier to take a class at the community college, I registered for Spanish 121, the beginning Spanish course. My log was called "My poor overwhelmed brain," and this was when I really got into learning, and learning about, languages.

Initially I only intended to write about, and sometimes write in, Afrikaans and Spanish, but I added Finnish in the spring, and then Swedish over the summer as well. I mostly wrote in English, but I did sometimes write in the other languages, but mostly I wrote in Afrikaans and Spanish.

Why take up Swedish? A few reasons: first I was listening to a song on YouTube called "Vi kommer att dö, samtidigt du och jag" (We're going to die at the same time, you and I) sung by Annika Norlin under the name "Säkert!" Despite the the name, it is actually a humorous pop song and I loved hearing it so much I just had to learn the words. I also found out that Swedish is an official language of two countries (Sweden and Finland) and that these countries had an intriguing history, since Finland was actually part of Sweden for many centuries.

I took the Spanish class in January and this time I actually did learn it. I knew that the textbook and other class materials were not sufficient for me, so I also listened to music I found on YouTube and sometimes attempted to read articles and books.

Where I am now and general comments on how I learn languages
Keeping the log was itself a learning experience for me. I did keep it going all year, but there was an unplanned 3 week break due to computer problems, and you may have noticed that I seem a bit disorganized, choosing languages almost on a whim and admitting that my progress with Finnish is slow.

The reasons for this are that I became very curious about languages in general, and would do things like try to learn a phrases in Hungarian, Romanian, Limburgish etc., or attempt to write Chinese characters. Sometimes I would daydream of devising a master plan to learn 10 or maybe 20 languages by a certain age, but naturally I could not maintain a consistent effort trying to learn so many languages.

My reasoning was "What if I traveled to Budapest met a charming Hungarian woman in a café, and she spoke very limited English while I spoke very limited Hungarian? Our conversation would not last long, nor would we get acquainted at all. This is not a judgment or criticism of others who can, and often do, learn many languages; rather it's an admission that I have many interests and goals in life, some of them directly pertain to languages, and some do not. Thus, in October 2009 I decided that I needed to focus on the four languages I've already mentioned.

For 2010 I started a new TAC log http://how-to-learn-any-language.com/forum/forum_posts.asp?TID=18662 and I thought up a more detailed study schedule (though I don't strictly follow it, which is why my Finnish, and Spanish, are coming along very slowly). This log was intended to have more messages in all 4 languages using very little English, but lately it has more Swedish messages.

Right now, I am most intrigued by Swedish and I want to be even more focused. I used to be bothered that I take a long time to learn languages, but now I am comfortable with this slow pace. Besides, I've spent my whole life learning English and am still learning it even now, and I assume this is true for other languages. I can't afford to travel yet, and of the languages I'm learning, Spanish is the only one I know I can use without moving abroad; so I don't need to be in a hurry.

Regarding the best method or program for language learning, I would say that there isn't just one. One technique, book, class etc., by itself probably won't work; so it is necessary to find a combination of techniques, books/programs and maybe even a class that you like and try to be consistent. I constantly need to remind myself that each individual language learner has different reasons for learning languages and unique goals, therefore, how *they* learn may not work for me (and how I learn may not work for them) and that's fine. I mostly use the Teach Yourself and Colloquial series language course books and many websites, but the links are too numerous to list here.

 I believe that languages (at least written languages) have three basic components; in no particular order these are: Sounds, Writing system, and Grammar.

Sounds includes phonics, intonation, stress (what part of a word or sentence I should emphasize). This may be the least important thing since I'm not convinced that I can achieve a native accent in any language (and in fact i'm sometimes told that my accent in English is a little unusual).

Writing system comprising the alphabet or character system as well as the spelling system, which is important when studying languages and/or dialects which are similar (such as Dutch and Afrikaans, since one noticeable distinguishing characteristic is the slightly different spelling systems).

Grammar, which I will describe as being word order in a sentence, pronouns, verbs, adjectives, adverbs, prepositions or postpositions, plural and diminutive forms of words, and negation, and (assuming these things exist) case endings, verb tenses (including conjugation patterns), and genderization.

The first thing I want to do is get an idea of how a specific language should sound, so I start looking for both recordings and written explanations of how to pronounce letters (I haven't begun to learn any language that does not have an alphabet, so I can't say whether this is a good strategy for Chinese, Japanese, etc.) and words.

I am somewhat of a musical person so I then find songs and radio broadcasts online in the target language. I do this because I want to get my brain accustomed to the sound and rhythm of the new language, with the ultimate goal being to being able to spontaneously think in the new language. At first I don't care that I won't understand anything I'm hearing, but after a week I try to find lyrics for the songs I listen to and try to discern distinct words while listening to the songs a few times.

I don't try to produce the sounds I hear initially; I'd rather wait until I can hear the song or letters and words in my head first, which usually takes me 4 listens. I then try to speak or sing along simultaneously with the recording. I usually look for songs on YouTube. Song lyrics, and poetry, are not a good way to learn grammar because often to make words rhythmically flow the phrases are not grammatically correct ,but that doesn't matter at this stage because I just want to hear languages as they are spoken and sung.

After a week or so of spending at least an hour a day listening, I figure it's time to learn basic vocabulary and grammar. This means things like greetings, pronouns, and a few verbs and nouns (I try to learn the same words in every language, because I'm the same person regardless or whether I happen to be writing or speaking Afrikaans or Spanish) so that I can give a brief introductory message. To do this I need to know a little about word order and the most basic tenses. My introductions could include things like my name, my age, where I live, what I do during the day, my interests, hobbies, and maybe a little bit about why I'm learning the language. Next, I learn about how to introduce myself verbally; then I start listening and repeating recorded dialogues and making up my own simple sentences and deconstructing them by translating them into English using the word order of the target language.

When the above activities start to feel like unnecessary reviews, then it's time for finding authentic material to read. Authentic material could be poems, stories and newspaper articles. I like to have a bilingual dictionary at this stage, but I don't think it's absolutely necessary and I have only two, one for Spanish and one for Dutch. I can't find any good bilingual dictionaries for Afrikaans, Finnish or Swedish at a price I can actually afford right now.

First I try to read the material and see how many words I

actually know without looking them up. Then I might try to do Professor Arguelles' scriptorium technique, which is to find a written text (preferably a book but newspaper articles may work better at this stage), and read it aloud one sentence at a time. You read each sentence 3 times, the first time reading out of the book (or article), the second time writing and pronouncing each word (don't worry about how awkward it feels and sounds to do this) separately, and finally reading the sentence as I wrote it down.

Scriptorium is probably a somewhat advanced activity, and I've only done this for Afrikaans,(although Spanish is definitely next), but I like it because it helps me get over being self-conscious about speaking, reading and writing a language all at the same time. I learn more grammar and vocabulary gradually as needed. For example, Afrikaans may have 9 tenses (though I can only find information on 4), but I only know 3 of them, past, present and future; I don't need the other 6 yet. Spanish has at least two subjunctive tenses.

Conclusion

I have not yet spoken Afrikaans, Swedish or Finnish with anyone yet, so I don't really know if I can. I do feel that I must attempt to do so soon, because I want to know if my techniques have actually worked and what things I still need to learn. I sometimes make random comments in Spanish and get praised for my pronunciation, but most of the praise comes from English speakers so I'm uncertain how well I actually pronounce Spanish. However, the most important thing for me is to treat learning these languages as a never-ending adventure.

I initially subscribed to Alsuvi's Channel on the recommendation of a friend, and also to hear what Catalan sounded like. I have not regretted it...

Tune into his YouTube Channel at:
http://www.youtube.com/user/alsuvi

Having watched many great videos on YouTube featuring quite a few people amazingly speaking so many languages, I began thinking about how many languages I could learn to speak myself, with the aim of someday posting similar videos on YouTube. At present, I may say that I can get by in four and a half languages: Catalan, Spanish, English, French and Italian, even though I do not feel I have the same level of proficiency in all of them. But let's start at the beginning...

My name is Albert Subirats, and I am from Barcelona, Catalonia, in the north-east of Spain. I am a privileged person because I was born in an area that has its own language (Catalan) and culture alongside the Spanish one, so I have grown up using two languages or interchangeably—in other words—as a perfectly bilingual person.

In Catalonia around 47% of the population speaks Catalan, but everyone also speaks Spanish. Among those who have Spanish as their main language, some of them also speak Catalan, while others understand it but cannot speak it. A smaller percentage neither speak nor understand it.

Usually, in a bilingual environment one language prevails over the other; that is, you can effortlessly speak both languages, but you feel more comfortable with one of them. In my case, I may say that I think more often in Catalan than in Spanish, but at any rate I consider myself a perfect bilingual because I have always spoken Spanish with my mother and Catalan with others. Thus, I feel equally comfortable in using both languages.

When you live in a bilingual environment, there is always a lot of contact between both languages, and there is some inevitable vocabulary transfer. In other words, because Catalan and Spanish are quite similar languages (both are Romance languages), most of the grammar or spelling mistakes we make are due to the influence of the other language. Is this too confusing or does it imply that we make more mistakes than, say, a monolingual Spanish speaker? No, not necessarily. It is just that the kind of mistakes we make are mainly because of the influence of the other language. I utterly understand that people tend to defend their own language, but I do not understand why some people prefer to be monolingual instead of bilingual or multilingual. As I said, I consider myself to be privileged and I am very proud of being bilingual.

The other two languages that I feel more or less fluent in are English and French, but I have a really different experience with each of them and I have learned them in quite different ways.

I will start with English, because it is my first foreign language and the one I have been studying for the longest time. At present in Spain students start studying English earlier than I did, even though I am not sure this means they will do better in the future. In my time as a student we started at 6th (more or less at 12 years old).

The foreign language teaching here is really unproductive and not the best way for one to learn the real language. Fortunately, I was one of the few privileged students that had a native speaking English teacher for the first two years. She was tough and strict, but I learned a lot (even if I was taught in the traditional way); to the point that I consider that they were indeed the only two years in which I really learned something about English in school.

From then on, I just had several average teachers that just repeated the same boring and utterly useless things year after year. Maybe it was just a coincidence, but those first two years with that native speaking teacher, I was in no way a brilliant English student; in fact, nothing could be further from the truth!

However, in the years that followed (High School), I was one of the best students in my English class, although I really did not do anything to deserve that "title," as I did not really study a lot.

There was no Internet or anything similar available to us, so we did not have the amount of resources that we have at present. Apart from the little bit that you got at school, it was hard to get any materials with real English content of any kind, aside from the occasional movies playing in some small old-fashioned cinema from time to time.

At the University, I studied Translation and Interpreting,

and I had English as my major and French as the minor (I started French from scratch). So in the first year I had some classes in English with native speaker teachers, but they were more focused on general culture and history rather than on actually teaching the language.

I finished my degree, and did a postgraduate degree in localization (the adaptation of computer software for non-native environments, especially in other nations and cultures) and I started to work as a freelance translator. I've been working in this for the last 8 years (apart from also proofreading and translating between Spanish and Catalan).

Reading and translating, reading and translating...

Contrary to popular belief, translating is not about communicating (in its interactive meaning); it is about understanding an original text and trying to say the same things or express the same ideas in your own language, and in a natural way.

So what happened after a few years of just reading and translating? My speaking skills got worse and worse. I also forgot a lot of basic, everyday's vocabulary because I just read technical English.

A couple of years ago, at a friend's party, I met a German guy and when I tried to speak to him in English I felt really uncomfortable and a bit embarrassed, especially when I told him that I was a translator! "Yes, I know, it's weird, I'm not really fluent in English, but you know, I just read boring technical manuals all day...."

Oh God, it was a disaster! It is true, I do not need any speaking skill to do my job properly, but anyway, for my personal pride it was unacceptable.

Therefore, my first move to change that situation was to spent a month in an English speaking country, such as Ireland.
After spending four weeks there I could not say that I became fluent, but it was a first step towards losing my fear of speaking. It was the first time I had ever lived surrounded by English, and I had to use the language everyday in order to survive there. It was a great and very useful experience.

When I came back home, I decided to keep on improving my English, and after a lot of research (and dismissing the traditional grammar approach offered by most of the language schools here), I came across LingQ on the Internet. I am not going to explain here how it works, but I just love its approach to language learning. It has been really useful to me since I started using it, about a year and a half ago.

I also believe, however, that there is not a magic formula for everyone, and that you must choose what works best for *you*. In the beginning, I only used LingQ to study their lessons and to improve my vocabulary and reading comprehension.

After a few months, when I felt more confident, I started to sign up for one-on-one conversations with native speaking tutors. Eventually, I began to also participate in group conversations (which I personally think requires a higher level as you should be able to take part in a discussion with several people simultaneously).

Right now I am using LingQ mainly to improve my speaking or communicative skills by participating in individual and group conversations. I also review some vocabulary from time to time, but I use a lot of content from outside sources such as the Internet. I watch and listen to a lot of content in English, such as YouTube videos, TV shows and movies. I also read a lot (I think that all the novels I have read for the last year have been in English) and I try to write to as many people that I can, whether in forums or corresponding with friends.

So where am I right now? I feel fluent and confident enough to hold a conversation with a native speaker. I understand most of what I hear, and I can even understand a lot of jokes and some kinds of irony. Have I reach my goal? No yet. There are still a lot of moments in a conversation in which I do not find the words I want to use so I have to try to express myself in another way. I still have to expand my active vocabulary, but I am really satisfied with my progress so far.

My experience with French is completely different. As I said before, I started learning French at the University, and after just one year of traditional learning, by my second year I had the opportunity to take an Erasmus grant. In contrast to many of my friends who went to England to improve their first foreign language, I decided to go to Toulouse, in the south of France.

My experience there was just remarkable in all aspects,

both as a personal adventure, and as a language learning one. Learning a language can be just amazing, because you learn from every input you receive, whether watching TV, hanging around with friends, etc. My wife often tells me: "You are not studying English, you're just watching the television" My response is that "The TV show is in English, so I'm learning English."

Oops, I'm digressing—back to the topic. In my first month in France, I made the same mistake many Erasmus students make: I only associated with Spanish speaking people. You still learn something, because you sit for your classes which are taught in this foreign language and you are surrounded by it when going to the supermarket, etc., but your progress will be much slower.

Thankfully, after just a couple of months I had the good fortune to hit it off with a French guy. I spent a lot of time with a group of 5 or 6 Spanish friends, but this French guy was also with us all the time, and he was really patient and helpful, and my French got better very quickly. In just about half a year I felt really fluent in French—almost to the point that I almost forgot my ability to speak English (which in theory was my major foreign language)!

A couple of months before coming back to Spain I took a trip to Norway to visit a Spanish friend who was doing her Erasmus there. I flew to Oslo and then I had to buy another ticket for Bergen. So I found myself in front of a desk trying to buy a ticket and speaking in English. I was having quite a bad time of it; to the point that I was unable to ask a simple question such as "How much is it?"

The kind and helpful sales assistant suddenly asked me: "Do you speak any other language?" As you may guess, the normal predictable answer should have been "Spanish?" Not for me in that moment. I said "French!"

I felt really relieved when she said "Sure, no problem" and I could buy my ticket in French. I can say I had acquired an extremely high level in French. Unfortunately, until a few months ago, I have not spoken French for many years, and my level of fluency went down and I forgot a lot of vocabulary.

Right now I feel more or less fluent, as I can hold a conversation with a native speaker, but my pronunciation is far from what it was and I often have to think hard to find a particular word or think of another way to express an idea.

The good part is that thanks to Facebook, some months ago I again met my French friend and we have spoken several times, so I have both rekindled a friendship and have found the motivation to begin improving my French so as to be able to communicate with him with the same or almost the same level of fluency I had many years ago.

To sum up, which is the best approach to master a language?

From my personal experience, I have to say the second one. In less than a year I acquired a level of fluency in French that I had never had in my many years studying English. However, it is not always that easy to spend a year abroad, especially when you get older and have a family. But can you improve or master a foreign language just studying it from at home in your own country? Sure you can! Especially nowadays, with all of the excellent resources that we have available. It may take longer, or require a greater effort to do so, *but it can be done*, as I hope to demonstrate in the coming months as I continue to improve my English.

Finally, the "half language" I can speak is Italian. I say "half" because I studied Italian in a language school here in Barcelona many years ago, but just for one year. Anyway, Italian has a lot in common with Spanish and Catalan (and even with French), so it is an "easy language" for me to learn. Of course, there are no truly "easy" languages, but I could say that it is far easier for me than, for example, German.

I can understand Italian more or less if the speaker does not speak really fast or use a lot of slang, and I can say some basic things in Italian.

Another similar example would be Portuguese, which I have never studied and I don't speak, but because of the similarities with my languages, I can more or less understand a conversation. For example, I remember when I went to Lisbon for a week of vacation some years ago—I could made myself understood and I could ask some basic things, having just learnt some very basic vocabulary (like hello, goodbye, excuse me, thank you, coffee, milk, etc.) Of course, I do not consider Portuguese as one of my foreign languages. Or at least, not yet. However, maybe after dealing with German and improving my Italian... who knows?

Felipe's piece shows how language learning can have a surprise benefit: it can straighten out your life...

Polyglot Project Essay

Felipe Belizaire
YouTube Channel: Newstylles
http://www.youtube.com/user/newstylles

Male,25

American

I am truly honored to have this opportunity to partake in the *Polyglot Project* created by Claude. I should begin by saying that I am not a Polyglot, but this journey of language learning has opened opportunities, given sight and has enriched my life beyond my measures of expectations thus far. I've studied Portuguese, Creole, and Tagalog. Although I am not well experienced with foreign languages yet, the process of learning brings happiness and occurs naturally for me, and I've made the decision of incorporating languages—along with cultures—throughout my existence forever.

The Starting Point:

I was born in Miami, FL within a multicultural society to parents of Canadian and American backgrounds. I have a younger sister and older brother from my mother's side. My mother was born in Toronto, then later relocated to Brooklyn, New York, where she met my father. My parents' choice of moving to Miami was structured, for the most part, around "the   weather." My mother basically raised us as a single parent and would stress the importance of education to us every time we sat for dinner.

As a child growing up in a city which is predominantly Cuban-American, Spanish was the most exposure I had in regards to foreign languages. My mother learned Spanish through her co-workers, all of whom were of Hispanic backgrounds. At home, she would speak to us in English and would only revert to French when she was upset about something, or when her friends would call....but she never spoke Spanish at home. My brother and I could understand all of the hissing and fussing words in French but could not respond back.

Out of the three of us, I was the only one who was always surprised and curious about how my mother was able to communicate in two different tongues. Speaking other languages never held any interest for my brother or sister. My brother has always been a math guru..his forte. Although she told me that I would learn both French and Spanish in High school, I would still question her every time she said a word in French (at home) or Spanish (outside). The curiosity of how she learned languages was killing me. Maybe it's a trait of some sort because my siblings and I have different fathers.

You see...my brother and sister have the same dad but I don't. I met my dad for the first time when I was 14, and to this day the only inherited attribute from him that I am truly thankful for is his interest in foreign languages. I remember sitting down listening to him tell me stories about how he's been to numerous countries all over the world, and how he speaks 6 languages without issues. He rattled off a few phrases in Jamaican Patois, Spanish and Russian, and then told me he needed to practice the other '3' languages he knew, but he never told me what they were. I haven't really spoken to him much since.

Middle School days:

I never liked this city very much while growing up. Everything here seems so backwards. Growing up in Miami actually molded me into the person that I am today. I attended public schools and found myself involved with the wrong crowds of people during my last year of middle school and my freshman year of high school. Everything one may see on television about Miami is all factual, and at that time my mind wasn't focused on education but on materialistic items and false aspects of life. I took Spanish for the first time in middle school and received a "D" in the class due to my lack of confidence, motivation and trying to fit in with the "Cool" kids. English was dominant. Foreign languages were not widely heard amongst students in my school. We discovered who spoke Spanish, Creole, Chinese or French only when that student's parents would come to pick them up. Even after finding out who my bilingual peers were in class, I wouldn't dare try to question them about their language or ask them to speak it because that wasn't what the "Cool" kids were doing. So even though I may have wanted to, I convinced myself not to.

High School Days:

I began high school on the wrong note and my freshman year was a complete disaster. During my sophomore year,

I enrolled into French 1 and realized that I understood a great deal of basic French. Without much effort, I was soon pronouncing words accurately and receiving good test scores on speech. Grammar was a totally different monster of its own. Although I made high marks in my classes, my drive and hunger for learning languages still wasn't there.

Looking for a hobby in order to better utilize my spare time, I started to produce music with computer software and eventually became known as the guy who makes beats in school. I enjoyed playing keyboard and fooling with synthesizers in order to create odd sounds, but began to feel like I was wasting my time. I never wanted to become a musician, but the field of computers was always something I loved.

It was only during my senior year of high school that things began to completely change. My brother told me about a club in school called "Robotics," and suggested that I should try to join before graduating. I joined the club and it was very, very diverse. There were students from Columbia, Singapore, Brazil, and China to name only a few places. Everyone spoke English in the class, but the two students who were from Brazil spoke to each other in Portuguese. It was only then that I became aware of the passion, urge and love I had for languages. With its smooth, cool sounds, Portuguese instantly became my favorite language.

My journey thus far:

I noticed when listening to native speakers speaking their language that I would get very curious to find out what they were talking about. I made a decision to that I would learn a language on my own, without formal classes while in college. During my first year of college, I began looking for materials to self-study Portuguese and found Pimsleur. I thought to myself…. Audio only? Will this really work? Being that this was my very first course in a language of which I had no prior background knowledge, I was a bit skeptical about giving the course a try. After spending countless hours online looking for material, I decided to check YouTube for reviews on Pimsleur and other learning tools for the language. To my surprise, YouTube made a profound impact on me with the sheer amounts of language channels and foreign language communities! I watched Polyglots from different parts of the world speaking languages they did not grow up with! I was astounded and truly amazed. So I started collecting as many resources as possible for Portuguese... especially Brazilian Portuguese (as opposed to European (Continental) Portuguese).

When I started studying, I used Pimsleur's Brazilian Portuguese audio course for the first 2 months. Pimsleur comes with 3 Levels for Brazilian Portuguese, with 30 units per level. So that's 90 lessons in total and they are about 30 minutes each. It should take you about 2 to 3 months to finish the entire series. I basically listened to 1 unit per day and eventually moved on to doing 3 units per day until I finished them all.

Afterward, I started using Books and Audio courses. The first one I used after Pimsleur was "Teach Yourself Brazilian Portuguese" by Sue Tyson. This book is extremely good! It comes with 2 audio CD's and contains 18 chapters. I would play the dialogues while reading along aloud each day. I worked on a dialogue for 2 days max before moving on to the next. After working on 13 chapters, I got anxious to see what the other courses were like so I opened up the Colloquial Brazilian package that was sitting on my bookshelf. The course was put together very well and would help anyone who is at an intermediate level progress into an advance level. I used it for 3 months and learned many colloquial, informal terms (which Brazilians use most of the time when speaking). I did the same as with the Teach Yourself course: I would listen to each dialogue and read along. Two additional books I picked up were the "501 Portuguese Verbs" and a phrasebook. I basically carried the small phrasebook with me everywhere so I could skim through and learn new phrases while out working during the day.

Learning languages in general is a life changing decision. My routine was basically work, school and language study. It was complicated for me at first but now is OK, and the rewards of being able to communicate are well worth it in the end.

John Fotheringham's welcome addition to this book succinctly and effectively details what is required to learn a foreign language. I'm so glad he submitted it...

Why Most Fail in Language Learning and How YOU Can Succeed

By John Fotheringham of *LanguageMastery.com*

The vast majority of language learners fail to reach fluency in their target language even after years and years of study. Most learners account their failure to one or more of the following excuses:

1. "I'm just not good at languages."

2. "I had a bad language teacher."

3. "I don't live where the language is spoken."

4. "I don't have time to study a foreign language."

5. "I can't afford language classes."

Each of these alleged reasons is in fact a fallacy:

1. The ability to learn languages is innate and universal (except for those with mental or physical disabilities).

2. Languages by their very nature cannot be taught, so it matters not how good or bad your teacher is. Teachers

and tutors can be helpful, but the ability to learn a language well lies primarily in your court.

3. Using readily available online and offline tools, you can learn *any* language *anywhere* in the world.

4. If you spend even an hour a day, *every* day on a language (10 minutes here, 15 minutes there) you can reach oral fluency in less than a year.

5. You don't need to attend formal classes to learn a language well, and in fact, the classroom is often more of a hindrance than a help as it gets people thinking *about* the language instead of actually spending time with the language itself.

Fortunately, each of these misconceptions can be easily overcome by adopting the right language learning methods, having the right attitude toward language learning (and the target language itself), and utilizing the right materials.

Methods

If you have ever studied applied linguistics or T.E.S.O.L, you know that there are myriad language learning "methods" or "approaches". All of these, however, can be distilled into two major camps: *formal* and *natural*.

Formal vs. Natural Language Learning Approaches

1. **The Formal Approach.** Most people's experience learning foreign languages is of this type. It involves sitting in a classroom, studying grammar rules, memorizing

vocabulary, translating to and from the foreign language, and taking lots and lots of tests. While some people do enjoy it (and enjoyment trumps all!), the formal approach to language learning has proven to be highly ineffective and inefficient for the vast majority of language learners.

2. **The Natural Approach.** This is the way all of us learned our first language and his how most successful learners acquire *foreign* languages. It involves getting massive quantities of listening and reading input and massive quantities of speaking output once the learner has established enough passive fluency (this usually takes about 6 months to 2 years depending on how many hours a day you spend with the language.) There is little to no attention spent on conscious study of the language's grammar rules, and one's abilities are measured not by tests or "levels" but by the whether or not they can actually understand and communicate in real life situations.

The Dismal Results of Formal Language Education

So what are the results of teaching and learning languages in a formal, classroom-based way? Most of my experience learning and teaching languages has been in East Asia and North America, so I will use these two regions as examples:

East Asia: After 10 years of English study, the vast majority of Taiwanese, Chinese,Japanese, and Korean students graduate from university unable to speak the language fluently, if at all.

North America: And if you think this is just because East

Asian students of English lack the proper environment, consider the case of New Brunswick, the only constitutionally bilingual province in Canada.

To help boost the French skills of Anglophone citizens, the province created an early immersion program starting in the 1st grade. After 12 years of daily study, and living in a French-speaking region, only 0.68% of the students reached an intermediate level in French! (Source: www.cbc.ca via Steve Kaufmann.)

Obviously, formal language education simply doesn't work for most people. But why? The reason is that *knowledge* and *skills* are completely different beasts.

They Key Difference Between Knowledge vs. Skills

Formal language education fails because it treats language as an academic subject, not the physical skill it truly is.

This fact received little attention until a certain Dr. Stephen Krashen put forth his now famous Acquisition-Learning Hypothesis.

This complex sounding theory can be explained with a simple metaphor:

"Learning", a conscious process, is like memorizing the owner's manual for your new car. "Acquisition", a sub-conscious process, is like being able to drive well (but not necessarily knowing how the car works.)

Most people never reach fluency because they spend far too much time learning *about* the language (reading the manual) and not enough time actually acquiring it (driving the car).

To learn "how to drive" in a language, you need to spend as much time as you can behind the wheel. This includes three main tasks:

1. **Listening.** This is the primary task involved in acquiring a language. It is how you learned your *first* language and is how you will also learn your second, third, fourth, fifth, etc. When you are just starting out in a language, listen to relatively short segments over and over again until you can get the basic gist of what is being said. As your fluency expands, begin listening to longer content such as radio and TV shows, movies, etc. Many people suggest listening to music in foreign languages, but I find this to be of little help since people don't sing when they communicate in real-life (unless you're trapped in a musical…)

2. **Reading.** Try to find transcripts of your listening materials so you can both back up what you hear and easily look up and save new vocabulary for later review. I suggest podcasts from LingQ, Praxis (the makers of ChinesePod, SpanishPod, FrenchPod, ItalianPod and EnglishPod), and for English learners, The Get-it-done-Guy and TED Talks. Once your level permits it, buy both audio and ebook versions of your favorite books in the target language. Be careful, however, not to fall into the trap of reading more than you listen. Many learners do this, leading them to overly rely on the written word and

leaving them unable to understand spoken conversations.

3. **Speaking.** Once you feel ready to begin speaking (and no sooner if you can help it!), begin talking with native speakers. If you don't live where the language is spoken, this can be accomplished easily and cheaply through Skype or Google Voice. Tutors and language partners can be found using online language learning communities like *LingQ*, *LiveMocha*, and *Busuu*.

Why Formal Language Education Has Survived So Long

So if formal language learning and teaching methods are so ineffective, why have they survived so long?

There are three main reasons:

1. **The Weight of Tradition:** Though there have been many "cosmetic" changes over the years, languages have been taught in the same basic way for millennia.

2. **Ignorance & Arrogance:** Most people don't know (or won't admit) that there are better ways.

3. **Vested Interests:** Textbook publishers, language schools, teachers, and even politicians, all benefit financially from the formal education status quo.

But even after we push all these factors aside, we are left with yet another obstacle: the individual learner and their attitude towards language learning and the foreign language itself.

Attitude

"In language learning, it is attitude, not aptitude, that determines success."
~Steve Kaufmann, Creator of LingQ.com and author of *The Way of The Linguist*

Mental Foundations for Success
To ensure that you consistently spend enough time engaged with your target foreign language, and get the most out of whatever time you *do* spend, you must be:

Interested. The more you like the content, the more that will stick (and the more time, in turn, that you will likely spend with the language!)

Motivated. Motivation is fueled by interest, enjoyment, and perceivable progress. Which is why it is essential to choose materials you like reading or listening to. (*Perceivable progress* is discussed under "Patient" below.)

Goal Oriented. It is not necessary to have serious, pragmatic goals, but you do need a direction to aim in. Whatever your goals, make sure that they are "SMART": **S**pecific, **M**easurable, **A**ttainable, **R**ealistic, and **T**imely.

Consider these goals for example:

1. I want to speak *perfect* Chinese.

2. I want to finish this Chinese comic book by Sunday.

Number 1 is *not* a S.M.A.R.T. goal. The word "perfect" is extremely subjective and cannot be accurately measured when it comes to language learning. If you mean, "sound exactly like a native speaker", then it is certainly not a timely goal as this requires many years of massive language input and practice, while the ability to communicate can be reached in a matter of months.

Number 2, however, *is* a S.M.A.R.T. goal. It is very specific, can be easily measured (your finish the book or you don't), it's certainly attainable if the comic is not too far beyond your ability level, it's a reasonable objective, and the time frame is short.

Patient. Language learning isn't hard, but it *does* take time. And since progress in physical skills can be hard to notice, it can really help to monitor your progress through monthly or quarterly recordings (via audio or video). I do not recommend using standardized tests or completion of "levels" to measure your progress, as both do little more than show what you've memorized, not what you've actually *internalized* and can put into use.

Calm and collected. Try not to get frustrated when you make mistakes or people can't understand you. Both are a natural part of learning a language, and negative emotions like fear, anxiety, anger or boredom significantly reduce one's ability to learn (and perform) physical skills like speaking a language.

So how can one remain relaxed and confident in language learning? There are 2 keys:

1. **Don't speak until you are ready.** For most adults, speaking too soon leads to anxiety, inhibition and frustration when you can't communicate your needs, wants or thoughts. It also tends to produce "fossilized errors" in your pronunciation, grammar and vocabulary usage that are very difficult to undo later. Be a baby instead. Infants spend about 2 years actively listening before starting to speak. During this time, their brains are busy subconsciously organizing what they hear. If you want to learn a foreign language well, you should go through a similar "silent period".

2. **When you are ready, speak as much as possible.** If you don't have any friends or colleagues who are native speakers of your target language, find a good tutor or language partner to speak with. "Good" means that they are friendly and patient, can speak a foreign language themselves (so they can empathize with you), they let you choose your own materials, and they don't try to "teach" you the language.

Disciplined. Some days you will rather zone out and watch Prison Break, and spend time reading or listening to the target language. But if you only do things when you feel like it, you won't get very far in any kind of skill-based endeavor.

The good news is that you can strengthen your discipline just like a muscle. Every time you complete a task that requires discipline, the stronger you become and the easier it is to complete the next task you aren't in the mood for. Here are 2 prime examples:

1. **Not a morning person?** Force yourself to wake up the instant the alarm goes off. You will then be that much more likely to study that day.

2. **Trying to watch what you eat?** Each time you say no to pizza or beer, it will be that much easier to say to sitting down to a nice cold glass of foreign language input.

Now that we've covered effective methods and the necessary attitude to learn a language, let's turn to last (and perhaps easiest) problem to fix: *materials*.

Materials
Beyond a complete lack of efficacy, the formal language learning model has 2 other major disadvantages:

1. **It's expensive.** Textbooks, CDs and tuition can add up quickly. Many would be language learners give up because they simply can't afford formal classes, textbooks and CD-roms.

2. **It's location and time specific.** With jobs and families, it can be really difficult to schedule formal language classes. And even if you do, chances are that more urgent commitments will arise. Fortunately, modern technology and media distribution has solved *both* of these problems, while providing far more engaging and personalized content to boot!

Podcasts

Perhaps the best example of modern media is podcasting. Apple iTunes alone has more than 100,000 free podcast series available at the click of a button, with something sure to match every interest, ability level and language. iTunes is available for PCs, Macs, iPhones, iPod Touches, and iPads. Other podcast directories include the Zune Marketplace, Podcast Pickle, and Podcast Alley. Android can use Google Listen.

And with the advent of high-end portable media players, you can carry all this content around with you wherever you go. You can literally learn *anything, anytime, anywhere.*

YouTube
Another great resource for free, short, interest-specific content is YouTube. From stupid pet tricks to how-to software tutorials, there is something for every appetite. Most episodes are between 5 and 10 minutes in length, making them perfect for repetition.

Choosing Content

But with such a plethora content available today, how should one choose what to listen to and read? There are 2 key criteria that your language learning materials should meet:

Interesting. Choose topics that you enjoy listening to and reading in your native language. If you are not interested in finance, then don't waste your time on financial news in the foreign language.

Comprehensible. If you can't grasp at least 80% of the content you read or listen to, choose something easier.

Most adults choose overly difficult content thinking that it will help them improve faster (and look more intelligent). In the end, this just slows progress and leaves you unmotivated to continue learning.

There are two exceptions to this rule, however.

1. In the absolute beginning, nearly all materials will be mostly incomprehensible. Once you progress from newbie to beginner, you should be able to find plenty of materials and easily apply the 80% rule.

2. If you are really interested in the topic, it doesn't matter as much how difficult it is. I often read business and technology magazines in Mandarin Chinese that are far beyond my ability level, but I enjoy slogging through because I enjoy the topic so much.

Conclusion

If you adopt the right methods, attitudes and materials, *anyone* can learn a foreign language in a matter of months, not years or even decades as is usually the case with formal learning methods. Moreover, if you follow the advice above, you can actually enjoy the language learning journey, not just the destination.

So download some podcasts, stick in your headphones the next time you are doing the dishes or riding the train, and do what millions of adult learners fail to do every year: learn to speak a foreign language well.

"It's too expensive" and "I don't have time" are no longer valid excuses!

Fang from Singapore has submitted this most welcome addition to the book...

What language learning means to me

Learning a language feels like being given wings to fly and see the world in a whole new way. It changes the way we think about things and people.

Learning a language feels like being given a pair of spectacles to see things more clearly. It gives us an opportunity to learn everything that is related to the language. It makes us understand that everyone in this world is different, that everyone hold different opinions. Yet in spite of all these differences, we are still the same deep down. We have hopes and dreams and we also have fears.

Learning a language seems like fighting an inner battle. There are moments during the learning process when one is uncertain and tired. Yet something at the back of your head seems to be saying, "Go on, you can do it! You enjoy this! Go on! Persevere!" Yep, it's that fight to overcome the inner demons and proceeding to the next stage.

Learning a language is also very much a self-discovery process. It's learning to be responsible for oneself. It's learning to be in control of one's learning process. It's learning to get out of one's comfort zone and trying things in a new language. It's learning what works for oneself and what doesn't. It's learning to be humble. It's learning that there is no end to learning. It's learning to make use of all senses to enjoy the process. And it is also learning the importance of having a sense of humour. It's learning that it's alright to commit mistakes. And it's also learning that we all have to learn from those mistakes and move on. It's learning to be sensitive enough to put oneself in others' shoes and looking at the world from a different view.

Learning a language makes us a child again. We start from scratch. We become curious about everything about the language.

Learning a language is seeking out companions who share the same beliefs. Though what everyone wants to achieve in language learning is different, yet those people who share the same passion motivate you during moments of uncertainty during this journey of language learning. Other times, we might unknowingly inspire others to persevere and continue with their learning.

Learning a language feels like finding a key that unlocks a box of priceless treasures and many doors. One can gain so many valuable things and good friends along this journey. The most valuable thing along this journey is gaining more self-awareness. Learning a language is a never-ending journey filled many memorable and enriching experiences. Every experience that we gained in language learning redefines our lives.

This journey is filled with many emotions, yet many times, it's filled with happiness and joy. We grow and we change in this journey. We are never the same since the day we started on this journey to learn a language.

And with this, I have to say that I have never regretted any moments with learning Japanese. Learning Japanese has enriched my life in so many ways that I can never imagine, from knowing great Japanese friends, to enjoying Japanese literature, music, culture and so much more. Though I'm still far from fluent in Japanese, but I am really glad that I have learned SO many things on this journey. Learning Japanese has also led me to learning Korean, and it has also helped me rediscover more about my mother tongue, Chinese. I know I will continue to enjoy this journey and will be able to discover more things in time to come.

Fang from Singapore

http://creativityjapanese.wordpress.com

Cody may be only 19, but he has already taken on some challenging languages. He can be found on YouTube at: http://www.youtube.com/user/Codylangaugesblog

Cody Dudgeon
Polyglot Project

It has been said that knowing one language is like living in an enormous mansion and locking yourself in one room. This "mansion" we all live in is the world. The world is full of languages and cultures that are just waiting to be explored. I have left that lonely room and ventured into other rooms, learning about languages and developing my own methodologies. I have found, throughout my life, that the benefits to learning languages are endless.

The first time I ever became aware that there was such a thing as another language, I was only about 2 or 3 years old. I was visiting my great grandparents in Vienna, South Dakota, which was a big trip for me at the time since I was living near the Twin Cities in Eden Prairie, Minnesota. My great grandparents were both full-blooded Norwegians, whose ancestors had made their way from their cold, wet Scandinavian homeland, crossing the Atlantic Ocean to settle in North America.

Even though my family has been in North America for a few generations now, they still speak some Norwegian and have held firm in their Norwegian attitude and values. I remember being both confused and fascinated the first time I heard them speaking to each other in Norwegian. I

321

remember my great grandmother teaching me how to say "thank you" in Norwegian, and thought it was the coolest thing on earth! I remember that moment vividly because they passed away shortly thereafter.

My great grandparents are always in the back of my mind. They introduced me to foreign language; they were my wonderful, Norwegian speaking great grandparents. Since they spoke so much Norwegian at home, my grandma naturally picked it up and can speak it to this day. It brings her great delight when I express myself using Norwegian words and phrases. Because I had this experience at such a young age, Norwegian is a language very close to my heart. I hope someday to speak fluent Norwegian and to visit Norway and see the land of my ancestors.

The second time I encountered another language was when I was 5 years old. I was visiting my paternal grandmother. I remember playing in her backyard, when I saw a man with a large beard come out of her house subsequently followed by my dad and my grandparents. This was my grandmother's brother Jerry from Germany. I had always known that I had relatives in Germany, but this was my first time meeting an actual relative. I don't really remember much about my interaction with him, but I can tell you what he looked like and what clothes he was wearing. I know that was the day when my grandma first introduced me to the German language. She taught me some of the words she knows and I was very interested. That was the day I learned the German word "Danke." At the time, I was only a young kid and did not think much more of the encounter, but I never forgot that word.

Later on, when I was about 12 years old, I had another experience with German, having by then become interested in music. I was, at the time, really into "hard rock" and "heavy metal." It was then that I had come across a German band called "Rammstein."

Rammstein is an "Industrial Rock" band from Germany. Their unique instrumentals and lyrics instantly got me hooked. It was their influence that motivated me to explore more about Germany and German culture—and I discovered that I really liked it! I decided on the spot that I would start learning German. Of course, at that age I had no idea as to how to go about learning a foreign language. At the time, I had already taken half a year of Spanish in middle school. That was the only experience I really had when it came to intentionally learning a language. With Spanish, I did not achieve success, as I was uninterested, unmotivated, and unsatisfied with the teaching methods.

I began to wonder: "How am I going to learn German?" I discovered that the CD pamphlets of my Rammstein albums contained the lyrics to the songs. Alongside the German lyrics on their CD "Sehnsucht," there was also an English translation. I began to listen to the songs on the CD's and read along with the lyrics, even though I had no idea what most of it meant. Eventually, I began to find similarities between the two languages and discovered what some of the words meant. I found some websites with basic German lessons and German-English dictionaries. I began to be able to understand the lyrics; they became ingrained in my mind from continual listening to the Rammstein songs. Later, I found and began to watch movies in German. I also began reading German children's books, and saying basic things in German with my family when they came to visit. During my first two years of high school, I began to acquire some books about learning the German language. It soon became my secret hobby. None of my friends during that time knew any other languages, or had any interest in Rammstein.

In my third year of high school, I was able to take a German class. It was an "ITV Class," meaning that it was a video course presented on a television monitor. Basically, the instructor had a camera with audio on us at all times, while we had the same on her. It was similar to Skype. I studied German in my junior and senior years. Although I learned some grammar and vocabulary, most of the fundamentals I had already learned on my own prior taking the classes. Still, it was well worth it, as I had a really fun teacher who was wonderful at her job. To this day, I am convinced that it would be next to impossible to find another language teacher who could surpass her teaching skills.

After my senior year I wanted to make sure I did not lose my German. During the summer, I studied hard and felt really satisfied with my progress. I still feel quite confident with my German. At the same time, I was thinking about learning another language, so I could say: "I speak 3 languages—I am trilingual." I also wanted to have the fun, life-enriching experience of learning another language again. I figured that since I had so much fun with German, it should be just as fun to learn another language. I began to try out other languages to see which one interested me the most. I soon encountered a problem: *I enjoyed them all!* That made it increasingly difficult to choose just one.

After trying out Russian, French, Norwegian, Swedish, and Dutch, I concluded that learning another Indo-European language would be too easy. It would probably be even easier than learning German, which to me came very naturally. As a result, I began to focus on languages that did not belong to the Indo-European family. I was interested in both Japanese and Chinese. I eventually chose Chinese over Japanese because it sounded the most foreign to me and seemed harder to pronounce. I thought that this will be a fun challenge.

It was around the time that I chose to learn Chinese that I began to search on the Internet about language learning. I was curious to see what methods people were applying to language learning. It wasn't until I searched on YouTube that I was able to find any useful information. I remember one YouTube session when I was searching "how to begin learning a language," and came across a video with that exact title made by Steve Kaufmann. I came away thinking that this guy is a genius, and genuinely knows what he is talking about. I started watching all of his videos, and through him discovered Moses McCormick (Laoshu), and through Laoshu I discovered Loki. I was (and still am) completely amazed by these 3 people. Coming across the YouTube Polyglot Community forever changed my life. It motivated me to learn more languages and make my own YouTube channel called "codylangauges."

Not only did I start learning Chinese, but I also decided to learn Swahili. I had wanted to learn an African language eventually, but was motivated to learn it sooner that I had planned. I had met a Kenyan in my College Algebra class. I asked him what language they spoke in Kenya and he told me that it was Swahili. I thought that was cool, and told him that I wanted to learn Swahili. Next thing I knew, I had ordered a *Teach Yourself Swahili* course and a Swahili phrasebook. Chinese and Swahili are still the languages I am currently learning.

I am now entering my sophomore year of college. For the fall semester I have enrolled in a Mandarin Chinese class as it is the first semester that my college is offering this language class. I am both eager to take this class and weary of the methodologies that will be implemented by the professor. I have always been an autodidact at nature and have taught myself many skills and hobbies. I have always been weary of formal instruction, because it has not usually been as successful for me as learning on my own. I am nonetheless curious to see how the class will be taught. I know that as difficult as learning a Sino-Tibetan language such as Mandarin Chinese is for a native speaker of English, I will not give up on learning independently from formal teaching. No matter what, I am going to learn Chinese, so I have no fear of the class being unsuccessful for me.

Once I am confident with my level of Chinese and Swahili, I will continue learning more languages. I am pretty certain that I will continue to learn languages for the rest of my life. As for how many, or which ones, I do not know. Although nothing is certain, I am reasonably sure that the next language I plan on learning will be Arabic. I have concluded (after my experiences in trying to acquire Chinese and Swahili simultaneously) that were I to attempt to learn two languages simultaneously again, they should belong to the same language family—such as Spanish and Italian. I do not think I will attempt to learn two languages together again unless they are both from the same language family.

What methodology you use when learning languages is important, but what is **necessary** is the right attitude. **Attitude is everything**. You must have an **open mind** and be willing to accept a foreign culture and language. Like a parachute, the mind cannot function unless it is open. Also, some people are worried that embracing the foreign language would hurt their identity, or in some sense make them "less American," etc. In reality, it just means you are an American who is bilingual and has a special spot in their heart for a foreign culture. It does not make you any less American.

Having the love for the culture, the country, and the people is really important in learning any language. It keeps you motivated. I was so motivated to learn German that I would be willing to learn any German word I would come across. I did not care if it was about a subject that I was completely uninterested in, because I loved the culture and language so much. Maybe you're not necessarily interested in the culture, but you have some other motivation. I know people who want to learn a language simply because that is their favorite author's mother tongue, and they would want to read their works in the original. Whatever the motivation, it must be there. **If you aren't motivated and open-minded, you will not have success.**

I think that most people forget why language was developed—it was developed for communication.

Communication should be your goal when learning a language. Being able to communicate successfully is more important than being perfect.

"If you want to improve, be content to be thought foolish and stupid."
-Epictetus

As adults, we tend to be more afraid of making mistakes when speaking. If you make a mistake, it is far from the end of the world. It may be a little embarrassing, but because it was embarrassing you will not forget the little mistake you made. Life will go on, and you will have learned something new as well. We don't need to have perfect grammar or perfect pronunciation to be able to effectively communicate in a foreign language. People should focus on communication first, and once they can comfortably communicate, they should work on the little details of perfecting their language skills.

"It is not how much fixed knowledge you can accumulate, but what you can apply livingly that counts."
-Bruce Lee

In real life, you will want to be able to get your meaning across instead of knowing 25 verbs in past and future tense.

If you want the most success while learning a language, you need to be learning on your own. Try to be independent, so that way you can follow your own interests and keep yourself motivated.

He who depends on himself will attain the greatest happiness.
- Yi Jing (Book of Changes), 2nd Millenium BC

You know how you learn best more than anybody else. You should seek out the subjects that interest you, which are in the target language. With the World Wide Web, you can find an article in most any language about any subject. Whenever I read an article or watch video about something that I am truly interested in, I tend to more readily remember what went on, what new words I discovered and so on. Many people find retaining information difficult to accomplish when they are just beginning to learn. When you are at a beginners level you must simply stick it out, and in the future you will open yourself up to many interesting articles that will be comprehensible to you. I think that is crucial to learning a language, and every language learner should try to implement it.

As a beginner you should try to get a lot of input. Do not focus on grammar. It's not really important at this stage. You should just try to understand what is going on, and maybe every once and a while be able to say something relevant to the conversation. I'd also recommend that people try to focus on pronunciation right away. They should try to learn the new sounds that might not be in their language. I do not mean to really focus hard on pronunciation, but just enough to be understood, because that is what is important.

I have always told people that if they would like to begin learning a language, they should try and get some language manuals that are made for the beginner level. Some good language manuals or course books would be the *Teach Yourself* and the *Colloquial* series. Those are my personal favorites, but if they do not work for your learning style, do not worry. There are many other great publications out there. Assimil is a French made language manual that is known for having funny illustrations and wonderful audio recordings. Pimsleur is known to be quite good for more exotic languages like Thai, Indonesian, Arabic, Japanese and Chinese. No matter what course book you choose, it will definitely not hurt. If it is not exactly perfect for your learning style, it is another resource to help you learn.

People usually say, "Well…if I read this book, then I will know the language…right?" The answer, quite simply, is *NO*. It won't make you fluent, but it will bring you to an intermediate level, and you will be able to pick up new vocabulary and engage in basic conversations. Once you learn the basics of the language, all that is left is increasing your vocabulary and perfecting the small details. There are countless ways to do this. I like to get phrasebooks in the beginning (alongside the course books) because they usually have essential words and phrases for everyday communication. A "must have" when trying to increase your vocabulary while learning a language is a good dictionary.

You can never have enough dictionaries for the language you are learning. I started out with a simple English-German pocket dictionary, but definitely plan on upgrading to a better one. My favorite foreign language dictionaries are made by Oxford. There are many online dictionaries out there as well, which usually have examples in context. Movies, music and YouTube videos are also great ways to increase vocabulary. The more resources you make available to yourself, the more vocabulary you will pick up.

I think people usually have the misconception that learning a language is a very difficult thing that requires a lot of hard work, but this is simply not true. You can be really lazy and still learn a language. If you are constantly exposed to a language in real-life situations, you will learn it no matter what, whether you want to or not. The German citizen Khalid El-Masri was on his way to vacation in Skopje, when Macedonian border guards stopped him because his name, in the Arabic script, was spelled the same way as the suspected terrorist Al-Masri. He was given to the CIA. He was held in various prisons across the world and he was interrogated and tortured. During this time his American captors constantly exposed him to English. He learned English to an advanced level while falsely imprisoned for a year. He spoke English well enough afterward to do many interviews about his captivity. He never intended to learn English. He never wanted to learn English, but because he was always exposed to it, he naturally picked up the language.

Our brains are designed to notice patterns, and if we allow those patterns to be noticed, we allow ourselves to learn. It does not require a lot of serious study to learn a language. It just requires exposure to the language on a regular basis. Whenever I am doing household chores, driving, etc., I am always listening to the language(s) that I am learning. Even when I sleep I have something on in the background. I usually listen to the dialogs from my *Colloquial* and *Teach Yourself* books. I put them on my MP3 player and listen whenever I am on the go. By hearing these dialogs over and over again, they become stuck in my head much like a favorite song would. Through repeated exposure, I can memorize certain words and phrases to the point that they become automatic. I soon start to think in that language due to the constant input. You literally do not have to do much of anything except listen. *You can be lazy and still learn a language!* I think this should be a tactic for every language learner. You must make the environment one in which you are always being exposed to your target language.

To maintain or acquire fluency in a foreign language, you must be consistent and set some sort of a goal. The reality is, if you do not keep yourself exposed to the language, you will regress and forget it. I try to keep myself exposed to each language I have learned on a daily basis. Every day, I try to watch videos, or read something in the target languages. You cannot ever truly say that you have learned a language, because you are limiting yourself by doing so; learning is continuous.

Without a goal, you will not know how much time to put into your language learning in a day. Let's say you are just beginning to learn Japanese. It is a language that for native speakers of English takes a lot of time to learn because it is so drastically different. A language like Japanese will require a lot of patience. While in the beginning stages, you will want to devote more time a day to study than if you are at an advanced level. If your goal is to get to an intermediate level within 6 months, I'd say try to study 2-3 hours a day. Spend most of the time listening, but do not neglect reading, writing, and speaking. Without a goal or constant exposure, you will find yourself rapidly regressing in your language(s).

Another thing that people must consider when learning a language is that even partial knowledge of a language is quite valuable. People usually think that you must learn a language to fluency before it can have any value. This is blatantly false. Being at only a basic conversational level in a language can enrich your life in so many different ways. Just showing that you are trying to understand somebody's language will show that you are truly accepting of their culture.

À Rome, fais comme les Romains.
-French Proverb

People of that culture whose language you are learning will see your efforts and be more apt to talk to you and feel comfortable around you. You can also make new friends simply because you can speak a little bit of their language. I get plenty of enjoyment if I can understand only 60% of a movie in Mandarin Chinese or partially understand a German short story. People must realize that there is great value to having only partial knowledge in a foreign language.

Knowing a foreign language is the most beneficial self-improvement activity one can do. It will enrich your life in ways you would never imagine, and it will forever change the way you think about the world around you.

"Language shapes the way we think, and determines what we can think about."
-Benjamin Lee Whorf

Knowing another language is looking at life from a completely different viewpoint. You're not only learning the language but also about the culture and people who speak that language. You can't fully learn a language without learning the culture, and vice versa. When you learn another culture and language, you learn another perspective on the world. You can take things you like from that culture, further enrich your life and get a new perspective on many things.

A real practical benefit in knowing a foreign language is that it will always improve your prospects for employment, or at the very least, will not hurt them. It can improve your salary by making you more valuable to the company, since you are able to communicate with more people. I had a friend who spoke good Spanish. He got paid extra at Walmart because he could help Spanish-speaking customers. Even at a job like Walmart, it is beneficial to know a foreign language. It gives you an edge over monolingual applicants. There are many fields where knowing a foreign language can be extremely beneficial, such as government agencies, the travel industry, engineering, communications, education, international law, economics, publishing and advertising. The list goes on and on.

"Wer fremde Sprachen nicht kennt, weiß nichts von seiner eigenen"
(Those who know nothing of foreign languages, know

nothing of their own)-- Johann Wolfgang von Goethe

Research has shown that people who know a foreign language are far more effective at communication in their own mother tongue. They have better memory, test scores, and literacy. I have discovered that after studying languages my vocabulary has increased exponentially. It is like food for you brain. If it is good for you, why not eat it?

There are so many benefits to language learning. If I were to write about them all, I would have to write an entire book. Leaving my room in the "mansion" was the best decision I ever made. It has enriched my life in countless ways. I am so grateful for the experiences I had as a young child, which got me ready and geared up for learning foreign languages. Through the process of learning languages, I have discovered many things that have improved my language learning. I have discovered that it is mostly the attitude you have about the language, and how motivated and interested you are in the language that is most important. I hope and pray that all of you reading this will begin a new language learning adventure. So go out right now, buy a coursebook, and start studying.

You at least owe me that ;)

Edward Chien, an American, was bitten by the foreign language learning bug at a very early age. Read on to find out who influenced him. Edward's YouTube Channel is: http://www.youtube.com/user/propugnatorfidei

I have always been interested in foreign languages. When I was nine, I decided I was going to take up the study of seven different languages that year. Not surprisingly, all I ended up learning was "Wir kommen!" and "Comment allez-vous?"; and I don't even remember what the five other languages were. In any event, I did enjoy what effort I put into the project, and when I was ten I began a systematic study of Biblical Greek. However, at the time my ambitions were focused on learning the way of chess, and so Greek remained just another subject in my schooling.

In high school I added Latin to my academic regimen and progressed at a satisfying pace for one year. Through study of Latin, I accustomed myself to memorizing paradigms through frequent mental repetition. Tedious as this sometimes was, I cannot imagine that it was more tedious than it would have been to look at a Latin sentence and try to guess at the significance of the different endings. Memorization is a necessary skill in life, and there is no reason we should be averse to employing it in the study of foreign languages.

Toward the end of my first year in high school, the big event happened: my parents began the process of adopting an 11-year-old girl from Russia. Consequently, I began learning Russian with the plan of facilitating communication between my parents and my sister-to-be. It was quite difficult at the time. I had a sufficient background in synthetic morphology not to be put off by the giant mass of nominal inflections, but there were nonetheless plenty of challenges: the declension of numerals, consonant mutation, VERBAL ASPECT, and so on. However, I kept at it more or less studiously, and by the time my sister arrived six months later, I was able to say in Russian... not very much. But it was enough to be of significant use. Inept language has far more communicative power than even the most carefully coordinated miming, and I was able to provide translation services to my family regularly and to others on several important occasions—including one visit from the police, but let's not get into that!

Throughout the following year, which was my second year of high school, I made great progress in Russian by combining conversational opportunities with my sister with diligent personal study. In particular, I worked through a medium-sized Russian reference grammar two times and made it a habit to learn twenty new words per day. I started listening to Russian poetry, understanding small parts of it by following along in the text but mainly enjoying its acoustic beauty. I studied parallel editions of classic Russian literature. I sang Russian folk songs. I did just about everything! All this had two main results: 1) I became irresistibly attracted to the depth of Russian culture, and 2) I never got past Unit 1 in my geometry textbook. Hehe!

In any event, at the end of that year I decided to go to college so that I could avoid taking physics in my junior year. Strangely enough, this plan worked. I know, right?

So, wishing to continue my linguistic pursuits in college, I took placement tests in Latin and Russian. The Latin result is too complicated to explain here, but in Russian I was admitted into the third year course. In other words, if two semesters of a language in high school is supposed to be equivalent to one semester of it in college, I had progressed at four times the expected rate in Russian. This is due to two circumstances: 1) I had a Russian sister to converse with, and 2) I had been studying Russian independently, unencumbered by classmates and homework. It has always been my experience that good teachers are an invaluable resource, but almost every other aspect of formal education only slows one down.

In college, besides taking courses in Old English and Old Church Slavonic, things so happened that I was not able to pursue any language besides Russian. But Russian alone had been quite enough to significantly increase the experiences that were possible in my life. Russian has done so many things for me that it would almost seen unfair to select just a few of them for examples. Suffice to say, learning a language to fluency is much more than worth the time and effort it takes!

After graduating from college, I decided that I wanted to learn an agglutinative language. I narrowed the contenders down to Turkish, Hungarian, and Finnish, and, despite its significant disadvantage to the two others in utility, chose Finnish because I liked the way it sounded. I think that whimsical decisions like that are an important part of learning languages. The process should remain exciting and fun and not be allowed to become a chore.

I used an almost cultishly grammar-centric approach in learning Finnish: I studied rule upon rule, never exhausting the bountiful Finnish supply, contextualizing all of them with a total vocabulary of about twenty words. After the three months of that summer, I didn't yet know how to say "hi," but looking up most words in a dictionary, I was able to read a newspaper article. This is decidedly more significant in Finnish than in some other languages, as its agglutinative morphology can quite radically alter the appearance of words. For example, the past tense of *antaa* is *annin*, of *syödä* it is *söin*, of *mennä* it is *menin*, of *haluta* it is *halusin*, and of *valita* it is *valitsin*. If you don't know the rules for stem mutation, i-induced syncopation, and the rest, no dictionary will save you. And I can't imagine that it's easier to try to derive the rules yourself from the data than to simply take them as presented. Yes, at first it takes some time to connect the rules in your head with what's on the paper, but with practice the process becomes automatic and effortless.

At the end of the summer, I accidentally got a job as a Latin teacher at an elementary school. I know, right? Learning how to teach required the better part of my efforts for some time, and so, save a bit of German, I did not seriously study languages that first semester.

In December, I happened upon Stu Jay's interview on Joh Jai. What a set of clips! My language cravings went right back up to the same uncontrollable levels they'd been at during my study of Russian. I went to work the next day and told all my students about the videos immediately. "Stu Jay" became a term of common parlance among my upper-level students. A week or so later, school closed for winter break. I reflected.

After break, I went to school and told my students to forget about Latin and study whatever language they wanted. I'd help them find materials and explain to them how to learn a language independently, and then off they would go! Some of them ended up having experiences that could probably be included in this collection. Personally, in the course of the following several months I resumed German and took up Spanish, Thai, Malay, and Farsi. We had quite an atmosphere in my "Latin" classes, all of us sitting there studying everything from Italian to Middle Egyptian! Most of my students used a more balanced learning technique, but I continued to cover copious amounts of grammar first and worry about vocabulary later. By the end of the school year, I had reached approximately the same point in all the languages I'd started: with extensive use of a dictionary, I could read most texts of normal complexity. I also dabbled a bit in Hebrew, Inuktitut, Japanese, and Chinese, but didn't get anywhere noticeable in them.

Since then some of my languages have progressed and others have stagnated or declined. I've been a bit too busy to maintain all of them as I would like. Nonetheless, I have every intention of continuing to learn, and not just languages: I have set a goal for the next couple years of teaching myself all the math I should've done in high school. I wrote this piece in a hurry (I'm in the middle of preparing lessons for the coming school year, which starts next week), but I hope that it will encourage readers to always keep learning.

My Dutch friend Bart was kind enough to submit the following piece about his language learning journey. Bart can be found on YouTube at: http://www.youtube.com/user/Bartisation?feature=mhum

Trials and Tribulations: My humble story

about Language learning

First of all, this is not some sort of epic story about a person's motivation to learn foreign languages, nor is it about the glorious results I have achieved during the years. In fact, I've only just starting to get the hang of it, and it's only been a few months that I have found the right way for me to learn a language. However, I have already noticed the huge benefits that learning a foreign language can have on someone's life. Before you read my story allow me to introduce myself properly. My name is Bart Vervaart and I hail from the Netherlands, in the small village of Oudenbosch to be exact. My native language is Dutch. Besides Dutch, I also speak English fluently and some basic Russian. Currently, I am learning Polish, Russian and Finnish.

Primo Victoria: Learning English

My first victory in terms of language learning was my study of English. However, I can't even call it "study," because I haven't studied the language in a traditional fashion. I learned English from watching television, playing videogames and using my English while traveling abroad. I first came in contact with English when I was about five or six through watching cartoons. At that time, almost every cartoon was in English with Dutch subtitles. Not wanting to read the subtitles (lazyness, I guess..), I would frequently ask my parents what some of the words meant.

This was my first contact with English, and I kept remembering the words because most episodes were repeated often. The more I watched ,and the older I became, the more I knew. I was very curious about English, as I wasn't used to hearing it. To me, it sounded funny and strange, and that was the reason that I wanted to learn more about this new language. As I watched more shows and learned more English, I started to really get into it. I asked my parents to teach me how to introduce myself, and how I could ask people if they could also speak English. My parents bought me various English children's books which I loved to read together with them. Another item that really helped me with learning English was my old trusty Gameboy and the Pokemon Blue game (Thank you Nintendo!). Like television, almost every videogame was in English. It was baptism by fire, as the games used very complicated English texts (especially for a seven year old). However, this didn't stop me, and in the end I succeeded and it has truly enhanced my English. I played many other games but it was Pokemon in particulair that really helped me. By the time I was eight I could talk about basic stuff in English. I was seen by my friends as some sort of an intellectual juggernaut. Even if they could also speak a little bit of English, I was at least a year ahead of them and at this point I had never even had a single English class at school.

Many years passed, and I kept learning English by playing videogames and watching TV. I really felt confident and good about myself, mainly because of the praise I got from my friends which really motivated me to continue studying

English. However, the biggest motivation for me to learn English was knowing that I actually had family in an English speaking country. One of my uncles lives in the United States. I couldn't wait to go there and speak English to him and his family. It would take a couple of years before I could actually visit the U.S. In the meantime, we started to have some introductory lessons in English. It was very basic and easy. Everything they taught there, I already knew—which really disappointed me. I did have the opportunity to speak a little English with the teacher, but it was not enough for me. I wanted more! When I was twelve, I finally got what I wanted—a trip to the United States.

This was the first of three trips I would make to the U.S. I met my Uncle and his family, and I spoke a lot of English. I promised myself that I would not speak any Dutch unless my Uncle did not know the English word for whatever it was that I wanted to know.

This worked phenomenally well and I learned an incredible amount of English in a short time period. When I returned from that first trip to the US I was already at a high intermediate level in English. My second and third trips further improved my English to the point where I could call myself fluent by the age of sixteen. I later traveled to Scotland ,where I first came in contact with the Scottish accent.

I like to enjoy myself while learning a foreign language. What drew me to English was the funny and strange sounding words. To keep my interest in English fresh, I study English accents. I am particulairly fond of the Scottish and Irish accents. Also, Scottish and Irish slang is something I like to explore from time to time. I hope to visit Scotland and Ireland often in the future, as both these countries are really fascinating to me.

Downfall: High School Terror

Although I never, ever had to study hard for English (I didn't even study for my final exams and passed easily) during my High School years, this doesn't mean that I didn't study other languages during High School. In fact I had to take two years of German and five years of French.

In the beginning, I was really looking forward to learning those other languages. I had been to Germany before and I liked the sound of the Language. French, on the other hand, was really exotic for me. I knew how to say "bonjour," and that was pretty much it. So I couldn't wait to have fun with two new languages. However, it ended dramatically, as my interest in languages was brutally murdered by the grammar focused school system.

As a result, I lost my interest during the very first month, and I lost all my confidence in learning a language. I always thought that I was good at languages, and I had proof of this by being able to speak English fluently without ever having studied it. However, I had to study so hard to keep up with French and German that it wasn't even fun anymore. I couldn't even make it fun, since there were no cartoons in French (I refused to watch anything other than cartoons!) or German, and none of the videogames I played were in French or German. I was always able to pass the tests, but I almost forgot everything I had to learn. My confidence reached rock bottom, and I didn't know what to do.

Sayonara: Trying to learn Japanese

When people ask me which language I started learning after English, I usually answer: Russian. However, this is not really true, as in my final two years of High School I was began to play around with Japanese. During my youth I was always interested in Japan and it's history. Many cartoons that I watched where originally from Japan (Dragonball Z, Pokemon and my all time favorite--Gundam). Most videogames that I played were also made in Japan, so I hoped to adopt the same strategy I had used with English and learn Japanese. I also got my hands on *Pimsleur Japanese* and I listened a lot to it. Soon I started to feel my confidence growing again.

This wasn't the case, however, when I found out about the three scripts and the rather complex grammar. As odd as it might sound, I quit immideately. I couldn't even handle learning German (which is relatively easy for Dutch people to learn), let alone something as alien as Japanese.

I still know some phrases of Japanese but I can hardly consider it useful knowledge. However, what I did discover was the benefits of using the internet as a resource. I could download and find so many Japanese things which could have made my language learning efforts that much easier. But in the end it doesn't matter, because I never continued with Japanese and never used the resources that I downloaded.

After Graduation

Since I had failed at Japanese, I pretty much abandoned all hope of learning any other languages. I was preparing to do something with my English, as it was the only foreign language in which I was really good at. Even after so many years, I still had fun using my English when talking with people on the internet, watching movies and reading books in that language. Often, those books were from Russian authors. Russian sounded really cool; I frequently listened to Russian music and I liked the sound of it. However, I never really thought about learning it since I believed it would likely end up in failure like my attempt at Japanese. After graduation, I didn't know what I wanted to do next, so I signed up to do volunteer work. I applied for a program in Estonia to teach English at a Russian school there. I didn't need to speak Russian or Estonian for the position because they would teach me that once I arrived. I was almost certain that this was going to happen and that I would spend a year in Estonia.

My parents, however had encouraged me to find something else to do if the plans were suddenly canceled. So I chose to go to College to become a English teacher if the Estonia trip was canceled--which it was. This was upsetting, as I was really pumped and had already told everybody about my forthcoming trip to Estonia.

Laoshu

During the summer of 2010 I started to learn four languages: Estonian, Russian, Polish and Finnish. I was also playing around with Norwegian. And this time, I was doing it right. I knew exactly what I had to do to learn the languages. I got the right resources, had the right motivation and attitude. I was ready to learn not just one language, but many more. I desired to be a Polyglot! These major changes in such a short time were all because of one man—Moses Mccormick a/k/a Laoshu.

Everything I n now know about language learning I owe to him. He has been become my hero.

After a few weeks, I could speak high beginner Estonian and low intermediate Russian (which is the highest achievement I ever made). My Finnish and Polish were still in the beginning stage during the early weeks of the Summer. This was because at the time I still thought that I was going to Estonia!

When I found out that the plans were canceled, I focused more on Finnish and Polish, later Polish exclusively. This was because I was planning a two week trip to Poland in August. That August, in Poland, I would experience the benefit of learning another foreign language.

From Poland with Love: How one trip can change it all.

I knew only a little bit of Polish but I never imagined the benefit I would get from it. I was helped by a lovely Polish girl who taught me some Polish and showed me her beautifull country. I went to the South-East of Poland, in Tarnobrzeg to be exact. I met many nice and wonderfull people. I discovered a lot about Polish history, cuisine (Poles know their food!) and culture. I loved to just walk through the City listening to people talking to each other, hoping to find words I knew.

I was frustrated many times since I couldn't understand many things people said to me. However with the help of that lovely girl I was able to make myself understood. I had previously said that I was going to master Russian first, but after that trip I am sure now that it will be Polish. Not just because I absolutely loved Poland, but because my girlfriend (you guessed it, the girl who helped me) is Polish and I want to be able to talk with her family in their own native language. Polish will be my main focus and I want to reach the same level in Polish as I have in English, if not better.

There is a lot of work to be done before I can achieve my new goal. I will also learn Russian and Finnish, as well as many other languages in the future. But I will focus on Polish from now on. It's really interesting how one's plans can all change in such a short time.

The Future

I have only made my first steps towards become a Polyglot. I succeeded a long time ago in learning English without actually studying it, when having fun was the most important factor. During my high school years, I failed to really learn French and German and I didn't succeeded at learning Japanese on my own. However a cancelled trip to Estonia and the influence of Laoshu made me rise again from the ashes. I returned to learning languages, which resulted in the study of Russian, Polish and Finnish. This time, I know how to do it and how to succeed. A trip to Poland made me realize this, and was a huge motivation for me to continue studying foreign langauges. I will start my course of study to become an English teacher and hope to travel the world, teaching my students English as learning their languages in return. I cannot wait.

I want to thank all of my Russian, Polish, Estonian and Finnish friends, who helped me and motivated me to continue learning the languages. I really appreciate it!

I also want to thank all the Youtubers out there who are making videos about language learning. I watch every single video you guys make over and over again!! I love them so much that I started my own channel. I want to thank Claude in particular for coming up with the idea of the Polyglot Project. It's truly an honor to be able to contribute something for this project.

As you know, I only started on my journey to become a Polyglot quite recently. I hope this story interested you so enough to want to follow me on this journey. If so, I welcome you to visit my YouTube Channel, where I will

try to post new things as often as I can.

http://www.youtube.com/user/Bartisation?feature=mhum

Thanks for reading my humble story !

Bart Vervaart

Kathleen Hearons is a talented writer and accomplished polyglot, and I'm extremely pleased to include her submission in this book. Read her story, then be sure to visit her YouTube Channel at: http://www.youtube.com/user/katrudy7

Polyglot Project Submission:
"The Making of an Autodidactic Polyglot"
by Kathleen E. Hearons

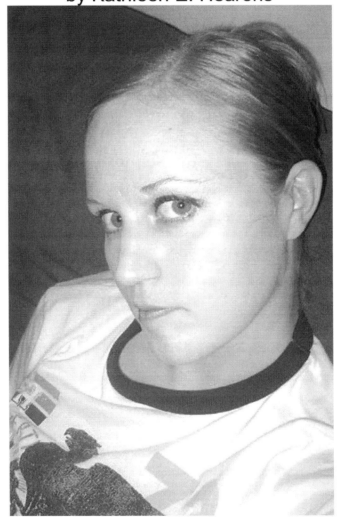

"The chair is *beckwem*," I said to my grandmother. She gave me a puzzled look, so I tried again, "*Beckwem*. You know, 'comfortable'?" The first-generation Bavarian German-American tilted her head back and smiled, "It's *beck-VAEM*." Her eyes smiled with satisfaction at my homage to her mother tongue. "Oh, *beck-VAEM*," I repeated softly and pensively. The gratification of seeing her light up saturated my mind, and that moment launched my insatiable pursuit of tearing down the proverbial language wall; little did I know then that I'd do that with a wrecking ball that I'd go on to design through my own passion and ambition.

I was ten years old, and I had chanced upon a pocket-sized German-English/English-German dictionary set in the living room of my parents' house. I knew that my great grandmother had come to the US directly from Germany, and that my grandmother had been raised in a German-speaking household, but that she hadn't gone on to teach my mother any German. The only foreign language anyone in my household knew was pidgin Spanish, since we all lived in a predominantly Mexican suburb of Los Angeles, in Southern California—a place that I lovingly refer to as 'Mexifornia.' In spite of that, I was engulfed by a fabricated sense of nostalgia for a fatherland in which I had never dwelled, and I chose to explore the language of Germany.

My nascent zeal to learn German led me to seek out language lessons from my grandmother, as if spurred by a desire to "reconnect" with a culture that I myself had lost. And so, she began to teach me to pronounce and read in German. She purchased beginners' books to help me to

351

build up a working vocabulary, and she spent an hour every Sunday afternoon listening to and helping me to read aloud to her from an old book that was printed in traditional German gothic-style lettering.

My childhood studies in German helped me to cultivate an authentic accent, but I had very little command over the grammar of the language; rather than to construct my own expressions, I was limited to mixing and matching the ones I had memorized from the books. My freshman year in high school, I had my first opportunity to study langue in a formal setting, and I was thrilled at the notion of finally being able to learn German sufficiently to speak it properly...that is, until I learned that I had to choose only between Spanish and French, as German was not offered at my school. I opted to take French, which I perceived to be the more "exotic" of the two, given that Spanish was spoken everywhere, all around me in my hometown.

After four years of diligent studies in French throughout high school, I developed a desire to learn another romance language: Italian. Once more, however, I was dismayed to find that no one in my hometown taught Italian, nor was it available to study at the local junior college. Thus, I had two choices before me: learn on my own, or not at all. In truth, the notion of taking it on solo wasn't the least bit intimidating, and, armed with gift cards for Barnes & Noble, I selected an audio-based beginner's Italian book/CD set and began training myself to mimic the sounds on the CD as accurately as possible.

At the same time, I was taking a French class at the local junior college. The only course available that semester was French 101, and although I knew myself to be well beyond absolute beginner's level, I enrolled in it for the sake of continuity in preserving my studies of French. To my surprise, however, I wasn't nearly as elevated above the novice level as I had haughtily assumed, and I was constantly learning things that I had come into the class believing I already knew. It was a commensurately humbling and edifying semester, to be sure, and my sharpened techniques in better acquainting myself with the syntax, phonetics, and semantics of French spilled over into my simultaneous autodidactic studies of Italian. I profited from studying the two together for just that reason.

I studied Italian for two to six hours a day, seven days a week. I simply couldn't study it enough. When I'd put my books down for the day, I'd find myself craving more and more learning, and I'd finally cave in to my assiduous gluttony for the serendipity that came with discovering that I could take something that I knew nothing about and digest it to the point of being able to use it as though I had known it since birth. I was working a part-time retail job at the time, and I was a full-time college student with a rigorous fitness schedule, so it wasn't as though I had no other way to occupy my time. But no matter how busy I was with required classes and ringing up items as a cashier, my drive to spend my time in a way that I found truly and deeply fulfilling overcame any urge to unwind at the end of a long day.

In my third semester at the junior college, I started taking German in addition to French. Once again, I took the beginner's (101) course. Unlike my experience with French 101, in the case of German I was delightfully surprised to realize that grandma had taught me a lot more of the grammar than I remembered. I did very well in that class, and my professor was tickled by having a bonafide fellow grammar-nerd as a pupil. She even assigned me extra homework—at my request—to push me to grow at a faster pace than the rest of the class; I did.

After having exhausted the meager extent of the junior college's course offerings in German and French, I received a full scholarship to study Italian in Italy from the director of a language school in Livorno, a port town in Tuscany. I had been corresponding with him in Italian over the previous year, and he said that he was so impressed by how rapidly my self-taught Italian skills had advanced that he wanted me to come and be one of his students, on his dime. And so, I stayed with a host family in Livorno for the summer of 2002. I brought along with me, of course, books to continue learning French and German throughout my stay. I couldn't dare put my studies on pause, lest I jeopardize the returns on my investments. And at the end of the eight-week program, I was certified by the University of Milan to have achieved a level of intermediate Italian, I had helped one of my host-sisters to pass the German portion of her university-entrance exam through speaking Italian with her to tutor her in German, and I had a French-speaking boyfriend who was in tears beside me at the gate to my flight back to Mexifornia.

Upon my return from Livorno, I had two more semesters left before graduating with my Associate of Arts. I decided to go ahead and finally learn Spanish and enrolled in Spanish 101. I remember my Cuban teacher correcting my Italian accent and substitution of Italian words for when I didn't know how to say something in Spanish. It took me a month or so to fashion a distinct Spanish accent, and I knew enough Spanish at that point to take advantage of the growing need in my hometown for English tutors who could teach English in Spanish. I took on four students as a private tutor, and in teaching them, my Spanish went from a conversational level to being advanced within another month or two.

Throughout this whole time, I was still setting aside 30+ minutes every day for French, German, and Italian, respectively. I then added to that roster Arabic. Learning Arabic was a common response by people my age to the terrorist attacks of 11 September 2001, and swaths of 20-somethings were underway training their brain to read from right to left. I dedicated one month to teach myself to read and write in Arabic, and then I delved into the grammar of the language. I progressed as rapidly with Arabic as I had with the Latin languages and German, because I was able to study it daily, and for as much time as I could set aside. Volition was a non-issue, as I was overwhelmingly self-driven.

Into my final semester at the junior college, I received a scholarship to study political science, my chosen major for my pending Bachelor of Arts (B.A.), in Prague, Czech Republic. In conjunction, a settlement with my father's construction company over his on-the-job injury had landed my parents an ample sum of disposable income, and they chose to bestow it upon me in order for me to complete my junior year of college in Florence, Italy. In a touching and selfless move, they said that they had wanted to reward all my hard work with making my dream of studying abroad come true. That they did.

While in Prague, I continued to set aside at least 30 minutes a day for each of my languages: French, German, Italian, Spanish, and Arabic. I learned some Czech, but I wasn't serious about learning the language as a whole; after all, I was only going to be in the Czech Republic for two months, and I didn't anticipate having any opportunity to use the language outside of that. I was able to practice my German with the older generation there, however, who had been compelled to learn it in their youth under the Nazi occupation of then-Czechoslovakia during World War II.

I left for Florence directly from Prague, and my former boyfriend of one year earlier met me at the train station there. He took me to meet up with my new university, and I soon found a room for rent with a native Argentinean who had come to Italy at the age of 17, landing the place at a steal of €500 per month (everything included) before any of the other students could by virtue of my fluency in Italian. I was able to practice both Italian and Spanish with the Argentinean, and not long after my arrival, I decided to learn Russian, for no particular reason other than the utility in acquiring a language whose geographic span included as many countries as time zones. I purchased books that were printed in Italian to learn Russian, and I set to work teaching myself to read and write in Russian. In between my English-language courses at California State University, Florence, I was also auditing Italian-language courses at l'Università di Firenze, where I studied French, German, Spanish, Russian, and Arabic with Italian students. This improved my Arabic drastically, and I was able to read Russian progressively better.

When I came back from Florence, I was informed that there had been a change of staff in the Department of Political Science at California State University, Northridge. As a consequence, only one of the courses that I had taken in Prague, and none of the courses that I had taken in Italy were to be transferred, as the new director refused to honor the decision of his predecessor to accept the credits. This meant that I now had two more years before I would receive my B.A.

Given that much time, and with my major emphasizing Middle Eastern politics, I figured I should start to learn Farsi/Persian. I added a 30-minute slot to my daily language regiment, and I kept up with French, German, Italian, Spanish, Arabic, and Russian as well. By this point, however, with a 120-mile commute and holding down three part-time jobs, my time was more limited than it had been while I was at the junior college. I had inadequate time available to me to really get into Farsi, and I was stalled out on pronouncing it differently than Arabic, which uses the same script.

And then came graduate school, along with a 3,000-mile move from Los Angeles to Washington, DC. If I thought I had mastered time-management in undergrad, I was put to shame in managing the astronomic workload of grad school. I heard the volume of labor best described as, "Think of how many chapters you were expected to read each week in undergrad, and convert that to entire books. Welcome to grad school." That tsunami of reading, having to write three to five papers a week that were anywhere from 15 to 50 pages in length each, and working a part-time job to pay for books and food (and living off of copious loans to cover the rest of my expenses) was merciless. Effectively, grad school had burglarized my language studies entirely. It was a shocking experience to me, since I had spent the previous six years studying *all six languages every single day of my life*. I was devastated.

I passed the Arabic exam at American University to receive my Masters of Arts in Middle Eastern Studies, with a minor in US Foreign Policy, and graduated in 2008. Eager to leave the plastic, hollow culture of DC behind, I trekked back to Los Angeles, carrying with me only that which could fit in my car; all else I gave away in a hasty one-week packing stint. However, after months of dreary unemployment in California, receiving email after email beginning with the mocking phrase, "Thank you for your interest," I realized that my pigeon-holed degree was as valuable in Southern California as were tire chains. It wasn't long before I received two interviews in DC after sending out about 15 applications to various consulting agencies. I accepted one of those positions and packed up the car once again, with my dad once more in the driver's seat, just as he had done three months prior.

Since we had a long drive ahead of us, and my dad would be at the wheel for the 13+ hours per day of sitting in the car, I decided to learn Hebrew while on our way across the country. I bought a beginner's book, and within two hours into our first day of travelling, I was already literate in Hebrew. For the remainder of the four days' trip, I proceeded with learning basic vocabulary and practicing reading and writing over and over and over.

By the time we got to DC and I started my new job, I had eight languages listed on my resume:

- *Advanced*: French, German, Italian, and Spanish

- *Intermediate*: Arabic and Russian

- *Novice*: Farsi, Hebrew

I kept up my languages to a fair degree—a far cry from a daily regiment that coddled each one with near maternal affection, but a strained effort to do as much as I could with as little as I had. One year later, I changed jobs and went from working 40 hours a week to 60 hours a week. The language study went from having the equivalent of a stomach flu to having the equivalent of cancer; prospects for survival were terminal. What was I going to do? I couldn't just stand by idly and lose everything that I had worked years and years to gain—not to mention the fact that learning language was the passion by which I lived and breathed, my veritable *raison d'être*.

Today, I ration my semblance of free time to best accommodate my struggle to sustain all that I have earned in my studies of eight languages. It will take changing jobs again—perhaps even a move to a career in language— before I'll be snuggled up against my books in leisure time again. All I can really do for now is use however much time is available to me, for however long it's available to me.

The utter asphyxiation of my one true passion routinely

injects a dreamlike denial in my thinking of how things turned out with my career. I feel as though my "real" life is on pause until I can get back to regular language study. It's an out-of-body experience, a palpable cognitive dissonance. But one that keeps a candle burning in the dark warehouse that holds all of the syntax, phonetics, and semantics of my eight metaphysical offspring. And so, I remain optimistically convinced that I can and will sustain my language abilities throughout this unforeseen hiatus. Sporadic spurts of 20-minute segments of one—if that— language per weeknight (as I work most weekends) serve as artificial life support to my comatose languages. I swell with encouragement with each condensed session of language study, though, and I know that, no matter how much time is lost, my *raison d'être* remains just that, and that it will still be there when I get back.

My friend Mike Campbell, known as "Glossika" on YouTube, is a linguist and polyglot who "walks the walk." If you are looking for the equivalent of a university education on how to learn languages, read on...

Becoming a Polyglot and Linguist

by Mike Campbell http://www.youtube.com/user/Glossika

Introduction

I'd like to start off by explaining that I don't believe in talent. If talent had to be defined, I would say that it is constant interest and exposure to a certain ability that builds upon itself year after year. When I was a child people talked about Michael Jordan a lot. One day I found out that this guy spent so many hours on the basketball court every day since he was a small child. Today we can say that of any of the best athletes out there, whether tennis, golf, ice-skating or of musicians, or anything. In all, the crême-de-la-crême in each of their disciplines have put in tens of thousands of hours--disciplined hours--of doing the right thing in the right motions to get to where they are. In each of the disciplines I pursue, I know my position and the distance I have to run, but I also know that the more I do in a particular field, such as languages or music, the faster and more efficient I become in learning new material. So after you've done your 20-30,000 hours in a particular field, you have an inherent ability for picking up other related areas, and I find that I can do this at a different pace than other people can. But I've seriously put in hours of every day into foreign languages since I was a young child. And the culmination of all those hours manifests itself in abilities that others can't fathom because they grew up or have studied under different circumstances. So here's my story.

Family Background and Growing Up

I come from a broken family and have two very different fathers. My biological father has never moved since I was born, is self-employed in manual labor, and has eight children, of which I'm the eldest. I would say he was quite successful since his early twenties, but managing a large family as a single father has been quite challenging for him. Although I find many striking similarities between the two of us, I have only spent several weeks' time with him since the 1980s.

When she left him (when I was only a couple years old), my mother was working for a government contractor in Sunnyvale, California, where she met my stepfather who was working for the US government in intelligence and defense. Soon after they married, we left the country and I have spent the time rest of my life, for the most part, living overseas. I grew up attending both (US) Department of Defense Dependents Schools (DoDDS) and local schools.

My exposure to foreign languages while growing up were mostly European and I was immediately fascinated by places, travel, and the languages I heard. I was not a very social child, and I didn't end up building strong relationships with other people since we moved around a lot. Looking back, I feel that the social dynamics caused a bit of an identity crisis for me and out of that I started to code-switch both culturally and linguistically.

Code-Switching as a Child

Our first overseas stay was in North Yorkshire (England) at a location called Menwith Hill Station. After a few months my mother made a big deal about the fact that I was speaking English with a remarkable North Yorkshire dialect, even using local vocabulary. Not only that, I couldn't seem to drop it even at home; I couldn't do anything about it.

When I returned to the United States for visits, it was equally awkward as I would be the only family member speaking in a strange dialect that few Americans had ever heard before. This was quite frustrating for my father and probably created a lot of distance between the two of us. But it usually took a couple weeks and my speech would shift again. Returning to Yorkshire was always a bitter experience because I was so ashamed of opening my mouth. I withstood days and weeks of shame and humiliation while the other children berated me every time Yankee sounds came stumbling out of my mouth. I had a lot of pressure to conform to the local standard.

After about a year of this, I had complete control over my ability to code-switch. I had no concept of linguistics or code-switching, in fact, I was not even aware of what I was doing at the time. I probably would not have understood if somebody mentioned it to me at that time. It was all happening very naturally under social and peer pressures with the various interactions I had between school and family. My mother was the only one who would joke about the quirky Yorkshire-isms that I said from time to time. But this only helped me become more and more aware of controlling the sounds from my mouth to the point where I could be a Yorkshire lad when I left the house and I could be an American guy upon entering my house and speaking with my parents.

Conforming Under Peer Pressure and Identity Crisis

I distinctly remember one day at British school something I had not been previously aware of. I was attending Grosvenor House all boys' school where we wore uniforms. There happened to be a new lad in our form and up to that point I had no idea that he was any different than the others. One day in the locker rooms all the other boys started mocking and bullying him over his West Yorkshire accent, and ended up pushing him into a toilet stall and doing whatever else to him.

This event left an indelible impression on me: this idea of conforming by speech. It seemed to me that I had conformed or at least they had all gotten used to me to some extent--I have no idea today whether or how much I spoke like the others, but I actually thought I may be the next one getting bullied into a toilet stall.

Perhaps here I should mention that my case of identity crisis was building greater on the home front, to the point that I was beginning to fear loss of face. If my mother took me out shopping with her I would literally fear her coming out--in her boisterous American accent--about this, that or the other, and I would have to put up with stares from other people; when in fact, I was just trying to be just as "Yorkshire" as everybody else. This crisis grew more and more over the years, from country to country, to the extent where I'd fear telling someone I was American. By the time I was a teenager, if I met somebody new or if I was traveling, I would always avoid telling somebody I was American mostly because of my identity crisis. Due to the circumstances, I did not fully understand or embrace a feeling of pride in one's own country, despite singing all those patriotic songs in DoDDS schools. But even when I did attend the DoDDS schools, I felt myself becoming more and more different than the other children, who were more likely than not living a very sheltered, baseball-playing American life living inside a bubble of American reality inside another country. My family, on the other hand, never lived on a "base," and I was constantly interacting with the locals I was exposed to.

I've lived in England, Spain, Italy, Germany and Russia and was exposed to all these languages (and several dialects) by the time I graduated from high school. I've also lived for short periods of time in the United States in both northern and southern California, Colorado, Indiana, Maryland/DC, and New York.

While overseas, our travels throughout Europe and Africa were extensive. I was exposed to a lot, and I was growing more and more conscious of language, my own idiolect, cultural interaction, sociolinguistics and the way people behaved differently from country to country. I was also paying a lot of attention to my own behavior (and whether I could mask my natural American behavior). I could start to identify what countries people were from not just from the languages I heard but from their facial expressions, hand use, and the way they walked. I also subconsciously studied and applied it to myself in order to avoid my identity crisis, and the weird looks I noticed people would give to my mother (who I always thought was completely oblivious to what others thought--which could have also been a good thing).

I'm currently under the impression that all these feelings I had growing up have contributed to my becoming a polyglot and maintaining a perpetual traveler lifestyle. This is the first media I've brought these feelings up and I'm curious as to whether other polyglots around the world have in any way or form felt similar feelings or not.

My Parents' Influence on Me

My father did not excel in foreign languages. My mother, however, excelled in Spanish and even spent some time in South and Central America perfecting her Spanish. Before the job I mentioned earlier she had been working as a court interpreter in San José, California, and had used both Spanish and English with me as a baby up to a certain point. But I always had a lot of exposure to Spanish growing up.

Believe it or not, the Castilian of Spain had a strange effect on my Spanish. Due to my identity crisis, when I realized my mother spoke "differently," I found myself wanting to repel her Latin American Spanish for the Castilian Spanish that I was exposed to in Europe.

My mother also had a love for foreign languages. I

discovered she had studied German, French, Russian, and even exotic and very strange languages like Cantonese, although I had no idea how or why. But by the time I had discovered Russian for myself, my mother could barely read the alphabet at that point, so I no longer turned to her for help to fulfill my own curiosity in language.

My stepfather was and still is a mystery: a serious man of a few strict words or none at all. But passively, I learned a great deal from him. I still have no idea about his language abilities. I do know he kept cross-reference dictionaries for more than a dozen languages, and once, and only once, on one of the rare occasions that I was out alone with him shopping in a German supermarket, did I hear him carry out a full conversation in fluent German with a clerk. And the clerk obviously had no idea he wasn't German. Suddenly, I had another eye-opening moment. Here was a man who didn't mind being with my eccentric mother and yet he could be a local when he wanted to be. Here I was with my identity crisis, and I learned that maybe it's okay to appear foreign all the time and then use the language to your advantage, because you can be a local unbeknownst to the locals themselves.

We lived for many years in Germany at a very small location called Bad Aibling (Mietraching to be exact) in Southern Bavaria (Oberbayern) within sight of the Alps and the Austrian border and not very far from Chiemsee resort, which I'm sure most Germans are familiar with. The location is about halfway between Munich and Salzburg, so I've spent a lot of time in both cities. My bedroom window faced Wendelstein, a 1848-meter tall mountain that we climbed every year. I attended high school at the

DoDDS Bad Aibling High School. I grew up with full exposure to this Maibaum culture, Bavarian *Freistaat* pride, and above all, the Bavarian language with frequent exposure to its Tyrolisch variant in Austria.

Although the US government has pulled out of the place, if you were to visit it today, provided they still stand, you would see over a dozen house-sized white balls called radomes and satellite antennas littering the fields next to Mietraching where the US intelligence, military and security agencies (and many contractors) did espionage and surveillance of Eastern Europe during the Cold War. Menwith Hill was (is) the same way but I was much too young to remember it clearly.

Due to his job and security, my stepfather was a bit limited with where he could travel with us as a family. After 1991 I took a lot of weekend trips with my mother to various eastern European countries. By the time I was a teenager and she realized our interests were different she let me run off and do my own thing while she basically just shopped as a tourist. I really enjoyed this and instead of visiting museums anymore, I started to try and interact with people I met wherever I was. Aside from some school trips like the week-long Model United Nations in the Hague, I rarely traveled to western or northern Europe, and as a result I've had very little exposure to French or Swedish. I have to say I was exposed to Czech quite a bit but by the time I left Europe French was still a much easier language for me to understand than Czech. Other than Russian, the only other eastern European languages I learned to speak a bit of were Hungarian, Romanian, Slovene and Croatian. My abilities in these languages have changed quite a lot since then.

Exposure as a Child to Professional Linguists and Training Materials

Around the age of eight, on weekends my mother would drop me off at the library on the American base while she ran errands. Since this was an installation used primarily by intelligence, military and security personnel (and the civilian families) I would say I had a rather unique experience in what I was exposed to from a young age.

Although language was only one of many interests, here not only was I exposed to a huge variety of foreign language training resources but I also met some very fascinating people, including linguists and polyglots. At the time I was completely unaware of what these people did for a living and didn't know there was such a thing as a linguist. For all I knew, everybody was a soldier who jogged around the base everyday, and that was about it. So I didn't ask any sensitive questions, but I did ask a lot about those languages and I got a lot of answers. I couldn't understand how anybody could master something like Arabic, but somebody laid it out to me how it might be accomplished using these resources.

Over the years I learned a fascinating amount of information from the base libraries as they applied to the professions of the people who worked there. I would say it was another education aside from what I was learning in school.

When I think back to what I was actually looking at at the

time was probably the FSI and DLI programs themselves, and I remember seeing all the tapes too. My mother wouldn't let me check them out or use them, because "I didn't know what I was getting myself into" (or maybe us kids couldn't be checking out materials that were supposed to be used by the military personnel), but books with other scripts or what not were okay, especially Egyptian hieroglyphics, which I pored over and loved.

I remember a particular library where I discovered a rather large collection of American Indian language material. I'm tempted to say it was at the Augsburg base, but I can't recall how I actually got to that library. Anyway, I spent a whole day in there looking at their extensive language collection, emerging almost awe-struck from what I had been exposed to. Unfortunately, I never had a chance to return.

I remember arriving in Germany. I asked my parents, inquisitively, "When am I going to learn German?" and I said I should get a book right away. They discouraged me by saying "you can't learn a language from a book -- you're going to pronounce everything wrong". But I'm glad they said that because it made me more aware that the writing perhaps had little to do with the way it was really pronounced. Or perhaps they understood my personality and knew that when I was told I couldn't do something I became determined to find a way on my own in the end. When I figured out the "code" --which was really the phonological system and their written equivalents, books were a huge resource, and I could prepare "conversations" at home a half hour before I actually went out and had them. I learned to anticipate what I would need to say for the day and I learned to speak a language pretty quickly this way and continued to use this method for many years. If my parents hadn't told me that, I may have fallen into that very trap of pronouncing everything incorrectly. Ever since then, I place huge emphasis on getting the sounds of a language correct right from the beginning. I have a good enough ear that I can catch my mistakes when I'm speaking and I usually correct myself on the spot and repeat it correctly.

At a young age I had witnessed a piano player performing live in a shopping center and I thought it was amazing. I thought music was so mysterious, much in the same way I was in awe with languages, but here was somebody who had some kind of *power* over music, and could create amazing sounds at his fingertips. I wanted to be able to do that someday so badly that that one memory followed me for the rest of my life.

Music and More Exposure to Languages

I told my parents I had wanted to learn the piano, but they were against the idea for several reasons, I think mainly because it would have meant having to invest in buying a piano that they were not keen on moving or selling, especially if I were to give the whole idea up. I don't think they were keen on the idea of having to hire a private teacher either. But since I wanted this so badly, it became a challenge that I overcame using a variety of methods (I found pianos at school or churches that I could use). I eventually got good at piano and at one point intended to make a career out of it.
Nevertheless, tackling challenging music on the piano

remains a very important part of my lifestyle today, much like the role languages do. More importantly, as a student the conservatories and music schools brought me together with other musicians who were also polyglots and gave me the opportunity to travel more and use a variety of languages. I learned a lot of invaluable things from the interactions I had there and learning music itself greatly improved my ability to learn foreign languages--they play hand in hand so to speak (hmm, that's punny).

In high school I recall one particular weekend when I was on my way home from the conservatory in Munich where I went every weekend for piano class. The advantage of living in Munich, at the crossroads of central Europe, was that I was exposed to the most linguistic variation I would probably ever be exposed to. This was just after the Cold War, so there were lots of eastern Europeans coming through as well.

I was on the S-Bahn heading out to Kreuzstraße (cross-street), where I'd have to transfer to the regular train. Sitting opposite me on the train were two blokes speaking some mysterious *Fremdsprache*. I sat there for a long time and couldn't put my finger on what it was. Now if it were something like getting Slovak confused with Czech or Polish, I could forgive myself for that. But this was not Slavic, it was not Hungarian or Romanian, and I'd probably be able to tell if it were Greek. It wasn't north or west European, so I gave up. Although they looked rather intimidating I politely asked and the response I got was Albanian. Another eye-opener for me.

That was a reclusive country and this was the first time I'd ever met anybody from Albania. For having seen as much of eastern Europe as I had, this was as mysterious as the interior of China for all I cared. But I thought that I must have unknowingly encountered Albanians during our stay in Italy before and just didn't realize that what I had been hearing had actually been Albanian (in fact, I was to meet many more Albanians after this encounter, mostly in Italy). But here they were, these exotic and unidentifiable sounds, now labeled and categorized in my mind as Albanian.

Identity and Social Interaction

Just a few weeks ago I ran into a former classmate of mine with some other friends, and she's now a performing artist, composer, and writer for a music magazine. It's always an exciting thing to meet somebody in this way after so many years. If you live a life like I've had, it seems that between the countries and the people that become a part of your life, every step of the way has been so separate and distinct from every other that they could have been mere dreams of a past life especially since most of these events originate from a time before emails and the internet. I was not a social child with a circle of friends, and every move only exacerbated this lonely existence, or likewise enhanced my ability to attain satisfaction in independence alone with my languages and music.

After growing up I have seldom seen or talked to family members. My parents moved back to the US when I went off to university. My mother divorced shortly thereafter and, sadly, I never saw or heard from my stepfather again (even though this was the father figure I grew up with).

One can only assume he is an elusive fellow.

I am a product of the circumstances that my family created, so I don't feel there's anything wrong with the way I live my life. However, I usually stay extremely low key about it all so I'm taking a big step actually coming out and writing about it here. I've thought about going back and trying to re-establish normal relations with my family and living where they live, but I've discovered I really dislike living an American lifestyle, and prefer to experience it only as a visitor. Every time I return to the United States, all I see is an incredible and distasteful amount of consumption everywhere--aren't waistlines proof? For a country that sounds like it's taking *green* seriously and making cuts on the use of natural resources, I just think that people were born and raised to live like this and nothing is or can be changed much in that regard, much the same way I have a hard time changing as an adult from the way I grew up. People are comfortable with what they grew up with.

I don't feel normal in America, as everything really still is very different from how I've lived everywhere else. And I'd rather live in a place where I'm readily acknowledged as different, and so perhaps that's why I feel comfortable *enough* living in Asia: I live for the challenge to become a local, but lavish in the feeling of always being different, and I can't dislike the fact that the attitudes towards my difference are almost always positive.

Memory and How We Remember

My sisters all have children now. Some of them have moved to far away states now, so some of the only memories that I have of them are when they were children, mostly under the age of 10. In fact those were the last pictures I had of them, as I didn't see them grow up.

I remember seeing one of my sisters a few years ago -- one moment I remember her as a spoiled child full of temper tantrums, the next moment I'm watching her as a well-articulated, responsible adult and mother; and with her husband -- as if I were meeting a "person" for the first time, and that little girl that I remember was somebody entirely different (or just a fragment of my imagination), as there is no connection between the two events. The contrast couldn't be greater. So for them, I am that "long-lost" big brother and uncle who speaks a gazillion languages, traipsing through the jungles of Asia and hanging out with indigenous tribes.

When I returned to San José and drove around town with my father, memories came flooding back into my head. I had been back to San José many times as a child, but each time was only a window, or a glimpse of a moment in time, frozen in my mind, as if I were a time traveler; but many of these shared memories and occurrences that I witnessed were completely lost in the flow of time for the rest of the family. Everybody else was living in the current reality, of events building upon events month after month, year after year, and my reality was completely different and I wanted to know, 'so what's happened in your life over the last 15 years?' or 'so what was high school like?', and that's just an absurd thing to ask. Where everybody else saw freeways or shopping centers that they've used for more than 15 years, these didn't even exist in my reality, and some of my more indelible memories are only fragments in the flow of my father's memories.

I can imagine what it must be like for an immigrant family, who may someday, maybe 50 or 60 years later, return to the place of their childhood for a visit. I'm only half that age, but I can already feel that kind of nostalgia. Imagine returning only to find upon visiting that their memories barely line up with the reality of everybody else in the contemporary. As if your memories stay frozen in time from a bygone era that few, if any, can validate. The only thing (and perhaps people) you feel you can connect to simply doesn't exist anymore, something that has disappeared with the passing of time. This is why the memories of running through the stone hallways of a schoolhouse predating the computer era seem as if they belong to a previous life, considering how young I am. It's hard to fathom how we lived our lives without computers.

But here's another discovery I made about our memories. Many of our memories are forgotten, or just buried under too much stuff in our heads. Like an overfilled hard-drive where you can't find your files anymore. Part of the reason for this is due to living in one location your whole life-- where each experience at that particular location may overlap or erase other experiences you had at the same location before. I shouldn't say erase, but it becomes increasingly difficult to distinguish in which year a particular event happened.

Let's say you have fond memories of a camping trip with your family, but it was something you did every year at the same location. If there was an accident or a funny event or some other indelible memory from one of those years, would that memory get confused with other events that happened at separate times, or does it remain completely distinct to that particular year? Most people would confuse that memory or blend it with events from neighboring years. But I do remember those trips and we didn't do the same trip every time I visited, so if I were to return to those locations I'm sure I'd remember some very exact events and details especially what year it was. But for me it seems that the location is required in order to recall the memories.

Because of the constant disruptions and uprooting throughout my life, the memories I get to keep don't blend with previous or later years so I can maintain clear memories from almost every month of every year depending on where I was. My memories of returning to San José may to some extent blur from one year to the next unless I specifically remember the size or age of my siblings when that memory occurred. But it seems that I can also remember specific events from as early as my first birthday.

I'd like to talk more about memory and its relation to language learning and what my Russian piano instructor taught me. I've done a lot more extensive tests on memory in the past few years with my Chinese students of English and intend to do extend this research for my PhD.

Exposure to Asian Languages

I left the United States after university and I've been in Asia ever since. It feels like I only just arrived in Asia, but I've now lived here longer than anywhere else I ever lived.

While still in university in the United States I took lessons from a private tutor in Vietnamese, tried learning Japanese on my own, and had a Korean girlfriend for a while. For school credit I could only take one foreign language class per semester, which happened to be Russian, as the foreign languages were offered at exactly the same time in the weekly schedule. Have you noticed that up to this point I seemed to be avoiding Chinese? Something in the back of my mind was telling me that I wasn't ready for it or that it was just too much of an effort.

But other things kept nagging me and were consistently pointing me in the direction of Chinese. First, I couldn't help but notice lots of cognates in Korean, Japanese and Vietnamese that were undoubtedly Chinese loanwords. Second, in my linguistics studies I was very fascinated with language change and development over time (historical linguistics), phonological change (as I was already familiar with European languages and was now discovering existed in the Sinoxenic languages), and dialectology. What was pointing me in the direction of Chinese here was the question of what was language and what was dialect. Was Chinese just a collection of dialects? Or were there a bunch of languages? Could it be measured? And so my interest in Russian and other European languages had just about dwindled and I had decided that I not only had to master Chinese and find all that I could about this situation, but I was determined to research the dialect situation as well.

Chinese Dialect and the Question of Mutual Intelligibility
(Note, all *pinyin* text here is written in Campbell Universal

Pinyin. The original article can be found at
http://language.glossika.com/definition-of-chinese-dialect/)

The question of dialect as it applies to the Sinitic languages has long confounded the linguist and layman alike due to a mismatch of translated terminology and the semantics of which have created dichotomous attitudes towards the definition of language and dialect. In the first half of this paper, I define the terms accent, dialect and language, and go on to propose a more accurate translation of the mistranslated term 'dialect' from Chinese; in the second half I deal with the problems that exist in determining mutual intelligibility and its impact on language and dialect.

A language barrier can be determined when the speech of two locations differs significantly enough in lexicon, phonology, grammar, and syntax to render it impossible for intercommunication. A dialect is assumed by many to be a different form of speech that is more or less still comprehensible. I have found that monolingual English speakers have quite a different attitude towards the definition of dialect than do speakers of many other languages partly due to the fact that the amount of variation within English is far less than that of other languages. On the contrary, I have found in terms of attitude that English speakers have a far greater tolerance of foreign accents than many other languages can tolerate due to its prominent use in the world. I would postulate that the some of the greatest deviation we find in English are merely in terms of 'accent' rather than 'dialect'. Dialects actually demonstrate slight differences in the four factors listed above, and although there are some varieties of English on the British Isles that differ in lexicon and phonology, few if any demonstrate deviations in grammar or syntax.

So if any of these four factors are similar in any way, we run into problems in determining whether the two forms of speech are accent, dialect, or language.
We normally refer to an accent because of the way it sounds. I've heard people refer to them: the Hoosier accent, the Jersey accent, the New York accent, the Cockney accent, the Irish accent, the Scottish accent, etc. But I've never heard them referred to as dialect. Upon closer examination, what really does differ in these so-called accents? There is for one, a phonological deviation that creates that perceived change in sound or twang we hear. Among American accents, phonological changes typically manifest in vowels, however on the British Isles accents not only differ in vowels but also in the amount of aspiration of consonants and particularly in the amount of use of glottal stops. In American accents, glottal stops only manifest from the letter [t] whereas in some British accents, they manifest from letters [k] and [p] as well (Andrew Spencer, 1996: Phonology, Blackwell Publishers, Oxford; see Chapters 6&7: Postlexical Processes in English, Stress and Rhythm). Another marked difference among English accents is the use of intonation and prosody (in Chinese we strictly refer to a strict tonal system as not much study has been given to prosody in Chinese–yet). As a fluent speaker of both English and Chinese I know that tone plays an equally important role in both languages and that certain expressions in English cannot be expressed accurately without the right tone. American accents tend to be spoken with a lower register

and prosody than that found in British accents. Intonation across the sentence also occurs in different places.

The greatest deviation I have found within English is perhaps Scots. In fact, it is known that the development of Scots from Anglo-Saxon happened independently from that of English and since there are so many similarities I have a question of whether English directly influenced Scots. Scots reminds me in some ways of how Bavarian is to German, a dialect I speak. There are some grammatical, phonological, lexical, syntactic and tonal differences in Scots. But the language by and large is the same as English. Suffice it to say, this deserves dialect nomination, but not language. It would take an English speaker (for example, an American) a few hours to a few days to accustom their ear to Scots requiring explanation of particular words or phrases to help one's progress.

Accents are prevalent everywhere and in every widely spoken language. The differences are primarily phonological in nature encompassing mostly changes in vowels, with few differences in consonants, but marked differences in prosody and tone. But from the typical speaker of a language, all else held constant **prosody and tonal changes do not affect comprehension**. Vowels only affect comprehension slightly but changes in consonants can start to distort comprehension to some degree. One important note about attitudes here: some groups of people are discriminated against by their accent or the way they speak, in other words, an attitude has developed which really has nothing to do with comprehension. As long as these two groups of people have had extensive exposure then they can comprehend

381

each other.

Dialects, on the other hand, are the same language by sharing the same structure in grammar and lexicon with few differences, but the phonology is markedly different and some of the syntax may differ. We find an example of this in European Portuguese and Brazilian Portuguese, a language I speak. The phonology is markedly different in these two varieties and there are some syntactic differences, particularly with pronouns. It is interesting to note that comprehension of Brazilian Portuguese accents is much easier than that of European Portuguese accents.

Fortunately for us, there are many skilled and professional linguists in China that have worked out the linguistic taxonomy of the dialects. I have read a great deal of this literature and even if I attempted to prove that one particular topolect has been classified incorrectly, I would come under heavy criticism and sufficient examples would be required to support such a claim. Linguistics is a mature field and western linguists should put their trust into the scholarly works that Chinese linguists have produced over the last three decades, particularly the newest findings of the last decade–Chinese publications outnumber western language publications on the subject by at least a thousandfold. I do not take any of my research from secondary sources published in the west but directly from the publications and findings of Chinese linguists in the field–I am only providing a gateway to the research that is out of reach to linguists who are not literate in Chinese.

The speech of each location in China differs from each

other slightly: many locations can be grouped together based on shared similarities (dialects) which can in turn be grouped together with other regional variants into individual languages.

The layman, either living within or outside China, usually refers to the speech of each location as a dialect. The confusion arises partly due to the semantics of the Chinese word 方言 *fangyan* and the English word dialect.

Linguists have found that within the Hàn (Chinese) population, the various forms of speech can be subdivided into separate Chinese languages. The reason for the discrepancy is that in Chinese all languages and dialects are called *fangyan*, which translates commonly as dialect (for the layman), but technically as topolect in English.

'Topolect' does not refer to a linguistic classification; instead it merely has a geographical reference, closely resembling the Chinese meaning of *fangyan*. We can describe a topolect as a form of speech spoken in one particular location. The Chinese *fang* refers to location (topo-), and *yan* to speech (-lect). So, *fangyan* is neither language nor dialect.

The use of the terms *fangyan* or dialect creates another kind of confusion regarding intelligibility. People who grow up in an area where several languages or dialects are spoken by different groups of people actually learn to understand these other languages and dialects through constant exposure. This has nothing to do with mutual intelligibility but rather with exposure and/or use of that language. As an example, somebody who speaks one of those languages but who comes from a different area of the country will not understand any of the other local languages due to lack of exposure. But as exposure to the varieties increases, so decreases the communication obstacle.

We can find many examples around the world where language and dialect are blurred. If one follows the dialect continuum from Germany to the Netherlands where German and Dutch are spoken respectively, one will find that each village can communicate with the next. But when you come to the end and compare that topolect with the one where you started, you will find two separate languages, however by my definition above perhaps these are still just dialects of the same *Sprachraum*.
In some countries there are different names for the dialects spoken there and so they might even be given language status. Many of the Slavic languages of Eastern Europe maintain various levels of intelligibility with each other, while each one of them claim language status. By my definition above, Serbian, Croatian, and Bosnian are dialects of a Serbocroatian *Sprachraum*.

Mutual intelligibility cannot really be measured in terms of percentage for the following reasons. If Speaker A says something to Speaker B and their respective forms of speech are different, they will not understand each other. But this has nothing to do with determining the relationship of these two speakers' speechforms. The chance of Speaker B understanding Speaker A is greatly reduced if only one part of the sentence is not understood. This happens even between speakers of the exact same speech form. For example, how many times have you not understood a friend or family member just because you missed part of the sentence? Comprehension declines rapidly to zero with just a few missing parts.

When Speaker B hears the different speechform of Speaker A and recognizes his speech and has heard it a lot before, Speaker B now has a choice upon which determines his ability to understand: 1. I recognize this speechform but I think speakers of the speechform are low class (or I don't like them and don't want anything to do with them), so I don't *want* to understand Speaker A; 2. I recognize this speechform, although I can't speak it, I want to understand it and communicate because of its business potential and prestige, so I will attempt communication with Speaker A.

Our ability to understand another dialect largely depends on our exposure to it, and our sociolinguistic attitudes towards the speechform.

If we've never been exposed to it, even though it is similar, we will lack vital information and our ability to understand it will decline rapidly to zero, regardless of our sociolinguistic attitude. Attempts to listen carefully and decode the speech will quickly increase our ability at mutual intelligibility with the speaker.

This leads to my next point: any percentage applied to mutual intelligibility statistics should not be considered as *how much* is understood, but rather *how difficult* it would be to understand the form of speech. For example, two speechforms that are rated at over 90% mutually intelligible does not mean they will be understood upon first encounter, however it does mean that because of their >90% similarity, they can be learned almost by ear with great ease. Falling below 90% but above 75% would require a much longer period of exposure and maybe even some proactive study. In this range, one would have to learn to speak like the others in order to be understood especially if they have had little exposure to your own speechform.

This has been misinterpreted many times and it is important to point out the fact that **mutual intelligibility statistics only indicate the distance and the amount of work required to understand another speechform, not how much can be understood on first encounter.**

Throughout history Chinese has been recorded in dictionaries, not by individual words of several characters but rather by individual characters themselves. This has lead to some misunderstanding regarding the lexical structure of the language. Chinese actually does not differ much from English in terms of lexical structure, but because English has impure etymology and its history complex it does Chinese justice to make the comparison with Latin which is purer in form. In Latin all roots have a specific meaning, whether in isolation or combined together in a word. The same holds true with Chinese characters: these characters are the roots and building blocks for larger 'words'. In European languages, our roots fuse together undergoing morphophonological changes making it a little harder to identify underlying roots. This does not occur in Chinese, however there is a large number of semantically similar roots in Chinese from which words are constructed and that occur between topolects. For example, topolects A, B, and C each have roots a, b, and c, as follows:

A: a, b, c
B: a, b, c
C: a, b, c

Furthermore, these roots can be attached to roots d and e. However, the way they attach could be different in each topolect as follows:

A: ad, be
B: cd, ce
C: bd, ad, ce

The chance of topolect A understanding the words of topolects B and C diminishes greatly and vice versa, despite all three sharing the same roots.

For example, each topolect shares the following roots: 開 (a), 駕(b), 駛(c), 車(d). To say the word "drive a car" (a/b/c + d), many topolects can say "開車" (ad) and it's even possible to say "駕駛車" (bcd) but in some, you'll find "駛車" (cd) (in Cantonese, Southern Min, and Hakka) or "駕車" (bd) (in Gan); of course in each case these roots take on their own pronunciations which I'll demonstrate below. So although Cantonese, Hakka, and Southern Min share "駛車" (cd) you'll find "saiqia" (cd) in Taipei Southern Min, "sëiche" (cd) in Guangzhou Cantonese, and "sïca" (cd) in Meixian Hakka. Here are the examples laid out below:

開(a), 駕(b), 駛(c), 車(d)
Taipei Southern Min: 駛車(cd) saiqia

Guangzhou Cantonese: 駛車(cd) sëiche
Meixian Hakka: 駛車(cd) sïca

Likewise, Mandarin has "kaichë", Wu has "keco", Xiang has "kaicë", Gan also has "kaica", Southern Min also has "kuiqia", Cantonese also has "hôiche", and Northern Min has "kyeqia" as laid out below:

開(a), 駕(b), 駛(c), 車(d)
Mandarin: 開車(ad) kaichë
Wu: 開車(ad) keco
Xiang: 開車(ad) kaicë
Gan: 開車(ad) kaica
Southern Min: 開車(ad) kuiqia
Cantonese: 開車(ad) hôiche
Northern Min: 開車(ad) kyeqia
Likewise, monosyllabic verbs such as 丟, 扔, 投, 溜, 甩, 拋, 摔, 拽 etc. all have the semantic of "throw" and all are most likely understood by each topolect speaker, however, they are not all interchangeable for every situation and some topolects use one term universally in discourse over all others. Other topolects use a specific word for a specific situation. And so it is easy to see how confusion can arise despite the similarities that exist on a lexical level.

The two same roots could be reversed in another topolect in turn creating unintelligibility. Take for example 喜歡 'to like'. 愛 and 中意 can also be understood as 'like' though not commonly used in Mandarin. As in Mandarin, Xiang says xihoN and Northern Min says hihuïng. In Northern Wu (Shanghai) we have a reversal: 歡喜 (huöxi), but not in Southern Wu (Wenzhou): sïxü 喜歡. Gan says fônxi, Cantonese funhei, Eastern Min huang-ngi, Southern Min

388

(Chaozhou) says huannhi, this one not to be confused with other Southern Min areas where the same word huaNhi means 'happy' and where 愛 'ai' is more commonly used to mean 'to like'. I lay out these examples below for easier comparison:

to like: 喜歡(ab), 愛(c), 中意(de)
Mandarin: 喜歡(ab) xihuan, 愛(c) ai, 中意(de) zhongyi
Xiang: 喜歡(ab) xihoN
Gan: 歡喜(ba) fônxi
Shanghai Northern Wu: 歡喜(ba) huöxi
Wenzhou Southern Wu: 喜歡(ab) sïxü
Northern Min: 喜歡(ab) hihuïng
Eastern Min: 歡喜(ba) huang-ngi
Southern Min: non-cognate: gah-yi, 愛(c) ai, but 歡喜(ba) huannhi = happy
Chaozhou Southern Min: 歡喜(ba) huannhi
Hakka: 中意(de) zungyi
Cantonese: 歡喜(ba) funhei, 中意(de) zhungyi

I find it of particular interest from the above data that the onset consonant of 歡(b) [hu] labializes to [f] in Gan but palatalizes to [ɕ] in Wenzhou Southern Wu and remains unchanged in the others.

Many researchers have done analysis of sound correspondences between Chinese characters to try and establish a level of mutual intelligibility between topolects. However, this approach leads to many mistakes of our understanding of mutual intelligibility and from such an elementary investigation this gives us the false notion that intelligibility is possible between these languages. Since I'm writing for an English-speaking audience, let's take

389

some examples from western languages: Latin has the prefix 'per-' and so does English. But was it borrowed? Or does English have its own native form of 'per-' or a cognate that developed individually from the Latin? Yes, it is 'for-' as in 'forgiven'. We can see that phonologically 'per' and 'for' are obviously similar and upon further study come from the same source. However, for the lay person or typical user of the language this is not immediately obvious at all. Nor is the Latinate cognate 'perdonare' (where don=give) noticeably similar to the English 'forgive', which in turn gives rise to the English loan 'pardon'. Even knowledge of this fact will not help an English speaker understand the more common Latin word 'ignosco' meaning 'forgive'. Just as an English speaker will fail to identify the cognate or mutually understand 'pardon' with 'forgive', one will again also fail to identify the underlying cognate roots in such word-pairs as 'drag' and 'train', or 'reign' and 'royal'. And these are just examples from within English. Because of the great number of sound changes possible over time and between European languages, it's easy to see how these words have changed a great deal.

In Chinese, however, roots are very seldom borrowed from other topolects. Normally, if one topolect shares the roots of another topolect and wants to borrow a word, the word's roots are "translated" into the local topolect's pronunciation. This can easily be seen in placenames: Hôkjiu in Eastern Min is pronounced Fuzhou in Mandarin. When roots are borrowed from other topolects, a second strata appears in the language. This is common in Southern Min where an older pronunciation of all roots exist as common colloquial pronunciations, and later a more northern pronunciation (*Táng* and *Wényán* readings) is borrowed into the language creating for many common roots two separate pronunciations. This is quite similar to what has happened in English with original Anglo-Saxon or Germanic roots and incoming Latin and French borrowings.

The real question is, what do we measure to determine mutual intelligibility? Several factors must be considered:

1. Lexical (common use of common roots)
2. Phonological (specifically, how deviant the sound correspondences are)
3. Syntactic
4. Grammatic (for example verb constructions)
5. Sociolinguistic factors: geography, business, exposure and attitudes

Lexical:

If topolect A has only one lexical item, and topolect B has the choice of two lexical items, this greatly diminishes intelligibility if speaker B chose to use the other word. In all other cases where phonological and syntactic conditions are constant, speaker A should be able to understand speaker B.

We can single out such a constant in the following example from English. Studies on learners of English as a foreign language show that they possess greatly reduced comprehension of phrasal verbs in comparison with Latinate-based vocabulary, for example: 'to challenge' is more easily understood than 'to take sb/sth on' for which the opposite is true for native English-speaking children. A simple explanation for this is that native speakers prefer to use phrasal verbs in speech which are rarely accounted for in dictionaries and not considered as proper speech. Further examination shows that phrasal verbs in English discourse are complex in nature and can be further divided into separable, inseparable, or both. Textbooks that teach English as a foreign language rarely teach these phrasal verb forms resulting in a great loss of intelligibility on part of the English learner. The problem does not lie in the understanding of individual lexemes "take" and "on" but rather in their combined form meaning "to challenge".

There are other lexical changes apparent among Chinese topolects and an example of this is the swapping of different noun endings (for example -zï becoming -tou, -a, -lei, -zai, etc). In the southern Sinitic languages there is significant borrowing of monosyllabic verbs from Zhuang and other minority languages which enriches the number of lexemes possible in productive constructions.

Phonological:

1. Prosody and tonal changes do not affect comprehension as long as they are not uttered in isolation. As a language changes over time or comparing from location to location, these are the first things to give way.

2. Vowels change easily but stay within their general areas, for example front vowels rarely change into back vowels. There are four grades of rhymes (the part of the syllable minus the onset consonant including glides, vowels and codas) which start with no glide, Y-glide, W-glide, and Ü-glide and these remain relatively constant throughout the Sinitic languages.

3. Consonants: Aspiration and voicing are the easiest to change. Next are general changes such as palatalization, frication, labialization, velarization, etc. These kinds of changes affect comprehension considerably as demonstrated in the "like" examples above.

Syntactic:

Syntactic differences can be confusing to the listener especially if phonological changes are involved as well. If speaker A encounters speaker B where both A and B belong to the same language and dialect, syntactic differences will be understood. If A and B belong to the same language but different dialect and the syntax is the same, everything else except phonology being constant, they will be understood. However, in this case, if the syntax is different, they will not be understood.

Let's do a cross examination of one sentence in various Chinese topolects: Give me a book (給我一本書 V-PRON-NUM-M-N) where V=Verb, PRON=Pronoun, NUM=Number, M=Measure, N=Noun, DAT=dative/indirect object. (All spellings using my Campbell Universal Pinyin and recordings of each location below is available on the webpage

Mandarin
Standard: 給我一本書 Gei35 wo213 i55 bën213 shu55. V-PRON-NUM-M-N
Jinan: 給俺本書 Gei55 ngaN· beN55 shu213. V-PRON-M-N
Zhengzhou: 給我一本兒書 Gei24 wo53 i24 bër53 shu24. V-PRON-NUM-M-N

Wuhan: 把本書我 Ba42 bën42 xü55 nguo42. V-M-N-PRON. 把本書得我 Ba42 bën42 xü55 dë nguo42. V-M-N-PRON

Yinchuan: 給給我一本書 Gû53-gû· vë53 i11 bëng53 shu44. V-PRON-NUM-M-N

Lanzhou: 給我給一本書 Gû53 vë442 gû442 i11 bëNn442 fu31. DAT-PRON-V-NUM-M-N

Ürümqi: ●一本書 Guë51 i213 bëng51 fu44. VPRON-NUM-M-N

Jin

Pingyao: 給我一本書 Jü53 ngiê53 yë'31 bëng53 sÿ31. V-PRON-NUM-M-N

Wu

Suzhou: 撥我一本書 Bë'5 ngëu31 yë'5 bën51 sÿ33. V-PRON-NUM-M-N

Northern Min

Jianou: 拿一本書吶我 Na42 zi42 bông21 sü54 na24 wê42. V-NUM-M-N-DAT-PRON

Eastern Min

Fuzhou: 書掏蜀本乞我 Zü44 do53 (s)lo'32 (p)vuong32 köü'23 nguai32. N-V-NUM-M-DAT-PRON

Southern Min

Xiamen: 互我一本冊 Hô21 ggua55 zit21 bun55 ce'32. DAT-PRON-NUM-M-N. 冊一本互我 Ce'32 zit21 bun55 hô22 ggua·. N-NUM-M-DAT-PRON

Taibei: 乎我一本書 Ho11 ggua44 zit44 bun44 zu44. DAT-PRON-NUM-M-N

Shantou: 挈本書乞我 Kio'2 bung24 zû33 kû'2 wa213. V-M-N-DAT-PRON

Qiongwen Min

Haikou: 要一本書去我 Io55 zziak3 'bbui213 du23 hu35 va213. V-NUM-M-N-DAT-PRON

Hakka

394

Meixian: 分一本書分● Bun35 it1 bun31 su44 bun35 ngai11. V-NUM-M-N-DAT-PRON
Taoyuan: 分●以本書 Bun24 ngai11 zrït2 bun31 shu24. V-PRON-NUM-M-N

Cantonese
Guangzhou: 畀本書我 Bei35 bun35 sü53 ngô23. V-M-N-PRON
Hong Kong: 畀本書我 Bei35 bun35 sü55 ngô13. V-M-N-PRON

Here is an example of mutual intelligibility: As a speaker of Southern Min (also known as Hokkien, Minnanhua, Banlam-oe, Taiwanese, Amoy, Holo-oe), I would easily understand the Xiamen and Taibei examples above, however I would not understand the Shantou example (spoken in neighboring Guangdong province). Although it is very similar, I believe I would need to stay among the Chaozhou or Shantou people for a few days to start to understand their way of speaking. With more exposure, it would be easier and easier to understand. As a Southern Min speaker, the Eastern, Northern, and Qiongwen Min examples above are completely unintelligible and although similar would require much more exposure before I'd start to understand.

During the process of mutual intelligibility, what would have to happen in someone's head to really understand some other speaker? Most importantly, they'd have to identify with the syntax of the sentence as demonstrated in the 19 examples above. If the listener is able to identify that, for example, in Cantonese that the noun precedes the pronoun in this case, then he is well on his way to understanding this sentence. But more challenges lie ahead.

Next, the listener would have to identify the verb which appears to be varying from language to language, and in some cases disguising itself as a dative form, or appearing in conjunction with a dative form. Now with the syntax out of the way, the listener would have to identify the sound changes in individual words such as the noun and the pronoun. In the Sinitic languages the first-person pronoun varies much less than the third-person pronoun so we could create a lot more confusion with this sentence by just altering the pronoun.

In this example, the "book" is pretty much universal, however if we were dealing with more complex vocabulary made up of more than one root, we'd be facing different orders of the roots or different choice of roots altogether adding completely to the confusion. If the listener is able to break through all these barriers or just guesses the right meaning by pure luck, then I shall shower him with praise.

Finally, the definition of dialect in the Chinese sense is quite different from the English usage and it's better to use "topolect" instead to better represent the meaning of the Chinese. In the English sense, it refers to two different speech forms that can mutually understand each other. Due to the large number of differences between the Chinese topolects, we can arguably say they are not dialects in the English sense of the word and furthermore we can group similar topolects in an area into a language group. But as demonstrated, some languages such as Wu can vary significantly from north to south, and at the time of writing no linguist categorizes Northern and Southern

Wu as separate languages although this is readily obvious from as little the amount of data as presented in this article.

In order not to do this topic any further disservice, I hereby make an appeal to all of you not to refer to the Chinese dialects as dialects any longer but rather as topolects or languages instead. If others do not understand your use of topolect then perhaps it's time you helped them add a word to their idiolect. (Sources for this article available in the original)

Taiwan is Great for Learning Chinese

I'm often asked why I came to Taiwan to learn Chinese. Since I had made up my mind, I decided I would learn Chinese properly and that meant learning traditional characters. I did not feel psychologically ready to live in a communist country and I wanted to go to a place rich with so-called Chinese dialects as well. Taiwan was also a financially stable place where I would be able to support myself financially. The only reasonable destination was Taiwan not to mention I had already befriended some Taiwanese friends in university and felt I could meet up with them when I arrived.

But I have since discovered even more reasons why Taiwan is a good place for learning Chinese.

Everybody in Taiwan speaks standard Chinese as mother language with the standard *Pǔtōnghuà* accent. Mainland China however is a hodgepodge of different accents, and one's personal accent is often different than the so-called standard accent. Oftentimes you'll meet people you don't understand at all even though they claim to speak standard *Pǔtōnghuà*–the problem is their regional accent– but they'll understand you just fine.

Taiwan uses traditional characters, and knowledge of these means you'll also pick up simplified characters very easily. In fact, if you put all your effort into learning simplified characters, you'll most likely get burned out and will never be able to become proficient in traditional characters at all. It's much harder if you learn simplified characters first so I don't recommend it.

The accent that Taiwanese have has prestige and sounds "good" almost everywhere in China because of Taiwanese businessmen, TV shows, famous singers and actors, etc. If you acquire this accent, you'll be easy to understand wherever you go and people will like the soft way you speak.

The Taiwanese are known for being successful businesspeople. Learning to speak like people in Taiwan gives you an advantage in business in Greater China and opens many opportunities to work with management. Oftentimes, establishing connections, or *guānxì*, with people in Taiwan means you'll have the resources to do all kinds of business on both sides of the Taiwan Strait.

The Taiwan government has realized that it has to compete against Mainland Chinese institutions to attract foreign students to come. What this means is that if you'd like to come to Taiwan there is all kinds of financial aid available to you through the right channels. You can start by requesting information from the Taiwan representative office available in your country. Financial aid is given priority to students who will complete their degrees at one of the universities in Taiwan.

I'd like to discuss Chinese characters for a moment here. First I'd recommend to anybody who wants to acquire Chinese that learning characters from the outset of your studies is not recommended as a prerequisite to what you are learning to say. What I mean by this is that you should not limit what you're learning to say by what you have learned in characters, otherwise your learning will be extremely slow. I only recommend learning characters separately, or in parallel with your speaking studies, but it should not take priority over speaking. In the long run, you're going to use your speaking and listening skills a whole lot more than reading and writing. And even if you do learn how to read Chinese fluently, it will still take you a very long time to be able to read it *at speed* as you would in your own language. It took me almost ten years to acquire this ability--and not passively--but from constantly reading texts aloud every day for ten years. So if you're not putting in that kind of effort it will literally take you decades to reach that kind of reading fluency. Think about your goals in practical terms. Is it worth trying to reach reading fluency with speed, or is character recognition enough?

Chinese characters are hard to learn, but with dedication coupled with your acquired speaking ability, it's entirely possible for an adult to have full character recognition in just a couple years. Recognizing them is a lot easier than writing them, and if you forget a character, you can always access it through a handheld device like a cellphone by typing its pronunciation.

I believe that if you're going to learn Chinese, you might as well become proficient in reading traditional characters, which is one of the greatest reasons for coming to Taiwan to learn. But also take the following into account:

- Traditional characters use the original radicals and phonetic compounds which get garbled and can even distort meanings and etymologies in simplified characters.
- You can significantly boost your character recognition with traditional characters, much more efficiently than with simplified characters.
- When you know traditional characters, learning to read and recognize simplified characters is easy. A few simple steps and you're done. The opposite is impossible to do: learning traditional characters after learning simplified could actually triple the time required.
- Traditional characters are more beautiful and have a sense of completeness, in the words of Chinese people themselves.

Problems with Learning Chinese

There are several linguistic tools that I used in mastering Chinese during my first year. I overcame pronunciation problems by using linguistics. And then there were the characters, which I took a more scientific approach to accomplish.

My confusion over correct pronunciation resulted in a wide

range of pronunciations I was hearing from native speakers. First of all, I didn't realize that not only did social status have an effect, but the speaker's background and mother languages also had an effect. I preferred to use a Latin-based system like pinyin which would save me time in the long run. In Taiwan they were telling me about some phonetic symbols as the answer and end-all to my pronunciation conundrum. Since all Taiwanese were required to learn them as children, everyone is adamant about their effectiveness and they continue to hold a very special place in everyone's heart. However, I discovered that it didn't matter if it were pinyin or phonetic symbols, I was still getting a wide range of pronunciations from informants. My answers instead were to be found in some linguistic publications I found in bookstores that mapped everything to the International Phonetic Alphabet, which of course I knew very well. I was relieved to discover what the real sounds were and couldn't believe I had to go through so much trouble just to find this out.

I think that pinyin is still a good system, but the letters have to be learned separately just as if you were learning some eastern European language. For example I was surprised to learn that the letters 'p', 't', 'k' were always aspirated and strong as in English, and that 'b', 'd', 'g' were not voiced as in English but were rather unaspirated 'p', 't', 'k' as you find in many European languages or as in these examples of English, the 'p' in "open", the t in "attic", the ck in "backache" (notice how these sound softer). Then there were the confusing parts distinguishing between the alveolopalatal and retroflex fricatives. But in every case I found that pinyin 'x', 'sh', and 's' were the base for building three sounds in those series: 'x' /ɕ/ to 'j' /tɕ/ to 'q' /tɕʰ/, 'sh' /ʂ/ to 'zh' /tʂ/ to 'ch' /tʂʰ/, and 's' /s/ to 'z' /ts/ to 'c' /tsʰ/. The letter r (ʐ) of the retroflex series was the only voiced one found. But it was good to finally know that it was quite different than a European or English 'r'. I also found that the way Taiwanese pronounced /ʂ/, /tʂ/, and /tʂʰ/ on the surface were actually closer to [ç], [tç], and [tçʰ].

The scientific approach I used for conquering the characters was that I was increasingly finding that a great number of characters were based on phonetic compounds than any other kind. A curious statistic states that exactly 90% of all characters in Chinese are phonetic compounds. I was curious to find some lists of these phonetic compounds. Since my linguistic pursuits had led me to notice many references to Karlgren's publications, I decided it was time to find these publications and read them myself. In fact, Karlgren undertook quite comprehensive coverage of the phonetic compounds and this itself played in part as one of the foundations of his reconstruction of earlier spoken stages of Chinese. Since I was also intrigued and eventually wanted to research all of this as well, I felt that I needed a strong understanding of phonetic compounds and the historical development of each character phonetically. I could readily see that the Cantonese pronunciations of characters often ended in stop consonants but none did in Mandarin, so I was fascinated with how these sounds developed into the various Chinese languages also leading to my gradual acquisition of Taiwanese (Southern Min), Wu (Shanghainese), and Hakka.

During my first year of Chinese study I purchased both Karlgren's *Analytic Dictionary of Chinese and Sino-*

Japanese and *Grammata Serica Recensa*, both published by SMC Publishing in Taipei, Taiwan (located across the street from National Taiwan University). Both of these were extremely valuable in my on-going acquisition of Chinese characters. I also picked up a remastered Chinese-language version of the Karlgren with more extensive indices and a copy of Karlgren's *Études* which can be found at the Linguistics library at Academia Sinica. I found limited use, albeit containing much extended range of rare phonetics, in 古文諧聲字根 (Gǔwén Xiéshēng Zìgēn). In subsequent years I also picked up the following books covering more of the historical development of Chinese pronunciation throughout the various Chinese languages: 入聲字箋論 (Rùshēngzì Jiānlùn) covering the phonetic development of all the characters ending in stop consonants, 汉语历史音韵学 (Hànyǔ Lìshǐ Yīnyùnxué) Historical Chinese Phonology, 上古汉语音系 (Shànggǔ Hànyǔ Yīnxì) Old Chinese Phonology, 汉语语音史 (Hànyǔ Yǔyīnshǐ) History of Chinese Speech.

So to tackle the unique problems I had with learning Chinese in the beginning, which were phonology and the immense number of characters, I relied on a scientific approach and at the same time learned more about the language than I ever could have from a mere language course. This is something that I would like to pass on to all other linguists and polyglots who wish to achieve similar results, no matter what the language is: be daring to ask the right questions, and be willing to go out of your way to discover the answers using a scientific method. As I mentioned before, just relying on the tales and explanations of a few informants will not get you the answers you desire.

Process of Learning Chinese

While learning Chinese I also wanted to record my progress in the language, especially with vocabulary and characters and speaking ability, so I took what I thought at the time to be meticulous records, although looking back today I think I could have done a better job. And for all of you who have sent me questions about how I did this, here are the results:

Since I had been exposed to East Asian languages prior to arrival, I had already started learning Chinese characters. But the way they're used in Japanese is quite different and Chinese has a lot of other more common characters like pronouns and grammatical words that aren't used in Japanese at all. For learning the Chinese characters, I bought a book by Rita Mei-Wah Choy called Read and Write Chinese. I laud this book for many reasons:

- A very good introduction on characters and tones
- Traditional characters
- Character strokes
- Definition of character in English
- Mandarin pinyin pronunciation
- Characters are listed by radical in the traditional order, which meant that once I got good at finding characters in this simple handbook, moving up to a harder or native dictionary was pretty easy.
- An index by Mandarin pinyin so I could look up characters by sound. However, since the characters were not listed in the index it often

meant I had to check each character until I found the one I wanted, so I avoided using this index as much as I could.

- Best of all for my learning is that each character has a star rating for frequency of use which meant I could focus on learning characters of importance before moving on to less common ones.
- It also lists Cantonese pronunciation and has a Cantonese index for all the characters which I found useful later on after having learned Mandarin. But I now use different dictionaries altogether for Cantonese.

As I used this dictionary, I ticked off the characters as I learned them one by one and reviewed the whole book every Sunday. If I couldn't remember the pronunciation or meaning of a character I was reviewing I would pull the flash card (which I used in combination) for review the following week.

So when I arrived in Taiwan I knew at least 500 characters. Six months later it was Chinese New Year and I knew about 1500 characters, and that's when I took off traveling around Asia for about a month. I came back and continued studying and by summer I knew about 3500 characters. By fall I was up to 4500 or about what you need to be considered "literate" in Chinese. I now knew more characters than I would possibly need for any conversation, so it was more or less a matter of improving my vocabulary (i.e. character combinations).

In terms of speaking and listening, I could only say basic

sentences in the first half year and I couldn't understand much of what I heard. The hardest thing was because of a low inventory of possible syllables in Mandarin, I had to determine which character every word was made up of in order to determine the meaning. I found myself constantly asking for "what's the character for that" in order to understand what I was hearing. If I didn't know the character, I knew it by the next day.

At about six months' exposure my speaking was already reaching a good speed and rhythm although I still had tone problems and lacked a lot of expression. My last half year after Chinese New Year took me to full expression ability and to what I felt was very solid fluency. In my second half year I had already started buying linguistics books written in Chinese on phonology and Chinese dialects, and I pored over them and translated them and learned all I could about the situation. During this period I also went through several Business Chinese textbooks to learn more diverse vocabulary.

At the end of my first year, I returned to Italy and Spain for a few months and then returned to Taiwan in the winter when I started doing more and more translation. I got a job translating financial articles and various other translation jobs and more or less built lots and lots of vocabulary by translating lots of technical documents, legal documents, technology manuals. It was only my second year but I now had a very strong foundation with most terminology found in business settings. I also bought a DK picture handbook encyclopedia as I found I lacked lots of common knowledge vocabulary like animals, physics, geography, etc, as these kinds of words I would want to use occasionally in conversation.

During my second year, I had been in a 100% Chinese-speaking setting every day for every waking hour, or about 12-15 hours per day, or 100 hours a week, constant input and constant confirmation of everything I had learned up to that point. I was also doing lots of translation and forcing myself to learn more and more. Whatever I didn't understand I would spend asking people I knew to make sure I got the absolute correct meaning out of it. I got about 5000 hours of Chinese use that year, and that continued for the next four years, for a total of 20,000 hours of fluent Chinese use, not including the first year. And another 10 years have almost passed as I'm writing this with few breaks from Chinese in between then and now.

I became aware of a book that came out called 中文字譜 (Zhōngwén Zìpǔ), Chinese Etymology, by Rick Harbaugh who had studied at National Taiwan University. His publication and the accompanying website, www.zhongwen.com, seems to have become one of the most popular among students learning Chinese. I highly recommend these resources.

At some point during that time I did start reviewing and practicing my European languages and learning more of them. I also started reviewing the Sinoxenic languages and made trips abroad, but for the most part I was focused internally on the situation within Chinese. With my frequent trips to China and Hong Kong I was exposed to many Chinese languages that I'd been researching and writing about. My online resource for Chinese languages and dialects became number one on Google and held that place for eight years, even after Wikipedia copied and (and ultimately expanded) on almost everything I had translated and put on my site. This site has since moved and I'm working on building a database behind it which will take more time to complete.

How Music Helped Me Develop Language Methodologies

I did translation for about four years while teaching on the side before I started focusing on developing more efficient language training programs. This is when I started to learn more and more languages to test effectiveness. I also did long-term studies on the acquisition process of my students based on various methodologies and I have come to several conclusions, which I found can surprisingly even be applied to technology such as machine translation (MT). For more information about this, please see my article titled *Sentence Databases: "Input" for Artificial Intelligence as an Improved Machine Translation Model*, found here: http://language.glossika.com/sentence-databases/ .

One day I discovered there was a link between what my Russian piano professor taught me in how to remember vast amounts of music. I recall the time when I walked into my professor's class and I felt frustrated by the amount of work I was putting into my music but only getting mediocre results. I asked him, haven't you heard of Godowsky and how could he possibly have learned the whole piano repertoire by the age of 25? --Memorized, no doubt. I mean, if you considered there were probably over 2000 pieces of music that had been written or worth learning to play, not to mention that he had mastered all the most technically challenging music up to that date, it just seemed like an overwhelming impossibility.

My professor went on to describe that he had exceptional memorization skills and practice routines, but that even I could train myself to do the same. So I asked him to train me and show me what I was doing wrong.

What I learned was that I didn't *really* know how to practice. I'd never had a previous teacher who had actually sat down with me and teach me the proper practice methods. All I was ever told was to go home and learn this piece and pay attention to this and that, etc. But what my professor did was explain to me, in Russian, how I could practice a page of music in a certain way that would enhance my technique at the same time as enhancing my memory. And it seemed that all of this was part of the Russian school. What and how I practice the first day will be adjusted slightly for the second day and the third day and so on. But his point is that I would have to progress this practice routine every day for a week without skipping a single day. He said the brain forgets some things the next day that need to be solidified, and the best way of doing that is getting back to them the next day. He also explained that practicing the piano for four to five hours a day was completely unnecessary if all I'm doing is practicing the material he's given me. Accomplish this task, and I'll give you a new challenge.

So, instead of always starting my music from the first measure at the top of the first page, I was now learning my music **from the ends of phrases and working forwards** adding notes and playing to the ends of phrases each time. Not only did this eliminate awkward pauses and breaks (that could become bad habits if practiced too often that way), but my brain easily remembered the ending of these phrases well enough that I didn't have to keep looking at the music. By the time I got to the beginning of a phrase, I could just as well play it to the end almost entirely from memory in only a few minutes of practice time. Incredible, just as he'd said.

The basic skills of looking at the overall structure, practicing and training the parts and putting them all together, literally gave me a breakthrough in learning everything else. By the time I went to college I felt I was armed with an arsenal of great learning techniques that I'd acquired from my Russian professor. And I undoubtedly continued to use these techniques in acquiring foreign languages.

Now skip ahead a few years when I started to test methodologies. It was now clear as day to me that most classroom time was spent analyzing language rather than *training* language, just as my Russian professor trained me how to practice the piano. Understanding the structure of things (like grammar, or a complete outline of a particular science like biology) was a basic fundamental, but I had to keep in mind that language was a participatory "sport" not unlike playing the piano. It required the movement of an important muscle, the tongue, and required it to move in certain patterns with high accuracy at high velocity, just like playing the piano.

So actually learning language was just like learning to play the piano, or any sport. Sitting around analyzing it all your life would never give you speaking ability or fluency. You'd have to train, train, train. And I took these daily practice routines my professor gave me and started to apply them as daily language training routines for my students. The routines changed slightly daily to enhance the memory and speaking ability.

Furthermore, I contacted one of the leading experts on memory, professor Alan Baddeley, and conducted more and more tests based on his recommendations and guidance. And I got some impressive results. Before I go on, let me give you a little more background.

Effective Language Learning

Back in the 1960s, the U.S. government researched and developed foreign language courses in about 60 languages based on effective language acquisition methods, built specifically for government employees dispatched around the world who had to learn a language in a hurry. Languages most similar to English, for example Germanic and Romance languages, could be taught much quicker than others. Those languages with the largest difference to English, non Indo-European, especially East Asian languages, of course require the most amount of training.

Using the U.S. government's effective method of studying these 60 languages, the amount of time required in traditional methods, such as typical classrooms, could be greatly reduced and are categorized as follows:
- Category 1 (most similar languages): ~600 hours of classroom study

- Category 2 (more complex Indo-European languages or genetically distant languages): ~1100 hours
- Category 3 (most difficult and distant languages): ~2200 hours

Source: http://www.nvtc.gov/lotw/months/november/learningExpectations.html

Students can undergo the government's language training at the Defense Language Institute located in Monterey, California.

Most language learners who attend classes, whether in or outside of school, do not have teachers who underwent some of the more efficient training methods for learning languages. Many of these teachers probably learned languages similarly to their students: going through a lot of hard work, laborious homework, written tests, etc. According to statistics, using inefficient classroom study with the disruptions of students and the teacher's classroom management, the amount of time required more than doubles in comparison with more efficient methods. With English and Chinese belonging to Category 3, you're looking at at least 4,400 hours of classroom study before you reach an ACTFL level 3 (not fluent, but proficient) in the target language. And if you only do 2 hours of study a week, it'll take you 44 years!!! No wonder it takes some people a lifetime of study.

If you were to continue using traditional methods of study, you'd find yourself investing huge amounts of time and money just to get the job done, and there would be no guarantee as to how long it would take you to achieve results.

People who are busy with their jobs, who have children, and all the hassles of daily life have little more than 2 hours a week they can really get alone to spend on studying a foreign language. Based on my experience I've also seen a lot of people actually stop going to class because they either can't keep up, or their life has become too busy to keep the language study in their regular schedule. It's a shame the amount of money wasted on such programs with little or no results. The casual language learner really has a dream just like anybody else to someday speak this language, maybe just to impress the people they know, but more importantly to open up new opportunities for themselves and for that self-achievement that we all desire.

Based on the way the brain works, there are two ways to learn a language: broaden your knowledge (good for paper tests) which means you can read, fill in grammar exercises, etc. The other is to train your listening and speaking, which is an ability completely different than "knowledge". The point here is that babies are born without knowledge and learn how to speak their mother languages long before attending school and having any knowledge. Babies don't need knowledge to speak. Neither do we. It's just like any other skill like dancing, playing music or sports, or riding a bicycle: you don't learn it out of a book doing exercises on paper; you learn it by **doing**.

Based on brain research in areas of long-term and working memory, any language program that meets once a week, or practiced once a week, is ineffective. Language has to be learned intensively so that the new memories in the brain are getting stimulated frequently enough to take root. But by intensive I don't mean you need to spend 10 hours a day. We can take your typical 2-hour a week class and stretch that out over several days so that you're spending less time in each sitting but practicing more and learning more in the long run. By spreading things out and teaching one lesson slowly over several classes, you're stimulating your memories more frequently, practicing your muscles more frequently (the tongue), and slowly building to conversational levels by reviewing the same material over several sessions.

The drop-out rate of students in language programs is so high, and most of the reasons point to an inability to comprehend or a lack of practice of previous material. As you learn new material, you don't want to have to be searching in a dictionary for the words, you'd like to be told what they are, and how to use them right then and there. In fact, the teacher (if you have one) should make the assumption that you're too busy to get homework done between lessons, and be able to cue you in the right places because the teacher knows from experience you'd have remembered and what you'd have forgotten. Through this constant cueing, reviewing, drilling and practice, coupled with engaging and interesting mini conversations, your speaking ability builds up little by little through each session.

From recent discoveries in neurobiology we now have a better understanding of the brain's functions, especially in areas of memory, skills, and language acquisition. But unlike other skills, language acquisition is natural for humans and theoretically easier to learn than many other kinds of skills. In the methodology that I have developed, I make the following assumptions:

1. Since everybody speaks at least one language, anybody can learn another language.

2. There is no "smart" or "stupid" in language learning and teachers who claim their students are not smart enough have failed to efficiently train the student. However, at the other end of this I've noticed that smart students who think too much about what they're doing tend to make more speaking mistakes and end up with slower progress. Saying "stupid" things in another language can be fun because we can learn to laugh at ourselves. It also helps make the learning process more memorable. I help act out some students' "stupid" mistakes too or anticipate their thought processes, why? Because I understand what the student is going through to learn the language!

3. The most effective way to improve your foreign language ability is to focus on enhancing your working memory through actual use. I do this through stimulating the hippocampus on a regular basis (this builds listening comprehension) and turning what your hippocampus has recorded into memory into self-produced speech (building your working memory and your speaking ability).

4. Our working memories are linked with our muscles: the more we move our muscles the stronger those memories get. Our tongue is required to move during language learning or else we acquire no ability whatsoever. It is not

until these movements become so natural that we will no longer have to "think" about how to say things in the foreign language–you can just follow your tongue's natural movements.

5. If you have the chance to use your language outside with other people, try to anticipate the conversations you're going to have with them. Prepare what you want to say, do it over in your head on the way, then act it out in person when you get there. One of my favorite things to do was just go up to a clerk and ask about something you're interested in seeing or buying. Have a conversation with the clerk in the process, and by the end of the dialogue you can just as easily say that wasn't what you were looking for, or that's not what you had in mind, thanks for your help anyway. Now if you go out on a Saturday or Sunday, how many stores are there and how many times a day can you do this? And how many interesting people would you meet and how many conversations may have developed because of it? The possibilities are endless and this was one of my strongest methods in learning Chinese.

I liken language learning to martial arts. Doing it is always better than just reading about it. The advantage with language is that you can learn it from books if you know how to turn the written material into training routines. And that is what you would have to do to become a polyglot or else you would create quite a financial burden for yourself. Take it from a friend of mine, Antonio Graceffo "*The Monk from Brooklyn*" (a published book), who has spent years touring East and Southeast Asia learning every kind of martial art out there and all the languages that come with them.

I'm currently working on a publication under the working title *Foreign Language Training Martial Arts Guide* which goes into great detail on how to train yourself in a foreign language. It covers both analytical and physical training. The physical training discusses in detail the following:

- different kinds of training schedules for different kinds of people,
- how to train people with different kinds of personalities depending on their strengths and weaknesses (handicaps),
- how to acquire a language from a native speaker who has no experience teaching it, especially for unwritten languages,
- covers about a hundred different training methods and drills, how to carry them out with examples from various languages,
- dealing with particular details and how to fine-tune yourself to notice those details,
- how to become a language trainer and train other teachers,
- how to document languages and prepare learning materials.

Whether you follow me from my membership sites, my YouTube, Twitter or Facebook channels, you'll find out about when this and any other book comes to publication.

Closing out these pages is this fantastic submission from David James, the inventor of the Goldlist method, a system which facilitates the placing of foreign language vocabulary into the long-term memory. David is another YouTube Polyglot who has become a good friend, and I have personally used Goldlist and profited from it. His YouTube Channel has over 1000 videos, and his Russian lessons, presented by his character Victor Huliganov, are second to none. Read on, then visit his YouTube channel at:

http://www.youtube.com/user/usenetposts

The Pursuit of Understanding

My Life so far as a Linguist and Accountant and How I Came to Invent the Goldlist Method

David J. James

0. Introduction

My internet buddy "Great Uncle" Claude kindly invited me to submit something for his forthcoming "Festschrift für die Philologie" called at the moment the Polyglot Project book. He suggested that I might want to talk about the Goldlist Method, a little invention of mine, which facilitates language learning to the long-term memory, and which is available on a series of YouTube videos on my channel, which is http://www.YouTube.com/usenetposts, as well as on http://www.huliganov.tv. It's also the subject of its own forthcoming book.

Now, Claude has been kind enough in the past to review this Goldlist method, and he gave it a public recommendation on one of his films. However, since an awful lot is already up online regarding what the method is and how to go about making a Goldlist in practice, and also there is a lot published on video by me about why it works, I thought I'd try and take a different angle for this Polyglot Project book, rather than duplicate the same things over and over. At the time of writing I have the unfair advantage of seeing from the published draft that some people have already filed their submissions, and I note that there is quite a lot of personal background, in there, of people who have become polyglots or who are well on the way there, and the reasons why they did it and how they went about it, what motivated them, etc. I thought that given that context, it might be a good thing to take this opportunity to say a few things about my own history.

Now, initially I was going to include this autobiographical information in the book I'm writing on the Goldlist method which is a work in progress, rather than encumber that book with information about myself, which may be of very limited interest to that audience. However, it seems to me that a place where different polyglots are comparing their histories of how they got interested in languages is a very good place for this history to belong. So this will deal with how I became interested in languages and how it was that

419

I was able to put together the different pieces of the jigsaw in order to produce this method which seems to have helped a good many people with dozens more starting to use it every month.

A number of people who have been helped want to know how it was that I was able to come up with the method, and also some skeptics about the method have come up with the question "how come you have managed to think up some better method than thousands of language teachers around the world?", and since the history of how the Goldlist method came to be is tied up in my own personal history, this is a good occasion to answer both those types of question, which I usually gloss over or give an answer which is too short to convey the full story.

For those who have neither seen me on YT, nor heard of the Goldlist method, I hope that there will be things of interest to other linguists in the tale and that it will repay your trouble to read it even with no interest in me personally, as in these pages you will see that the decision to follow the linguistic path can have life-changing consequences and is not to be undertaken lightly! To be a linguist is to seek to understand, and the quest for understanding is sometimes accompanied by pain as well as pleasure.

People have often wondered why I give the method absolutely free and wonder where the hidden catch is. The answer is that it is free, there's no catch, and this personal history will also make clear to you why I did so – in other words it will also celebrate the kindness of some people who helped me along the way and gave me to carry forward that torch of helpfulness and open communication which I note is one of the hallmarks of every true linguist, and which is certainly the spirit in which this book has been put together by the editor and the other contributors.

In order not to make the Polyglot Project be overly weighted by one piece, a shorter version of this, more focussed on how the Goldlist method emerged from my life will appear there, whereas the version kept on a page at Huliganov.TV will grow and be less uniquely concerned with the Goldlist question, and include some illustrations, so by all means check out http://www.huliganov.tv for a fuller version of this story.

1. Early days and schooldays

And so we begin with a little boy who came down from the north of England to a Hertfordshire town called Hemel Hempstead, one of the so-called "new towns" and a dormitory town for London (in fact, it was recorded in the Domesday book – but in those Norman days it was but a tiny fraction of its current population and area, thanks to the efforts of the Commissioners for the New Towns after the Second World War). My parents, who were schoolteachers, decided that the town was a good prospect because jobs were in abundance and there was "London weighting", meaning that you earned more in certain jobs like teaching or nursing purely because of the proximity to the capital with its higher prices for housing and entertainment. Hemel Hempstead was a very good deal in the early 1970s – it offered things like free parking (which soon went by the board) , and a cheap rail connection to the centre of London (which also went by the board but which became less and less attractive as time went by, anyway).

It also had a (then) leading industrial estate of its own (later the fame of this returned when Buncefield oil depot exploded on 11th December 2005 in what was dubbed the largest explosion in peacetime Europe – but thanks to the exemplary town planning nobody died) which in the fifties and sixties had attracted some big household names. Hemel Hempstead was home to Lucas Aerospace, to Kodak, and about 40 other names most of which you don't hear anymore today, as businessmen also like to try their hands at linguistics and frequently invent new names for their businesses. So my parents moved to this London fringe town of about 80,000 people, when I was about four years of age.

But I was a born Geordie, a word that refers to people who come from the area around the estuary of the river Tyne in northern England. It contains Newcastle, South Shields, Gateshead, Jarrow and several other towns that make up a conurbation which has its own accent which is unmistakable, ancient, and still reeks of Viking England and the Danelaw. If you want a sample of spoken Geordie, look up my persona "Peter Paczek" on YouTube. This is the accent they speak where I spent my earliest years, and not only that, but with my parents both working during the day I had been under the care of my great-grandmother (my mother's mother had died at an young age), and this Victorian lady was from the time before dialects had softened up in the age of ubiquitous radio broadcasts, then television programming and eventually (as the culmination of what media can be) podcasts.

As children will do, if anything I exaggerated her already broad Geordie accent, and so I was a speaker of a very pronounced English accent, if that's not a complete tautology. As a result of this, on my first day of school after we moved to the south of England, when my mother collected me after school, she asked the teacher how I'd got on, and the teacher said " He is a very nice little boy, but we can't understand a word he's saying". I couldn't understand much of what they were saying either, because to my little ears, the difference between Geordie English and Hertfordshire English was a bit like two different languages. I didn't like the sound of it, either. Why were they saying 'fevvah' but still writing 'feather' like we did?

Like any child, I went into the process of learning the new language, and before long, I actually would have had to work hard to produce any Geordie at all. At the tender age of about five, I think this event was the seminal event in making me interested in languages, even though in all truth, all these languages were, were different dialects of English. Nevertheless, the seed had been sown. My brother and sister were born four and five years later, once our family was ensconced in the south for good, and so they never had to go through the same transition in forms of English. Neither of them did much in the field of languages, so maybe this point alone is the main reason I turned out to be a linguist.

One highlight of my childhood years, once every year, was the Eurovision Song contest. For those of you not from Europe, this is a big annual event which engages usually unknown acts and certainly new songs from all over Europe with country competing against country. You can see plenty about it on YouTube. But these days it doesn't look much like it did in those days. Back then, unless you were somewhere like Malta or Monaco, you were obliged to sing in your national language, and I remember being absolutely fascinated by the sound of all these different languages being sung try to work out how it was that the song titles meant what the presenter said they did. If I liked the song I would memorise it in without understanding the meaning of the words I was singing.

Seeing and encouraging my interest, my parents allowed me to stay up late for that – in due course I even got to see the voting, which was not perceived as quite as unfair in those days as it is now, although the old friendships and rivalries between countries did show up a bit, even then. The reason was that the telly-land elite voted on behalf of their nations – as soon as they discovered how profitable it could be to cast paid tele-voting open to the public, that was to come in and objective assessment of music was to play second fiddle to the look of the singer and the politics of the country. In order to counteract that, all the nations were allowed to sing in the language of their choice, but thankfully in my childhood I got to hear the songs in the languages of the countries, and I cannot tell you how much that fired my imagination.

I also took an interest on the map and in all the different countries in the world. I wanted to know what it was like to be somebody from one of those countries. And I understood somehow intuitively that if you want to have the experience of being somebody from a different country, but the only way of really getting into their head is to know their language. And so I used to envisage myself speaking different languages even though of course I had no idea how to go about it at the age of six or seven. I fantasised about being able to speak and to understand a whole bunch of languages, but of course at that early age I had no idea whether the reality of that was even humanly attainable.

My father's father and certain of the teachers at school would teach me some words of Welsh, and my mother would give me some French phrases. I was also able to look at but the French lesson parts of the Arthur Mee Children's Encyclopaedia which I'd had handed down from my ancestors. Basically whenever I came across any foreign languages I'd simply take an interest in the words, how they sounded and what they meant.

One of the first Pakistani families to arrive in Hemel Hempstead was housed between me and my junior school, and I used to meet the one my age and his older brother on the way to school and just enjoy listening to their Urdu. I think it significant that the first word I learned from anyone from that world of their languages was "doost", the Urdu word for friend. And good friends they were! There was a group of bigger kids who had taken it into their heads to bully me, and I had been forced to give them a wide berth. But when my new Pakistani friends noticed them having a crack at me one afternoon they laid into them with relish (possibly mango chutney) and that was the last trouble I had from that bunch. Language learning could have unforeseen advantages, I saw.

At one point in my childhood, my mother got out the stamp collection that she had made over many years as a child, along with her big stamp catalogue by Stanley Gibbons. "The Rise and Fall of the Stamping Empire" I think it was called, or should have been if only its author had been more prescient about the effect of e-mail on traditional mail in the later part of the twentieth century. Watching me peruse with fascination the little tokens of colourful sticky paper from around the world, my mother said to me, "

David, how would you like to collect stamps with me and then you can continue the collection that I started when I was your age?" But my reply is something I can remember to this day: " You collect the stamps mother, and I'll collect the words that are written on the stamps." And that's exactly what I did, as it turned out, and many more words besides.

Azerbaijan didn't have it's own stamps in those days – in fact it even used the Cyrillic not the Roman alphabet for its language back then – but I would have liked this one if they had.

Nevertheless, I did not really have a formalised system for learning languages. I started to learn French in junior school but if anything that reduced my keenness, as the teachers had an immense talent for turning a pleasure into a chore. Later in secondary school with a year of Latin (which was like the First and Second Punic War going on between me and the Latin teacher, as I ran roughshod over his teaching method like Hannibal's famous pets and still scored highly in his end of year exam, a fine piece of *ad damnum adderetur injuria)*. I didn't like that Latin teacher, and I think the feeling was, *mutatis mutandis*, mutual, but I completed the primer he was using with us from cover to cover in the two weeks before the exam, and was able to learn the contents of a small primer in my short term memory in that time – the short term memory can do that – but needless to say I didn't retain any of it after the exam. In that respect I was just as unsuccessful as all his other pupils, and maybe 90% of all the people who ever learned Latin at a school desk.

Instead I went on to do German, which was a living language. In my school you couldn't do both, as subjects were grouped and you chose what you wanted under certain constraints. I didn't get to choose economics either, and sacrificed that to German too. And here I had a great stroke of luck, in that my German teacher, Methodist lay preacher (and soon-to-be missionary to the Lobala people as a Wycliffian – these are the Christian group of translators and missionaries who most actively seek to eradicate illiteracy from the world, at the same time placing the Bible into the hands of every tribe and nation on the planet in their own language).

Mr David Morgan was a slight man, young-looking and with what today would be called a 'nerdy' appearance and so the students were not slow in poking fun at him behind his back, and at times in front of his front also. But he was made of exactly the right stuff. He told it like it is, the way you don't hear many language teachers say it, and that was **"you've opted to learn this language, it's not obligatory like French, so it means you have a personal interest in it. So I expect you all to take ownership of the learning process and to keep vocabulary books properly. If you don't own the**

language learning process and simply rely on the lessons, you probably won't learn German, but if you do own the language learning process then not only will you learn German, but you'll be able to find the way to learn any language on your own whenever you want to later in life."

Well, needless to say, this idea fascinated me, and despite having had a number of years of French by that time and knowing French better than most in the class, I knew that what he said was true. If I hadn't done things my way I wouldn't have any French, and if I hadn't gone through the Latin primer in my own way I wouldn't have got a good mark in the Latin. So I started to take David Morgan's advice, and put the bit about learning how to teach oneself languages to the test – and for five years between the age of 13 and 18, I had the advantage of someone who actually understood the correct way to be a language teacher. And I picked his brains in that time, you can be sure of it. I think that when he ended up in the Democratic Republic of Congo giving literacy and the Word of God to the Lobala tribe, at least he could be thankful that he didn't have to put up with me asking him questions all the time.

At the age of 12-13, while the year of Latin was going on, I had been every teacher's nightmare. On report for 12 weeks, "done" for vandalising cars and aiding and abetting in various petty larcenies, I used to get drunk with my friends most nights, and also at one point I even ran away from home with a friend, after the school just found out – and informed our parents, that we two were the epicentre of a miniature crime spree. We got as far as Berkhamsted, and the cold, hard December rain was just too hard to put up with. We were drenched and it was a few degrees above zero. It was dark and there was nowhere to go. My friend rang his mother from a public phone box with the last 10 pence coin and soon after that both his and my mother drove up and took us to our respective houses bedraggled and morose, to witness their tears and recriminations. My father said angrily "look what you've done to your mother", and probably there was nothing more powerful that he could have said.

He managed it though, a few days later. He came to me in the kitchen as I was reading a book on tropical fishes – a major love of mine through my life but not really touched on here so that I can keep it all more relevant to what leads to the Goldlist method and said "I've come to the conclusion it's all my fault, son. I have been expecting you to do well and be the best, but you're just an average lad and I've put too much pressure on you. Now all I want is for you to just be average, just do what you can and it'll all be OK". I was truly shocked by this message. "I'll show you 'average' " was what I thought. But I didn't say anything. How he managed to keep a straight face through this piece of classic reverse psychology I know not, but he did. I thought he really meant it, at the time, and it was only years later he admitted he was using a secret grip on me.

I took a bath that night and I looked at the shadow of my face slightly distorted against the contour of the wall of the bath, with the nose looking upturned because of the curve in the enamel, and I told my facial silhouette that this was it. From now on, now more messing around. No more disruption, no more dishonesty, only hard work and application.

So from that new year I followed the resolution and things started settling down gradually. Things didn't happen overnight, especially not the wariness of me on the part of teachers and my previous enemies among the other kids. I made up for past dishonesty by being becoming brutally honest, which didn't always help, and tried to keep my activities wholly legal, with the one exception of a bit more underage drinking, and some of the lessons I still couldn't manage to give attention to. Others I stopped disrupting, and sat through maybe doing something from another subject if I didn't like the subject in hand. Knowing the reputation I came with, the teachers whose subjects I wasn't interested in were happy with just that.

It was only at the age of 14, though, that I decided that a complete change was in order, and I changed my circle of friends, gave up drinking (which I adhered to very strictly for the next 20 years, and I still rarely take any alcohol) and really applied myself to academic success in every subject. The fact of not changing my friends and not stopping drinking after the resolutions made in the previous year and held me back a bit and also represented a risk that I could slide back into anti-social ways again.

The aim was to get through the O level and A level exams and then secure a good university place, but I was also enjoying certain things that fascinated me, and of course the languages were still top of that list. At about the same time, I decided to try to do what David Morgan had said was possible, namely to learn a language on my own. The BBC Avventura course was going on at the time, and I had been attracted to the idea of trying Italian. But something else was happening to my body at the same time, something that was going to change the course of my life for ever…

Anyone who has watched any of my films on YouTube has probably noticed a couple of things about me. One of these things is an evident portli- not to say porkiness. But then there are a lot of portly personages on YT – it kind of goes with the territory of slouching about in front of a computer all day. The other, more unique thing that you will probably notice if you look at me is that I sport a pair of what the Japanese call "ゲジゲジ眉毛" or "gejigeji mayuge". In medical terms, you could call this "Scutigeroid Supercilia Syndrome", although I doubt whether anyone ever has. In any event, I was busy growing this pair at age 13-14 and was already was getting called Brezhnev by all the kids at school, and (me being me), I decided to play up to it.

So I used to act a bit like Brezhnev as he appeared on the news, and give stiff waves as from the Kremlin wall to people, and talk in what I thought was a Russian accent. (This is what passed for humour amongst our crowd of 15 year olds, but the surprise is I'm now 46 and people still enjoy the character!) But then it occurred to me that if I was going to try to learn a language, may as well set myself a decent challenge. Italian was not reckoned by folk around me to be a massive challenge, but Russian looks exotic, and at that time it was the language of people that we didn't know much about, and the Soviet Union was not far from our consciousness in 1970's Britain. On a world map, the area under Soviet control ended a day's drive from the shore that looks over to our land. And there were 270 million people in the Soviet Union, living life in accordance to totally different rules to ours. This was also the run up to the 1980 Olympics and there was anxiety over Russia's invasion of Afghanistan (we little thought that it would be us fighting the same people 30 years later and getting the weapons turned against us which Charlie Wilson sent to fight the Soviets!) so the Soviet Union was in the forefront of everybody's mind.

As part of my curiosity about the world and the sound of languages, as well as a love of speech radio which I had had since the age of 11, when I sequestered my Dad's little Phillips portable, and shortly afterwards bought an old valve radio with all the short wave bands, I had listened a bit to Radio Moscow, and had heard what I took to be Russian and liked the sound of it, both in speech and in music. I wrote down phrases of a language I particularly liked on a certain frequency, although I didn't know them. I wrote "gavareet radio stantsia rodina" and tried to ask people what language that was, only to be told by my own mother that it was indeed Russian, and that she knew this because she had been trying to learn it in night classes while carrying me, but hadn't got very far with it. On top of that, my pubertising person also very much liked the look of the Russian gymnasts on TV, and I imagined myself with one of these pretty Russian girls, even though they were far away and in a different system and on the whole forbidden fruit, which only served to make them the more attractive, and so I became motivated by all these things to choose Russian to teach to myself.

So I needed to buy a book. There was a book "Russian Made Simple" in the W.H. Smith store in Hemel Hempstead (which was in a different place then to where it is now – Marks and Spencers is now about where W.H. Smith was then) and this was about GBP 5.99, or thereabouts. That was several weeks' pocket money, now

432

that I wasn't thieving with that bad crowd any more –
(incidentally they all reformed and went on to become
respectable members of the community – I didn't have any
monopoly on pulling myself up by my bootstraps). So I
had to go to my mother and ask her for the money. "I know
why you want to learn Russian" she said. I thought, "you're
not gonna go on about my eyebrows as well are you,
mother?" but I said "really, mother? why is that, then?" "It's
because I told you that I had tried to learn it when I was
expecting you, and I didn't manage it. You just want to
show me you can do the things I couldn't do, don't you?" I
agreed, rather than get into an eyebrow discussion, or,
even worse, an Olga Korbut discussion with my own
mother, but it was true that that aspect had also entered
my head as a supplemental reason for learning the
language as I've always been quite a competitive person.
So needless to say, I received the finance for the book,
and launched myself into it the next day, at the age of 15.

I taught myself Russian from that book, from the Russian
Linguaphone borrowed from the local library, and from
Russian Language and People (a BBC course which you
can't find so far on YT although I asked them to put it up,
but I'm just a licence payer, so what do I know?), and
hasn't been seen for ages. But in the end the main book I
changed over to was Michael Frewin's "Teach Yourself
Russian" – one of the old series of Teach Yourself books,
before they dumbed down about seven years later. I
worked my way through it in the way the book itself
recommends, doing the exercises and trying to remember
the vocab lists. I would spend a week or so on every
lesson and only move on when I was convinced I
understood everything. I took about a year over it, but I still
didn't have anybody to talk to, and then I moved on to

other books, including the then Colloquial Russian, again from the old series, not yet dumbed down as Colloquial did, following the TeachYourself series' example.

After a year, when people saw that I was serious about learning Russian, they started looking around for people I could practice with. The local grocer found me an old lady in Briden's Camp near Hemel Hempstead, who was born and raised in pre-Revolutionary Russia, the daughter of the Times' correspondent to the Tsar's court, who had to leave in haste during the Russian Revolution and I was to take tea once a week with that lady up in Briden's Camp until she sadly passed on. I used to cycle up a very steep hill that seemed to go one and on, although now in the age of GPS I know it's only 50 meters difference in altitude, to get to her little old cottage. She was so kind in her help, and never dreamed of charging me a penny – on the contrary, Margarita Georgovna's tea and cakes were out of this world, and she always gave of them generously as well as of her time.

Then friends from school found me an emigree in Tring and I used to take the bus or cycle there every week to have an hour or so's conversation. At that time there were nearly no Russians to be had in Hertfordshire. Only two teachers were registered for the whole county, but they weren't actually teaching it. This lady in Tring had also an amazing story – the previous generation escaped Russia in the revolution and her mother, with her as a small child, were in Harbin in China when the Cultural Revolution happened. The Russian community in Harbin was large, and they feared that the Maoists were going to hand them back to the Soviet comrades, which would have meant transportation to a gulag, and so they went en masse to the coast and got vessels to whatever free country would take them. This lady's family went to Brasil, but were almost turned away when the authorities asked the priest who was their group leader what his name was. "Methodius" in Russian is "Mifodii", you see, which sounds remarkably similar to "mi fodi" in Portuguese, but thankfully the misunderstanding was cleared up and they got ashore.

This lady got educated at Brazil's top philological faculty, and ended up being the translator of James Joyce into Portuguese. If anyone has ever read "Finnegan's Wake" then they will see that the task of even understanding it in the source language is not to be sniffed at, and the idea of coming up with dynamic equivalents in another language is a mind-boggling prospect, but that is what she did, and that is what brought her to Ireland, in pursuit of the trail of her favorite author, and then to the UK. She was in many ways a mentor to me, for over a year, in literary ideas as well as linguistic ones. And again, she would not dream of taking a fee for all her trouble over me, it was simply her pleasure to share her language and thoughts with someone who appreciated it. All that Marina Buck expected was that I would be the same to others – a major reason the Huliganov Russian Course and the Gold List method are out there free of charge for everyone.

Our school encouraged sixth-formers (that was from age 17) to offer coaching to younger children for a few periods a week, and when I became a prefect in the school I offered Russian lessons to younger kids, and one of them who remembers that to this day is Dr Richard Grayson, the Liberal party candidate now for Hemel Hempstead. I was encouraged in the then lower sixth form, which is the age of 17, to take O level in Russian. At the same time I took O level Italian as we had had a teacher join the school who was Senior Mistress and she taught French and Italian, but the latter was her real passion. Under her teaching for a year, I was ready for the O level with my "prima di" sentences and "dopo aver" sentences, and a vocabulary of probably about 1,000 words, as well as some fine hand waving techniques which are the parts of Italian grammar you don't find in the textbook, which won me a B – and the ability comfortably to pass the time of day with the guy in the ice-cream van I knew.

But my A in Russian annoyed my Italian teacher Mrs Scargall – "Perchè? Perchè?" she wailed, true to her maxim never to use an English word to a student if she had already taught them its Italian equivalent, "when I teach you, you get a B, but when you teach yourself, you get an A, how does that make me feel?" I answered as best I could in O-level Italian that I did not presume to plumb the depths of feelings of such an artistic soul as she, and she pouted emphatically, "I feel I waste my time as a teacher if you can do better on your own". Well, I tried to console her with David Morgan's wise words about how you have to own the language learning process, but she was having none of it. If anything that seemed to make matters worse, and her whole raison d'etre as a language teacher seemed to have been put into question by the simple fact that the same student who studies under such an inspiring teacher as she was, should have got a better grade in a harder language when he taught himself, and there were no teachers even to be had.

But this little episode highlights an abiding problem in language education. Governments need to understand that teachers of languages need to be coaches in how to show kids how to teach themselves and then just help them with their queries and make sure they stick with it. Instead of French classes or German classes in schools, there should be lessons where in the same room 30 kids are learning maybe 20 different languages in the same space, each one the language which grabs their imagination, and for some it might be several languages.

Adoption of Goldlist method style learning by Education Ministers would accomplish this, and would enable children to come out of schools having spent the 500 or so hours given over to language learning actually being able to read and understand the language, and not, as it is now, with children all learning French for 500 hours and yet not being able to have a basic conversation in French in the case of most British school leavers. Of course, that would mean that the teachers would need to accept that they are not really the important ones in the process, all they need to do is empower the students, but getting them to admit that – even to themselves – that's the hard part. I felt sorry for that teacher, she had certainly put her soul into the lessons, but that's still not the same as self tuition. Self tuition wins out every time, especially once the learner is onto his or her severalth language, but even in my case for the first time, it was the same story.

So I went on to concentrate on the French and German (and English for that matter, but that already really means literature in the main) which I was doing for A level, but I did find myself distracted by casual attempts to teach myself further languages, and I had about 20 hanzi characters while I was still at school, as well as some few hundred words of Greek and one or two others. But I was focused on getting a good university place and I managed to win a place at Cambridge to study Modern and Medieval Languages, which was a total transformation, as I had gone from the nasty punky thieving vandal tearaway who would give good kicks whilst pogo-ing ("you dance divinely, sir" was the response of another punk who got a good one in the kneecap at one local disco in the middle of the punk era) to the "arch swot", complete with new spectacles, in quite a short space of time, although it was really months and years not days and weeks that did it. For my teachers, in any event, it was a transformation "devoutly to be wished", but not for everyone in the school, in particular not for some of my peers…

I still recall the tears of the girl who was the top of the class in the end of the year exams in the first four years of our school when she had to cede that place to me in the final year, and then I was the only pupil in the year to gain an Oxbridge place. I was not popular with any of the other students at the school, not with my old friends for abandoning them and not with the academic crowd either, for outdoing them, although I might have been able to win them a bit more had I not been so open about gloating at them whenever I beat them at their own game. At this time I was still not a very nice person anyway. As I had not been converted to faith in Jesus Christ at that time I was not very nice to the others anyway, and tended to regard them as fodder for my competitive streak, but not much else.

It really didn't concern me at all that I was probably the least popular among these students, and how I laughed when one of them had a party and invited everyone except me, pointedly, and the small group that were hanging around with me, and all those who did go were stricken with Salmonella because his mother didn't understand how to handle food for that number properly. The next day I was able to pick David Morgan's brains unimpeded by their interruptions, and their share of the time. In fact I was only converted the Summer I left the school, which was probably just as well as nobody would ever have believed that someone like me, entirely self-obsessed, could possibly become a Christian.

I used to walk home with one guy who went to the Church near where I lived, intending to undermine his faith in the Bible and generally make an atheist commie out of him like I was, and I figured that since this guy was not very advanced academically, and I was the great hope of our school, the one who had got into Cambridge, etc etc, it shouldn't have been too difficult, but God wasn't having any of that, and I was born again into Jesus Christ in August 1982 at 18 years and 3 months of age. All the preceding months had been one big theological debate where I had pitted the world views of just about any group I could find against the rigorous Calvinism of this Church, and found that they had more consistent answers and deeper meanings of life than any of the other ones I could throw at them.

And then, all of a sudden, I knew God. One August evening in my bedroom I was almost taken out of myself and confronted with the Maker and Redeemer. I felt dizzy and simply prayed for about an hour on the floor and gradually came back to myself. Skeptics have all sorts of clever answers in psychology for these kinds of religious experience of course, and they may be right or wrong. But I had "found a Friend, ah such a friend, who loved me e'er

I knew him" as the hymn writer says. From that day it was no longer a pure intellectual exercise for me, but something in which the heart was also bound up.

I began to read the Bible, pray, repent and try to live in a Christian way. With a character like mine, the last part of that wasn't at all easy, though, but this account is maybe not the best place for going into that, and I am mentioning this religious stuff, in case you are wondering, as it does become relevant to the story later on…

2. Gap Year and University

In any event, the language learning continued unabated, only now with a new zeal behind it, as languages were something that could be pressed into Christian service. I read "War and Peace" in the original Russian in my gap year to get a really literary standard in Russian, and plenty of German literature from the University reading list. For the first six months of my gap year, I couldn't get on an exchange programme, but I did some work to put money aside for University and applied the rest of my time to study and learning. I also got interested in Esperanto and learned that from the Teach Yourself Book and was a regular for that six months in the Watford Esperanto Club. I learned a number of other alphabets and also devised my own alphabet which was to be part of my own conlang. (I have written a couple of conlangs, but I never got them to a state which I was happy enough with the outcome to share it).

I went to Seelze bei Hannover in Germany from March to August of that year under the aegis of the Deutsch-Britischer Judendaustausch (which, subject to a slight name change appears still to be going strong) and worked in a warehouse office at Riedel deHaen AG (now part of

Honeywell) for six months, which helped finance the rest of my university time as well as getting my German up to a high level, and it was in Hannover, or Hanover as we say in English, that I first met Polish people. I liked the Poles that I met and decided to try to learn Polish from them, and I noted down the vocabulary they told me in an exercise book – I didn't get very far with it at the time, just a few pages, but I was to dig the same book out a few years later and work it forward, and it became, almost by accident, the prototype of the Goldlist method book. So whilst I tend to say that 1993 is when I started using the method, the first seed of it appeared in 1983, ten years earlier.

Hanoverians are noted, even among other North Germans, for being a little stand-offish and not easy to befriend, although if you do finally make a North German friend, then you have a very loyal friend, in my experience. On the other hand it was easy to fall into a kind of friendship with the Poles who were working there, and maybe be forgotten just as soon after I'd left. One of the things that interested me about them was the similarity between their words and the Russian. I didn't have that much practice in Russian, although the reading of War and Peace was helping me keep an ever increasing pace of reading comprehension. I found a Russian Baptist Church in Hanover on Pelikanstrasse right near where the famous Pelikan stationery was made, although Google maps are showing a Sheraton hotel there now, which doesn't surprise me as people simply can't bring themselves to leave things be, and that was all the conversation in Russian I got. But I did get into some quite interesting Baptist Church connexions and into an awareness of what was happening to the Church in the Soviet Union…

While in Hanover I picked up a bit of Calenberger Platt, which I don't speak these days for the simple reason that it "migrated" westwards when I took an interest in Dutch and it ended up with me understanding and speaking a modicum of Dutch without even studying it in the systematic way I would usually recommend.

At Cambridge University, languages are taught with reference especially to their literature, and so they expect students to read the literature of the languages. This would be all very well, as I love literature, but I didn't really like the way of analysing it which they wanted me to do at University. It was hard for me, with the zeal of the new convert, to react to or analyse literature while abstracting it away from the Christian viewpoint. Instead it seemed irresistible for me to analyse every work in the light of Calvinist theology, which tended to disparage a number of the ideas in the work in hand, whether for its worldliness or its wrong ideas about spirituality. Certainly it was difficult for me to go along with the Marxist structuralist approach that Cambridge was famed for, and some of the professors seemed to like my literature essays with their barely disguised underlying Evangelicalism just about as little as I liked the methods they were imposing on the writing.

Now it is quite difficult to get away from literature in the Modern and Medieval languages tripos, but one way to do it is to focus more on history of the language papers. I wanted to learn more languages and I didn't care if they were medieval and not spoken anymore. As far as I was concerned, those languages were wanted, dead or alive! So I did as much philology and as little literature as I could fit into the tripos. And in the end I would have had a first, my College's senior tutor informed me, if I'd stuck entirely to the philology and had not, for sentimental reasons, insisted on doing the German 20th Century literature paper, in addition to History of the German Language, History of the Russian Language, The Slavonic Languages, and The Germanic Languages, and this four were the four philology papers that I took.

I asked Professor Green, who was the senior professor in the Languages Faculty at that time, before choosing that set of papers whether he thought it was a good idea, and he said "**you will need to learn too many languages. You need to learn at least three additional languages for each of the papers, The Germanic Languages and The Slavonic Languages, so that is six extra languages to learn, in two years. I do not think it is circumspect**."

Well, I didn't think it was circumspect either, but it was my idea of fun, so I went ahead and did it following my own counsel rather than that of the wise professor. He clearly knew all those languages, and his philological lectures were nothing short of amazing, so I thought "It's all very well for you to inspire me and then talk about being circumspect", and so by the time I was through I had learned Old English, Middle English, Old High and Middle High German, Gothic, Icelandic and Old Norse as well as looking at some Dutch and losing my Calenberger Platt, for the Germanic side, and Old Church Slavonic, Old Russian, some Polish and quite a bit of Serbo-Croat, which has in fact become a dead language since I studied it but was alive and truly kicking at the time. Now there are four languages where there was one before, because every freshly emerging Balkan state wants to elevate its dialect to the point of a language, and so you can see people claiming to speak Bosnian and Montenegrin as well as Serbian and Croatian, but all of this was srpsko-hrvatski in my day.

I had the great pleasure of being taught by the now sadly missed Dr. Ned Goy, then Cambridge's sole Serbo-Croat lecturer, and there were three of us in the weekly sessions in my second year, but when I came back from my year out to my fourth year, which is the final year, I had this great character all to myself, and we went through "Горски вијенац" ("Gorski Vijenac" or "The Mountain Wreath") by Petar II Petrović-Njegoš. This epic poem is written in a style of Serbo-Croat which is delineated as Montenegrin today, and Ned Goy used to produce a pint of prawns for each of us to share in each of his lessons. So now I still remember him whenever I eat prawns.

The Germans call an underattended course at University an "Orchideenfach", and dear old Ned Goy was a rare bloom by that token, as by any other, and you can find obituaries to him on the net which show how valuable, and yet at the time undervalued, a mind he was.

One summer holiday, I took a student rail card and went to Peć in Kosovo to meet a Serbian pastor my pastor in Hemel Hempstead knew well, and ended up translating one of his many books in English from Serbo-Croat. It is called "The Tongue – Our Measure" ("Jezik - naše merilo") by Simo Ralević, and you can still find it on Amazon to this day, published by the Banner of Truth Trust of which he was a trustee. But the name of the translator was not given, probably because my pastor wanted to encourage me to greater humility, which was fair enough, I have to say quite honestly. I don't think there were more than a handful of students who looked at Serbo-Croat at university level in the whole of the UK in the whole of the time I was there, whereas now it has become, in its four derivative versions, the language of four states each of all could at any time win the accolade of membership of the European Union, or even greater than that, win the Eurovision Song Contest, as indeed one of them recently did, thanks largely to the voting system.

The level of learning required in the so-called "big philology papers" in the Cambridge tripos in the 80s (from the website of Cambridge University I gather that the amount of required reading of the source texts has reduced considerably since then, maybe in order to be more circumspect, I don't know – the Germanic Languages paper was even suspended after tripos 2008, that's how circumspect they have become now, but they do have a paper instead on Modern European film, so it would appear that Cambridge has done all in its power to emulate the down-market Universities and I wonder whether there is any way back once you start going down that route. Maybe in a few years time they will actually have a paper on YouTube videos and some of the folk contributing to the current volume will become 'set texts', who knows?) was to know sufficient in order to be able to identify and translate a passage from each language in the original into English in the exam room unaided, chosen randomly from a chrestomathy of work, which students had been able to buy and study in the final academic year plus the year abroad before that, and then to be able to gloss and parse certain words and phrases chosen by the examiner from the given text. You had to be able to do this for three languages chosen from about five or six medieval or modern languages. In Slavonic the tendency was to use the modern more, as there was less medieval literacy than in Germanic or the Romance languages.

So that meant a working knowledge of the grammar and a vocabulary of in fact not more than 1000 words in each of these languages. The grammars were similar in a number of languages so in studying them you could take one as a base and do a "compare and contrast" exercise on how the grammars of the next languages differed. After a while I discovered that the grammars of European languages contain a very finite set of problems and features and from a point of view of how the basic grammar works, each incremental language can be learned quite quickly. I wrote the paradigms out from the grammar books, glossed them, and returned in a few weeks to do the same again, concentrating on what I hadn't remembered so well.

But the problem was how to learn the vocabulary. That was what, in terms of sheer time involved, could put my plan for a good degree in jeopardy and early on I used to worry whether I would indeed learn the words that are in the texts on time. I worried about it and started to rack my brains for an effective way to do so, as after all my degree could depend on success or failure in doing so. If a person really knew their texts, then they could get great marks in the translating and glossing section and not need such high marks in the essay section, which could be much less predictable and harder. And I had indeed chosen the less circumspect route, so I had to use my inventiveness to get through the situation.

But that also was a step along the lines of thinking that helped me devise the Goldlist method – this was the point in time at which I realised one of the underlying ideas of the method – the fact that regular grammar can be learned in a small percentage of the time it takes to learn the vocabulary, and the irregular grammar, the exceptions, should be learned together with the vocabulary items as they come. Therefore 80% or more of the work needed to learn a language, especially more for one in a family you already know, is all in the vocabulary, the stuff you can progress into your long-term memory in a systematic way, line by line, using staged repetition, counting your achievement as you go in order to stay in control of the whole process and own the learning of your language yourself, just as David Morgan had explained to me so many years earlier.

Nobody else did four philology papers, all the other students thought I was mad. Literature papers were more of a doss, as we called it. You could always read the books in translation if you were short of time and just learn a selection of quotes for the exam in the original. That was the acceptable short-cut, which I myself never used. I always read the full original and if there was a translation then I used it instead of the dictionary, but it was the original I read, without exception. Just as I always kept the Sabbath at University, without exception. I did not work on Sundays, which was my Sabbath, as it is for most Christians, although I have every respect for those who keep Saturdays and these days I keep both if I can only get away with it. Anyway, whatever method I was going to use it was not allowed to compromise my rigid principles. I was definitely going to learn the languages or simply fail my degree or get a low grade in the attempt. And the faculty I had chosen was called "Modern and Medieval Languages" and not "Literary Criticism the Marxist Way", that's what I had come to study, and that is what I was going to study.

Well, I hadn't discovered the Goldlist method by that point, even though I had already arrived at some of the key ideas underpinning it, such as the fact that grammar isn't the most time-consuming and challenging thing about learning a language, but rather the committing – at least to passive memory – thousands and thousands of pieces of vocabulary, with their little exceptions to the main grammar rules, and also small fixed phrases. If I had had the full Goldlist method, or a close equivalent, then the process could have been done much more efficiently, maybe in even half the time, and if I'd known about the human memory and how it works the things I know now, I would have worried a lot less. But as it is I started to experiment to find ways to speed up the process of the task I had set myself. I knew how I had learned languages up to then, so that was the starting point. But I needed more. And so vocabulary books started to emerge which I hadn't done properly before, I also wrote out the ancient texts in my own hand, and later also read them on cassettes which I then listened back to over and over.

What I did was, without realising it, an effective staged presentation, as Ebbinghaus – whom I hadn't heard of then – would call it, to my memory of the material. That was a way of learning to the long term memory. That's why I can't remember any of the Latin I rush learned for the exam today, but if I picked up the texts I had memorised over those two years for my degree, I could still read them today and translate them sight unseen for a quarter of a century. This I know because of course I still have these books, and occasionally, very occasionally, nose at an odd random page I haven't seen since my student days, and it all comes flooding back.

This linguistic experience all in all gave me one of the three components of the knowledge I needed in order to devise the Goldlist method, namely the knowledge that someone has who has learned a good number of languages before, trying to be more effective and efficient, and probably being more or less successful largely because of chance.

I was asked at the end of my undergraduate studies would I like to stay and research, because the fact is that I would have had a first class degree were it not for the insistence in keeping one literature paper, in which I only scored a 2,2, as I was told unofficially by my Senior Tutor. The fellows knew what I had done in learning that many languages and they probably saw in me someone who could have been a contender for an academic career just on the philology side, because several of them sought me out in a way which I did not understand at that time, being ignorant as I was in the ways of the world and how organisations – and their funding – function, and had I done so I would know more languages today, but in all likelihood I would not have devised the Goldlist method, as the other components came from the very different life I chose after graduating.

But to talk about that we need to get into deeper, darker territory, namely what happened in my year out, which was in the Soviet Union, and really deserves a chapter all of its own, although it relates to the third of the four University years I've already described from the curricular perspective. If I were to talk about Cambridge from a full perspective and all the friends and discussions I had there, a whole book would not be enough, and this despite the fact that I must be one of a small minority of students there who never had sex in Cambridge, which was quite far from the student life I had envisaged when I first decided to try going there, and I was already far from innocent way back then. Suffice it to say, it is without doubt one of the best experiences you can possibly have in your life to go to a good university. You never want it to end, but at the same time you are aware the whole time just how short it is, and how quickly it goes by. Some people hanker after it for years after leaving, and go back visiting or just decide to carry on living in their University town, only to discover that they soon become regarded as irrelevant and even pathetic by the next years of undergrads coming through, and the only way is to move on, or else have a proper academic career, rather than being a University sideliner. And in the latter case, don't even think about having plenty of money.

3. The Soviet Experience

I knew a little bit about Communism. I had spent time with those Russian Baptists in Hanover in my gap year, I had also been in East Germany and had a good look at the Berlin wall, spoken to Germans whose families had been divided by the Iron Curtain, travelled alone in the post-Tito Yugoslavia while it was still Yugoslavia. So it wasn't as if I walked into the Soviet Experience with my eyes shut in 1985. But I felt that it was the only way I was going to get my Russian as good as I wanted it.

Because of the difficulties of the Russian-British student exchange, various alternatives existed outside of Russia – there was a place in Paris where a community of emigres gave Russian immersion courses and you could even go for the whole gap year, but the language was already not very contemporary and in fact I did have a certain dread fascination about going to Russia proper, and I would have felt I had chickened out if I hadn't gone there, just because so many people were doing time down salt mines and in gulags just because they believed precisely the same things as I believed, in particular that the Church of Christ should be independent from the state and not reduced to a controlled organ of state, taking its instructions not from God but from atheists in the Communist party – or any other party for that matter. In fact, there was never any doubt in my mind that I would go there, and I would also look out the unregistered Church and support it in any way I could.

I regarded that as an evident calling since I was converted at the point when I was already due to be going to Cambridge University and studying Russian. Prior to that conversion, of course, as I mentioned earlier I had been an atheist communist myself, and so when I first thought of going to Russia for the year out, I hadn't envisaged any possible conflict with their ideology.

For students at UK universities wishing to spend an academic year out at a Russian University, the exchange programme with Voronezh University was the only game in town. It was run on the UK side by The British Council, that fine organisation which has changed significantly since those days, and none of my comments here on the British Council refer to the organisation in its current form. I have plenty of friends in it now in a number of countries, and none of these people is referred to in any way with the events of 1985-6.

The British Council interviewed students going on the course very carefully, and I also answered their questions carefully. Somehow it seemed they could sense I might be a risky person to send, but they could not find any justifiable reason for not sending me – certainly they as a UK institution couldn't exactly exclude a student from going on the grounds of faith. Not back then, anyway. All they could do was to advise caution. They let us know how almost every year one of the British students spending the academic year in Voronezh was singled out by the Soviet hosts for "special attention", purely in order to enable the people of Voronezh, especially the students of the university, and the wider Soviet people, to believe that the UK could not resist sending its spies to Russia at every opportunity.

A couple of years before my year went, for example, one of the victims of this policy was a certain student who made no secret of his love of heavy ordnance. He liked it from what I understand mainly from a point of view of admiring the engineering achievements that fighter planes and tanks represented, and he had Janes books and posters even decorating the walls of his hostel room. He also had a camera. Well, apparently from the version of this which came to my ears, the Soviet students in the hostel – on orders from their KGB mentors – told him that they were organising a barbecue and that girls he liked would be there, and great food and drink, and that they didn't need him to bring any food or drink, but they wanted him to bring his camera because no-one else had one. They gave him a map and told him not to tell the other UK people about it. Of course, when he followed the instructions and went through the crack in the fence to a dark field with his camera, the floodlights came on and the police came in from all sides and he was in an airfield with Soviet military planes all around, and he was accused of military espionage and trying to photograph them.

I don't speak about the case of that person in particular for any reason other than that this must have been Voronezh KGB's finest hour. Every year they chose someone to present in an anti-western light, but this guy with his love of military weaponry was the ideal telegenic target, although had anyone stopped to think about it, they would have realised that the last thing a real spy would do is to plaster his walls with posters of Nato's and the Warsaw Pact's respective toys. Neither would a real spy have been allowed home so easily after his discovery.

The fact that these episodes always took place shortly before the close of the academic year and also that they released the students without formal charges shows what a charade this was, but nevertheless it was an unpleasant charade to be involved in, and we were warned not to trust the Soviet students who were living with us in the same rooms – two Russians and two UK students in each room in the 'obshchzhitie' – they were all selected to live with foreigners because of their high loyalty to the party. This was the history faculty anyway, where some of the heaviest pro-Soviet propaganda was being fed to the students, students who themselves were set aside to be the next generation of the propaganda machine – until, of course, it all collapsed and they all needed to take a second look at everything they had learned.

Now as you may already have deduced from the above, in my year it was me that was singled out to be the propaganda victim. This time, they were able to make a strike at the Church at the same time. I had (from the sources mentioned vaguely above but I will still not be drawn on any more detail) knowledge of where there was, in Voronezh, a Baptist congregation which did not figure on any of the official lists. It transpired that there was a group of six or more Christians in the thirty or so of us UK students that were there together. About six of us used to be able to pray together and have Bible studies, and we also used to go along to that unregistered Church, including sometimes even our 'starosta' or group leader, the charismatic Richard Nerurkar (now MBE, although he hadn't been awarded it yet back then) who did us all proud by competing for Voronezh in a pan-Soviet Union long distance running event and winning. He was a fine believing man, and his career of helping people afterwards absolutely doesn't surprise me. This Church doubtless had KGB moles in it and we were also tailed a good deal anyway, but before long we were closely observed and various students from the Russians were set on to try to find out who knew about the Church.

I myself was smitten with one of the Russian girls, Olga, whom I met some two months after we arrived, when a bunch of very pretty girls were moved into our corridor well after term started in what I now regard as suspicious circumstances. She reminded me of the test card girl you used to see on BBC during the day before they had all day programming, who had been my first television crush, to be joined later on by Lindsay Wagner and Belinda J. Montgomery. If television is not all about giving you crushes on people you are never likely to meet, then I don't know what it is for, unless maybe to make money out of advertising. When I first saw the test card girl I asked my mother what that thing she was sitting next to was. My mother said "that looks like a toy snail". Well, I certainly wanted one of those, but not the snail, let me tell you. And here, at last, she was, in the same corridor of a shabby obshchezhitie in Voronezh. A mix of the test card girl and

Olga Korbut and every girl I had ever wanted before in my life, and all in the exactly correct blend.

Anyway, this Olga remarkably became my girlfriend, and also in due course my fiancée, but clearly was placed under immediate duress to find out as much as she could about what we were doing in that Church, who knew about it and how. Certain scenes reminiscent of Samson and Delilah ensued over the following months. In Soviet Russia, love falls in with you, if it's told to, and then tries to make you say what her controllers are trying to find out.

I don't blame her for succumbing to playing their games as any Soviet citizen's fate was absolutely in the hands of the KGB, and at one point where it looked to them as though her heart was not in it, their house was "burgled" and the police informed them that they would only be able to get their valuables back from the "robbers" if they co-operated, as in, if their daughter co-operated. Whereas if she didn't, then all sorts of things might happen. There was no such thing as unemployment benefit in the Soviet Union because there was no unemployment – officially. But of course you could lose your job if you or anyone they could get to through you failed to do their patriotic duty when asked to by a valid organ of the Party. Neither would she have been allowed to finish her degree.

So clearly there was no choice but for her to co-operate and basically play the Delilah to my rather love-blinded Samson. That's why I have had quite a lot of fellow feeling for this Alex Chapman chap, the husband of the agent Anna Chapman – I've been there. On the one hand you have this relationship with a beautiful woman which seems real enough, on the other, she has her job to do, and no real choice in the matter. But it's a distressing and life-disrupting thing, I can tell you. Until that point in my life I had never loved anyone as strongly as her, and I would not have swapped her for a channelful of Lindsay Wagners and Belinda J Montgomeries. Whether I should have done is an entirely different matter, but you cannot command the heart. "Любовь зла - полюбишь и козла" as the Russian has it (literally "Love's unkind – you can even fall in love with a goat"), and indeed they don't make goats anything like this Olga – I think it no exaggeration that you could have placed a photo of her face among all the most beautiful faces of the most notoriously pretty women who ever lived, and she would not look out of place, so what was not to love? Her nickname was "the star", and we all know what that rhymes with, in Russian, but it wasn't like she had any choice in the matter.

I did not, in my relative innocence, always understand at the time what was behind her questions to me, but one of the things she asked was "if someone wanted to find out about a Church like the one I was going to, where would they be able to find those details?". In this context I mentioned to her the fully public institution Keston College, which catalogued information about religion under Communism. This was as far as I was aware a normal college at Oxford, founded by Rev Michael Bordeaux who himself had been an exchange student in Russia who had tried then to link up the remaining Churches. I did not, myself actually have my source of information from Keston, although I had spoken to Rev Bordeaux. But that was not the question I was asked. I was not asked, or at least if I was I never answered it, where I had the information from. I was asked and therefore answered the question where I thought such information would be available for whoever wanted it.

Olga seemed to think that my own Church's minister, John E. Marshall, was funded by the UK government to take an interest in the Soviet Union. The idea that this staunchly disestablishmentarian old-school Congregationalist minister could have been in the pay of the Government made me simply laugh, and the subject was dropped.

For a while the six of us who were involved with this unregistered Church had been welcomed into the Choir, but after a few weeks one of the Elders asked me into his room, and said to me in tears "what I have to tell you is very sad. There are some people in this Church who are monitoring us for the authorities. They are not happy about your group of English students being in the choir as they will make too strong private connections with Soviet citizens. I have to ask you not to continue with the choir". Now, in my life I've been chucked out of various things for various reasons, but that's the only time I can remember the person who was doing the chucking out being in tears over it at the time of doing so, although there may have been some who were afterwards for less noble reasons.

This was a pity, as we had all enjoyed it, but his distress at having to ask us this was clear, and we did nothing to exacerbate it, and simply left the choir. Shortly before we were to go home for two weeks one of the elders asked if we could bring microphones for use in the service and maybe some Russian Bibles for the Church. These items were hard to come by in the Soviet Union. Even a photocopying machine had to be licensed back then, and they were lucky that pens were not handed out with serial numbers and you had to account for how you used the ink – somehow it felt that if they had passed such a law, it would come as no surprise, and would simply be a logical extension of the other totalitarian laws. I wondered at the hypocrisy of this in a nation that was vaunting itself to be a peoples' paradise and how they expected to gain the hearts and minds of people when they needed to keep them in and control them with such blunt instruments. All the time I was trying to understand what this whole Communism thing was for and how things had ever come to pass that such a poor system existed. I began to feel a lack of understanding of economics, and thought that educating myself in that direction more might clarify to me a bit more the whole Communism/capitalism debate.

I came back after the February vacation break with what they wanted, but was intercepted at Sheremietievo airport. In retrospect it is clear that I was asked to bring the things only so that they could have something on me, but they let me on to Voronezh and no more was said about it for a while. I did find this experience hard, though, and the whole atmosphere of the second semester there much more oppressive. On the one hand we had some excellent teachers in the University – one even gave some of us a class in Old Church Slavonic and Old Russian just for the more advanced students. But I noticed that Russian students were forever appearing in our room or coming to meet me and asking me for my opinions on this, that or the other. I had been pointedly told even by the British Council before going that I couldn't go around evangelising in the Soviet Union, but this, where people came and asked me what I thought, surely they deserved a full explanation of what they ostensibly wanted to know.

So I got into debates about theology, in which I could hold my own, and then also history and politics where I had views but was less able to really defend them. This in itself made me wish I knew more of how the world worked. I tried to explain in terms of basic economics why the free market system was superior to the centrally planned economy, but I felt that I had too little true understanding of economics and of business to be able to argue my points against these Soviet students with more conviction. So I resolved to make good that lack of understanding – somehow and at some time.

And of course when the fullness of time came, the authorities carried out their plan on me as follows – we had been on a trip to Tallinn, and when we got back we were informed that there had been ticks on the train and we were all to go and get injections for something. When it was my turn, they gave me some different shot to the one they gave the other students. And when I succumbed to the illness they gave me, the diagnosis was "mononucleosis" or "glandular fever". Although there was no glandular fever reported anywhere else in the student population, and usually it comes out in bursts with several students getting it at once. Glandular fever is the scourge of students and is sometimes called "kissing disease". When you get it you can be rendered too weak to study for months on end and usually this results in the need to repeat a whole year. Since I had already been funded to the max to do the extra year out as a linguist, failure to complete the fourth and final year could have cost me my degree. So I was devastated as well as mystified by the diagnosis.

I actually started showing the symptoms of this during a trip they organised for us to Yerevan in Armenia. I was looking up at the Ararat mountain where according to the Book of Genesis Noah's ark came to rest and a new era of life on earth began, feeling decidedly unwell, but little thinking how much a change was about to take place in my own life.

This disease, anyway, enabled the Soviet authorities to take me once we were back in Voronezh in a very weakened mental and physical state. I had basically tried to simply carry on as normally with the disease, expecting it to go away after a few days and making the most of the Yerevan trip despite feeling lousy, but instead of feeling better I felt worse. Gradually I got a black tongue too from secondary infections and started being sick all the time.

When I was supposed to go to hospital, they came and drove me instead to the police station. There they said they wanted to ask me questions about my intention to marry a Soviet citizen, and they took Olga also, off to another room, which was the last I saw of her until years later, by which time too many things had changed and I never did end up marrying her, although in the meantime I had spent years intending to. There, in the interrogation centre, they used Olga to play her off against me, and to try to extract more information about what I was doing with the Church.

They brought out then the episode with the microphones and Bibles which had been confiscated in February, four months earlier. They showed me pictures of them, not the original things I had brought. I expect someone sold those things to line their pockets, such was the corruption in that old system. They accused me of having been planted to stir up grievances against the Soviet state and making anti-Soviet activity because of the arguments I had had with these earnest students, all of whom were simply carrying out the will of the KGB.

They said that as I had already good Russian I never needed to go to their country to study, therefore my coming as a student was a mere pretext, and that I was a spy for that reason (I heard that in former years they had used precisely the opposite argument on one or two of their victims, stating that as they had not bothered to learn Russian properly, they must have been coming just to spy, so you really couldn't win with them, if you were the chosen one for that year). And they also said that they had just been told in the other interrogation room by a bewildered Olga (of course rather less bewildered than they were making out but by no means happy about the state of affairs, as I believe to this day) that I had been given the information about the unregistered Baptist Church by Keston College.

Well, I did not wish to deny the information as to do so would have led to the inevitable question "if not from them, then were did you get this information?" and so I simply held my peace. I was told that I would never be allowed to marry Olga if I did not co-operate, and I held my peace. I was very sick anyway, with this form of mononucleosis they had given me, and that seemed to anaesthetise the whole situation and make it somewhat divorced from reality.

I was asked had I had anything to do with Keston College, and I answered that I had written to them once or twice. I was asked who I thought ran Keston College. I said "Rev Michael Bordeaux". Did I know Michael Bordeaux? Had I ever contacted him? Yes, I had spoken to him. Was I aware that in fact Keston College was a branch of MI6 and was paid for as part of the British intelligence budget? I said as fair as I was aware, the one had nothing

461

whatsoever to do with the other. They said, "you would say that, wouldn't you?" I neither confirmed nor denied their assumption that I was a Keston College functionary – to say anything was simply to invite more inquiry, so I let them believe what they wanted to believe. But everything seemed to be twistable to speak against me – even the fact that my British roommate and I had sometimes spoken Welsh to each other so that the Russian roommates wouldn't be able to invigilate, even that was a good indication that I was not to be trusted, apparently. Thankfully they left him and also the other five who went to Church with me in peace, and didn't even ask me any questions about those folk, which I found reassuring. Evidently they just wanted their propaganda piece, and my realising that took the pressure off me quite a bit.

Then they made me sign a statement and read it out in front of a camera, and finally they took me off to a "hospital", but in fact it was the Tropical and Infectious Diseases hospital, under heavy guard, with me as the only patient I saw in the entire place. Truly, healthcare in the Communist world was far in advance of anything in the west – I have never had a whole hospital to myself in the west, or known anyone short of royalty to have it. Even my later mother-in-law from my first wife, who was a proper aristocrat if ever there was one, even if totally unrecognised by anyone outside her immediate family, had to share her ward in the Kensington and Chelsea with Jane Birkin's mother. But I was treated like a prince, a saint-exuperian prince, with a whole hospital to myself, and yet not able to enjoy my privileged healthcare status to the full as I felt so weak I could barely leave the bed to use the lavatory, in fact most of the time I used an "utka" – the only time in my life so far I've needed that – in fact I don't even know the English word – and although I had an English Bible with me, with a hymnary added at the back, I was too weary to peruse it for solace for more than a few minutes at a time.

But every day one or another of the other Christians in the UK group, who found out where I was being held, walked under my window and whistled the tune
"Meine Hoffnung stehet feste, auf den lebendigen Gott", calling to my mind the wonderful words of that hymn by Neander, as translated by Robert Bridges:

> All my hope on God is founded;
> He doth still my trust renew,
> Me through change and chance he guideth,
> Only good and only true.
> God unknown,
> He alone
> Calls my heart to be his own.
>
> Pride of man and earthly glory,
> Sword and crown betray his trust;
> What with care and toil he buildeth,
> Tower and temple fall to dust.
> But God's power,
> Hour by hour,
> Is my temple and my tower.
>
> God's great goodness aye endureth,
> Deep his wisdom, passing thought:
> Splendor, light and life attend him,
> Beauty springeth out of naught.
> Evermore
> From his store
> Newborn worlds rise and adore.

Daily doth the almighty Giver
Bounteous gifts on us bestow;
His desire our soul delighteth,
Pleasure leads us where we go.
Love doth stand
At his hand;
Joy doth wait on his command.

Still from man to God eternal
Sacrifice of praise be done,
High above all praises praising
For the gift of Christ, his Son.
Christ doth call
One and all:
Ye who follow shall not fall.

I wept whenever I heard this tune from outside the barred window. They did not know which window was mine, they simply whistled it around the whole building, like Joshua's trumpets. That tune called to me as if straight from the Neanderthal. I don't mean Neanderthal man of course. I mean the valley where pastor Joachim Neander used to love to stroll in as he composed his hymns in the seventeenth century and which was later named for him, long before people started finding pieces of Pleistocene personages in there. The song called to me from the seventeenth century and was still as strong and true then and will always be, saying as in Robert Bridge's English version, "ye who follow, shall not fall". I couldn't get up, and I had certainly stumbled, but I hadn't fallen.

Anyway, days went by in this incarceration disguised as a hospital visit, and once the disease passed enough for me to be able to walk around, they took me out of the hospital and I had to collect my belongings as quickly as possible from the Obshchezhitie, and no Olga was to be found there, to my dismay. She had been home outside Voronezh ever since the interrogation. I was accompanied by the excellent Richard Nerurkar to Moscow, (scenes of me going on the train were filmed without my being aware and were later included in the propaganda film they made about me to encourage good Soviet citizens to avoid friendship with foreigners from the west – if only I could get a copy of that one for my YouTube channel!) and handed over to Mr Peter Liner, then the second attaché of HM Embassy in Moscow. He kindly took me to his home and left me there reading his copy of Brewer's Phrase and Fable, until it was time to take me off to the airport. He was told that I had to be escorted to the plane, but in fact it was only possible to escort me as far as the passport desk.

I did not receive any mark of "persona non grata" in my passport, (although the parting shot of the KGB man who had interrogated me was "if you're lucky you'll be deported, and if you come back there'll be 'niepriyatnosti' " - which means "unpleasantnesses". This term is, needless to say, not defined in any tomes of international jurisprudence I have since perused, but I didn't think it wise to try to find out what these 'niepriyatnosti' might mean in practice – simply the fact that I didn't know whether I'd ever see the woman I loved again and trying to work out exactly what her role had been in all of this left me completely drained, on top of the disease they gave me) neither did any formal charges get levelled at me, but a letter of complaint went from the Russian side of the Exchange to the British Council, demanding to know why they had allowed MI6 to infiltrate their Exchange programme. In the next section I will explain how I got to know about that detail, and several more interesting facts about the aftermath of all this, and how it caused a change in plans without which the Goldlist method would not have been invented, or at least not by me.

Although I was in the Soviet press in the aftermath of this, neither I, nor the British Council, nor the University had any interest at all in bringing the matter to the UK press. I just wanted the whole thing as discreet as possible really for Olga's sake, and because the whole episode had weakened me. Incidentally, one month before the incident happened not far to the West from us the Chernobyl event had happened, during which we were advised by the British Council to leave and told we could if we wanted, but none of the students in our group took up the offer, and I'm not aware that any of us got sick from that.

Despite the difficult political situation and the squalor of the conditions we lived in, there was a resonance between us and the Soviet students, and even more so some East Germans who were there and who befriended us in outright bold defiance of the instructions given by their group leader, and the numerous "Stellungnahmen" they had to sign promising to minimise their contacts with us and use them only to educate us about Marxism-Leninism (how we all laughed when they told us about these!) and the general feeling was, if our friends cannot run away, neither will we. At least, not until the end of the academic year, when the departure was originally planned. If it had been a question of staying there for ever, I don't suppose anyone would have been so resolute.

People have asked me whether I am bitter about what the Communists did and how in some ways you could say that they ruined my life by doing what they did. It felt at the time as though my life had been ruined because they took away the woman I loved and wanted to be with for the rest of my life. It could, however, just as well be that by the same token they saved my life. These days I am utterly persuaded that, as the Bible says "all things work together for good to them that love God". Certainly I don't wish any ill on those who were part of the oppression – individually they were also the victims in what was a diabolical onslaught on the human race. I just think that what happened to me was a tiny taste of the oppression that happens to Christians, and that we've all got to be ready to see returning at any time, and which to have was more a privilege than a matter to moan about, or feel bitter. Even in the space of time that I've been working on this narrative, North Korea has executed two church leaders and sent 23 members of their families off to work camps for doing pretty much the same things as I was doing in the Soviet Union. We all prayed hard and the Soviet Union finally fell, but for some places we all still have much praying left to do.

4. Final year at Cambridge

I've covered some aspects of the final year when speaking more panoramically earlier about the academic content of my degree, but now I just want to go back and look at that year in some more detail, especially the upshot of what happened in the Soviet Union, my expulsion, and the complaints that had been issued by the Soviets to the British Council and by them onwards to my alma mater and to certain other places which we shall come to in due course…

I was sent back in June a few weeks before the end of the course, and the received wisdom was that the Russians did this so that the British would not have time to retaliate. My parents were there to meet me at Heathrow, and just put a John Denver tape on in the car driving back. When it came to "Country Roads" I sang along, but replaced "West Virginia" with "Hemel Hempstead" – which is how I prefer to sing it to this day. I was very glad to be home, on the one hand, but the object of my heart was not there so it was not such a perfect feeling, to be back, as it would otherwise have been.

As I mentioned above I felt very sick with this mononucleosis, but when my GP sent off my blood test the result was not recognisably mononucleosis or glandular fever. There was something there, but they did not know what it was. Perhaps it is still there, so if anyone has the wherewithal to investigate, let me know, and I'll let you take some blood if you have a proper lab for analysing it, assuming there's any trace of it left a quarter of a century down the line. But I had a lot of worries that when I got back to Cambridge I would be in trouble for what happened in Russia, maybe even sent down for it, but certainly given some hard words from the Senior Tutor. I knew that the British Council were not happy, and had complained to my University, but I had no word from them on what they thought of the matter. I had feverish dreams some nights on that Summer Vacation of going back up in September only to be told I was sent down, and I looked at starting the final year with genuine trepidation.

On top of that the whole financial situation had changed. My grant had been cut for my final year down to a small proportion of what it was, because it was measured on previous years' business of my mother plus my father's earnings. My mother had had to give up her business and

468

go back to teaching, though, and at the same time they had to start paying for my younger siblings to go to their universities, too. So I had to work in the holidays. I forced myself to work over the summer before returning in the general contractor's office of the BP European HQ (as it was for a while, but then BP moved on) which was being built in Hemel Hempstead. I was covering for the normal clerk who ran the copy room with its two photocopiers and its OKI dye line printers while he was away, and as long as I had no work in the queue I was allowed to study, and I remember having my old, non dumbed-down version of "Teach Yourself Polish" with me there, learning that language towards the "Slavonic Languages" philology paper I spoke about before.

But also I was far more curious about the world of work and business and I wanted to know everything. My curiosity about the whole of what I was doing appealed to some of the people working for Mowlems, the general contractor, and they took time out to chat with me about their business. They also suggested that I should come back after my studies and start to work with them, which was kind, although I decided in the end to do something different, not because of any reservations about Mowlems or their branch of industry, but really because I wanted a financial education, and a professional qualification.

Gradually I got my strength back so I was all in order by September. But I had to make do through the year on very little money, and I had to work through each holiday and I also was given a loan by another student who had more than he needed. That former fellow student's name is Stephen Carson-Rowland, and I believe he lives in Australia now. Should you happen to know him, please tell him that his kindness then will never be forgotten.

And now I want to tell you what actually happened when I returned to Cambridge. I was at Fitzwilliam College, which had been building a long-awaited new court, called, unsurprisingly, New Court, during the year I spent in the Soviet Union, a significant milestone in the history of the college. It was designed by the famous architect Sir Richard MacCormac (whom I had occasion to meet briefly when he came around to see how the students where using the spaces he had created) and a very fine building it was too, although after the Voronezh obshchezhitie even the digs I had had in my second year (still the subject of nightmares for me, let me tell you, but I won't go into details here as it is not tangential to the theme) would have been a cozy spot, let me say. I was hoping I'd get a spot in one of these new room, but what I wasn't expecting was to get the best room in the New Court, and for the same price as a standard room. "We heard all about what happened to you" the Senior Tutor Professor Lethbridge said by way of explanation, "and we considered you deserved to have this to even out some of the trials you've had". So there it was – not only was the College not going to discipline me for what had gone on in Russia, they even were rewarding me! I cannot describe how touched I was by this gesture.

That was the College, but what about the Faculty? Wouldn't they be annoyed that now the British Council would be looking hard at the Cambridge Russian students of the future, accusing them all of being undercover Government operatives scuppering all their good relations with the Russians? Not a bit of it. The professors in the Slavonic Department were soldarity incarnate. "Join the club!" one of the most senior boomed. "Just about everyone in this Faculty has had a run-in with the Soviet authorities, old man!". Ned Goy, delighted to have me back, especially as he had been student-free the previous year and therefore threatened with cuts, told me a few tales of his time, and his particular run-ins, which I shan't repeat in detail, but they involve him being questioned by a certain country's police for drawing butterflies, which they claimed were coded maps of certain installations. Ned Goy, by the way, bore a passing resemblance to the actor John Barron's "CJ" in the original Reginald Perrin series, although he didn't make me sit on flatulent chairs, and as I mentioned always used to share a pint of prawns with me in his lessons. Well, in one of the lessons we didn't do Serbo-Croat - instead he'd fished out from somewhere one of the propaganda articles written about this shady character "Dzheyms" in the Soviet Press, and we actually did a textual study on that, during which he deconstructed all their propaganda techniques and weasel language. It was a great accolade for me, apart from a very useful lesson from a philological standpoint.

I can only say that the whole of the University made me proud and touched me with their care and consideration and also solidarity with me in the year I got back from the Soviet Union, in a way I never expected, and will never forget. When I compare this with the stories of neglect, indifference by lecturing staff and poor academic practice I hear continually from University students around Poland and the Czech Republic – some of whom do not even get to borrow books from their faculty libraries and barely get the chance to have time one on one with their professors, or even in groups small enough to get meaningful discussions going that will stretch their minds, or

471

considerately marked work with a proper debriefing on how to improve their essays, or their perspectives on a topic – I feel absolutely sorry for them and realise how immense the Oxbridge privilege I had really was, and I dearly hope still is and long will be despite what successive Governments have done to education in my country.

I was obliged to work in the Christmas break and the Easter break of my final year (in Cambridge you were not allowed to work in term time, but to give yourself wholly to the University. You were not even allowed to leave the city overnight without an 'exeat' form signed by your tutor. But I had no longer the financially comfortable position I'd enjoyed in the first two years, and so I asked the college to allow me to be a waiter in these holidays, for the conferences that take place out of term time. I did not know that one of the conferences to come, of all places, to our college, was the British Council's own internal conference. So what a coincidence that was, as if I believed in coincidences…

So, one day during the Easter holiday, I was, unbeknown to Professor Margot Light, (I'm not sure she was a Professor then but now she is Professor of international relations at the London School of Economics, so I'll leave the title in for the sake of due respect even though it may be anachronistic) serving her table with food as she was saying to her colleagues "… of course this is the colleague of that student from the Voronezh group, David James. ….. yes of course we sent the letter complaining but no doubt neither the college or the University took any action. … it's unbelievable what he did…" and then I think she must have had cause to wonder about the nature of this world and who is really in control when the waiter she hadn't noticed said, "yes, Margot, but if you believed what I believe, you would have done what I did."

That pretty much put paid to that discussion, at least at that time and place. There is of course no answer to what I told them. Or at least, if you think you do have an answer, let me suggest it's possibly not a very good answer. Actually Margot's best answer might possibly have been to counter me with the same "Yes, David, and if you believed what I believe, you also would complain about someone acting like yourself the way I complain about you", and although she didn't say that, I will say it for her, putting words in her mouth, if only with the best of intentions. That is actually why I don't have any bad feelings for Professor Light, even though she was the most vocal of my critics back then. If you have views, you should act on them. That's what I did, and that's what she appears to me to have done. I can respect that more than apathy. She also writes thought-provoking papers trying to give a balanced view on European affairs, and seriously I cannot fault her for that. In the period since the fall of communism the west of Europe has failed to produce an effective bridge to certain disenfranchised countries in the east as well as Russia itself, and Professor Light's is one of the few voices crying in the wilderness about that matter, and the more she gets that message out, the better.

That was not the only odd "coincidence" related to that matter that I had in the year. Now every year Cambridge University has a huge careers fair, to which final year students are invited. It is quite normal for UK students to delay making the final choice on which career they will do for as long as possible – moreover an open-mindedness about that matter is encouraged by academics, expect in the minority of vocational degrees like law, medicine and veterinary medicine, where you have normally decided what you want to do before embarking on that course. It's also normal in the UK for people to be accepted into careers totally unlike their degree and this is welcomed by many employers as it gives more rounded personalities in the MP. Countries like Germany do not tend to do this – usually a German has an idea of his career before going to University, and knows that taking this or that course will box a number of options for him or her, and has to accept it. Little wonder then that the Germans have given rise to the term "Fachidioten", and in truth their Firms are often characterised by having plenty of specialists who can solve complex problems in a closely defined framework, but little ability for various experts from different fields to be able to communicate with each other and make a high performing team by combining their knowledge from various fields.

So for this reason the Careers Fair is always popular and well frequented, and I went along just to get ideas. Most of the ideas I had had before about my career I had recently discounted, as I explain in a moment. Now one of the traditions is that some branch of Her Majesty's Secret Services is present at that career fair, and true enough, GCHQ had a stand at the one I was at. So I thought,' I know, I'll take this chance to practice my Russian – and see how good their Russian is'. So I went up and addressed them, and the response was "Aha, you must be David James". I said, "Golly, you guys are good. How did you know?". At this, they said "Why did you claim to be an MI6 agent?"

So I explained to them how I had neither confirmed nor denied, in order not to have to disclose where I actually knew the Church's address and service times from, that the information came from Keston College, and that I was working with Rev Bordeaux and that he was in the pay of MI6, therefore I was MI6. I found out that the Soviet exchange organisers wrote to the British Council accusing me of being MI6, and that they, the British Council had then written a letter of complaint to MI6 never thinking to even check whether the information was true or not, telling them not to put their agents on the academic exchange programmes. So I had a good laugh with them about this, but although they were a likeable lot, there was no talk of me joining up even if I had wanted to – if ever a cover was blown before the agent even got recruited, that cover was mine. In the end, as an auditor and due diligence specialist, I do quite sufficient information gathering and recording to suit the nosiest man on earth, so no big loss that I ended up doing it for business, and not for any government. That certainly suits my view of earthly government more. The less you have to do with them, the better. They may have plenty of interesting and nice people working for them, they may, in their way, be something of an elite – too much so, in fact. But in the end we have another Master, another State, another Country to serve.

> "And there's another country, I've heard of long ago,
>
> Most dear to them that love her, most great to them that know;
>
> We may not count her armies, we may not

see her King;

Her fortress is a faithful heart, her pride is suffering;

And soul by soul and silently her shining bounds increase,

And her ways are ways of gentleness, and all her paths are peace."

(Sir Cecil Spring-Rice, British spy in Russia, British counter-espionage against Germany in Sweden, British Ambassador to America 1913-1918, and best man to President Theodore Roosevelt)

I was enjoying the study in the final year and I was confident in having learned enough of the languages I had set myself to be able to get a good showing on the Philology papers I had chosen for my part II. I also had the most wonderful and kindly friends in the Christian Union, some of whom have gone on to become quite notable people and I could easily link you to where their footprints are in various parts of the net. Sharing study days with these people was a tremendous blessing. I also saw Prince Edward cycling about with his bodyguard in tow a few times as he was there concurrently, and one time I saw Prince Phillip the Duke of Edinburgh too, but that was more a curiosity than a blessing, I suppose.

All the time, though, I had a great heartache because I had no contact with Olga, which I hoped was because of intimidation by the authorities, and later on I found out that this was indeed the case. I probably spent at least a quarter of my waking time just brooding about her and what had happened to me, and what I could possibly do about it. It appeared to me that the answer would be in having some status, or some wealth, and that neither would be achieved just by studying languages alone. I could no longer envisage the things which I had been toying with as careers before then, such as University professor like some of the ones who had so inspired me, or a minister of religion like John Marshall, or a missionary, like David Morgan.

In my final year of Cambridge I was privileged also to be a member of a small group of people who set up a new Presbyterian Church in Cambridge. The <u>Cambridge Presbyterian Church</u> appears to be still going strong. I took an interest in Church planting and at that time would have loved to be a missionary, but felt unworthy and not senior enough also. I needed to work first. (In the event I have planted accountancy practices in various countries rather than churches, but in some respects the issues are similar. The guidelines per se are usually straightforward enough, the problems emerge as soon as you put human beings into the mix. But naturally that's when it gets interesting and that's where interpersonal skills of which languages or linguistics are a major component, are a sine qua non.)

It seemed to me that I could always go back to those Church related careers later if I had a calling (how wrong that was – quite the opposite was going to happen), but right now I needed to get into business, but I didn't understand how. I knew even from those old debates with *studsoviet* goons that I didn't have a good enough grasp of economics, and I started to ask the people in my college studying degrees in Economics how best to break into the subject. I received a nice reading list, but most of all, I received a critical piece of advice, which I followed and which turned my entire life in a new direction, one that I certainly don't regret, he told me to do a training contract as a Chartered Accountant. At least to do the Graduate Conversion Course, an intensive 15 hour a week study while working course culminating in 6 three-hour long exams all of which must be passed first time or the student was counselled out of the audit profession, and was usually sacked from their training contract. If I made it through that year of study and passed, I'd be able to do the rest of the training contract with less stress and probably become a Chartered Accountant, which would open all sorts of possibilities of better earning and high-profile jobs, whereas in the worst case, if I didn't make it, at least it would be the best way of learning something of the things I wanted to learn.

I was sold on that idea, and applied for a training contract to various Firms of Accountants. I got a bad vibe from a few of the Firms, notably Peat Marwick and Grant Thornton, who both came over to me as high-handed and arrogant. The staff partner from Peats who met me, once his secretary had brought coffee, said "I've given you some coffee but you won't be able to drink it as I am going to give you a proper grilling now, and you'll have to talk so much you won't be able to". Presumably he wanted people who could talk without the need to stop and think. However, the firm Peat Marwick isn't around, per se, today, so I cannot ask them whether that was the reason for their interview policy or not.

However, BDO Binder Hamlyn who gave me an offer seemed to be a very courteous and considerate Firm and it was with some misgiving that I turned their offer down in favour of a local accountant in Hemel Hempstead, in fact the one who had been looking after my mother's business. It was a boutique Firm, ten partners, seventy staff, three offices in Hemel Hempstead, Watford and Harrow, and the best of it was that, as it was just around the corner from where my parents lived, while I was qualifying I could live at home, take an active part in the life of the Church, and still easily do my 15 hours study per week. I didn't believe that I would be able to study on the train to London – I knew what those trains were like, you were lucky to get a seat. So no London Firm for me.

I made the right decision, though. This Firm, Hillier Hopkins, gave me an excellent training, and were very patient with me. I think they expected that I'd be cleverer than I seemed when I turned up, after all, I was a Cambridge graduate, but as I kept on reminding them, I was a languages graduate, which in might case meant I could talk about nothing much at all (except, of course, Calvinist theology, which, despite its rigor and wholesomeness for the soul, is sadly of limited use in business today) but talk about it in ten or so different languages. Yes, languages add value to what you can do with your career, but unless you combine them with something else, all you can do is be a teacher (and as I mentioned, I believed these teachers are in the main not really needed) or a professor (which I ended up doing on YT anyway as Huliganov, just for fun) or a translator.

But a translator only translates other people's ideas and business and is himself invisible, and that certainly was not what I had in mind for myself. I was going to present my own ideas and give people professional advice that was going to save them money and help make them successful, and then when I had that workshop in my own language, I would be able to offer it internationally, and work with clients in many different languages. And that's exactly what I did, and exactly what you should do, dear fellow linguist, unless you are content to translate only the words of others or teach their children or occupy some low-paid University role, in the pleasant, hallowed halls of academia, but always with a rather constrained budget.

And so it was that I came out of Cambridge University after studying Modern and Medieval Languages with only about half the language knowledge – or let's say lexical stock – I have today, but put language learning practically on hold for some years. I had been given the hints from professors that there would be a provision for me to stay on and do a doctorate if I wanted it, but I really wanted to learn something different, that would maximise the commercial value of the languages that I had, and also enable me to have financial independence and stability and status, all of which could be necessary if I was to get Olga out of the Soviet Union somehow.

But this was also a necessary step to give me the things I needed to discover the Goldlist method, as I shall explain in the next chapter. In sum, so far in my life I have given about half of my learning effort to the learning of languages purely for pleasure and about half to the learning of accountancy-related topics, in order to have a decent professional career, be paid, do interesting things, really understand how the world works, be of genuine use to clients and add more value than anyone else could have done in certain situations, and, not least of course, use the languages. Had I not done accountancy, I would perhaps know 40 languages now, but I would still be able to talk in these languages with nothing like the understanding of the world and of useful subjects and so the learning would not have been fruitful. I also would not have readjusted my brain to start thinking in the numerical way that was also a necessary prerequisite for the discovery of the Goldlist method.

Another amusing piece of aftermath from the Russia episode also happened around the time I was finishing University. The history teacher in my old school organised for his pupils a trip to Moscow as part of their learning about the Russian revolution. One of the pupils who went along was also called David James (he is also probably teased these days as much as I am about a certain England goalkeeper!) and he got pulled out and interrogated when the group flew into the Sheremietievo airport. They had discovered that spy David James from Hemel Hempstead smuggling himself back! Or so they thought.

Then gradually it dawned on them that this person didn't look like me, refused to even acknowledge his command of Russian and also was making a very convincing job of looking 15 years old! So the teacher was called and the authorities apologised – "Sorry for scaring your pupil, but there is an Anti-Soviet agitator from your city who also has the name David James. We just wanted to be sure." "Yes", said the teacher, "I know him. I was his history teacher. He's about eight years older than this boy, and totally unrelated." "You were **that** David James' history teacher? Should have made better job. Maybe he would then have understood bit better our glorious revolution."

5. "I want to be a Chartered Accountant"

One of the things that tends to happen to University students in England, probably especially at Oxbridge, or at least, if it doesn't happen now it certainly did in my day, was that everyone comes along and flatters them that the world is their oxter and roll-on the day they graduate, and that when they leave University they will be welcomed into the job of their choice with open arms and life will be a cinch. Maybe there are such societies in existence somewhere on this planet, I heard tell of such an experience in Japan, indeed that is what George Mikes claims in his humorous book "The Land of the Rising Yen". Certainly, once students do leave their hallowed hogwartian halls in the UK, many of them are in for a rude awakening if so be they ever fell for the flattering lines fed to them by their own lecturers, by visitors to University societies, by visiting ministers of religion (with the exception of my minister who when he visited seemed to do the opposite which students perversely seem to like, but I think they sense that this guy wasn't feeding them a line like everybody else) and by the recruitment mill. Once the students join the ranks and filing clerks of your typical accounting, banking, actuarial or other office, then the motto is " forget University — **this** is your University!"

Hillier Hopkins was (and I assume still is) a very fair firm to its employees, and clients also. Many of the people who were there when I arrived 23 years ago are still there today, and I recently had the pleasure of speaking again to the very same accountant who have given me my first training course, Robert Twydle. His induction course was one produced by the Institute of Chartered Accountants in England and Wales called "Mann of Moorgate" – which was a clever reference to Moorgate House, the head office of the Institute in London. Despite the fact that Hillier

Hopkins was really, as I can tell even more clearly in retrospect, the ideal place for me to go and learn about accountancy, I still didn't find it at all easy at first. It took nearly two years for the penny to drop with double entry bookkeeping, until that time I just couldn't think in terms of debits and credits.

The problem that I had was that I had been dealing solely with language and not with numbers ever since the age of about 16 and now I was 23. I had done no study of mathematics at all for the last seven years, and are basically existed only very rudimentary familiarity with numbers in general. And what I may have known for O-level that certainly got very rusty by seven years down the track. For example, I was amazed and not a little horrified to discover that when I took 20% from 100, I got 80. But when I went and added the 20% back again, I only got to 96. Somebody had removed four of my original hundred in the process, and search as I might, I couldn't work out where those four had gone. These things don't happen in linguistics. If you turn some word order round, for example to make a sentence interrogative, and then you turn the same words back to the way they were again, the original meaning is restored entirely, and so I found it rather confusing that mathematics wouldn't work the same way.

The answer basically is that different parts of the brain are used when dealing with language to the ones which are used when dealing with questions of numeracy and pure mathematical logic. And these latter areas in my case had become totally atrophied. And at first I couldn't really link in numbers to the better developed language centres of my mind at all. And it wasn't until I started to realise that accountancy is also a kind of language, the language of business, with its own grammar which is the double entry system, the verbal aspects – being the balance sheet and profit and loss account respectively (these days we say silly things like "Statement on Financial Position" for Balance Sheet and "Statement of Income and Expenditure" for Profit and Loss Account – which goes to show how linguistics pervades even the most non-linguistic subjects) and its prepositions which are the operators +,-,/,*,^, etc that something clicked in my brain and I started to make progress.

That really took more than one year to do, but in any event I passed the Graduate Conversion Course (maybe largely because the amount of conceptual things included in it of the sorts of things that the linguist can easily understand, but also because I genuinely wanted to understand how the world worked even though was not easy for me to get to grips with it with my very one-sided education until that point) and sometime in the second year of trying to become a chartered accountant I finally began to justify Michael Kent's decision to hire me. He wrote in my record book at that point that I was making definite improvements after "a diffident start".

I think the use of the word "diffident" was a fair description of my start, although was never my intention to be anything other than confident and go getter in the area of accountancy, the problem was that my brain simply didn't have the apparatus to be able to grasp the ideas quickly, on the other hand I never liked to simply bluff neither was I encouraged to do so by the very professional people I was working with. At first I think that I shocked my colleagues by knowing so little even though I had told them all along that I didn't know anything and I had come to learn. If I hadn't had the good sense to come in freely admitting I was a tabula rasa as far as anything in business and finance was concerned, but eager to learn, they would have teased the life out of me. I think that and the fact that I accepted with good grace a larger share of the coffee-making, the bun-runs (as in the local parlance we called going out of the office to fetch sandwiches for everyone in the room), the archiving and the clearing of snow (not there was much of that in Hemel Hempstead!) helped my survival.

In due course I did start to pay back their kind investment, though. I could handle all aspects of the work by the third year – we were mainly looking after the small and medium-sized businesses of the local area, as well as some from further afield is not everybody likes to have the people who really know their business living too close to them and their families and friends! We did incomplete records, as well as more sophisticated sets of books. In once case, for a very traditional client, old leather-bound ledgers had to be written up by hand with a calligraphic fountain pen, and as I had always been stubborn about the use of a fountain pen in my work, so I was the ideal candidate for that.

We had computers in the team, but personally-issued laptops only really emerged after my training course was over and I was qualified already. While I was training, we had to book time in the computer room and sit in front of an amber screen, booking onto these huge computers journals which had already been prepared in full by hand, and where all the analysis had already been done on paper. I really enjoyed making big analyses and I got more comfortable with numbers in the course of doing them, and in some cases I used to tape together three or four sheets of A3 accountancy analysis paper to produce the sort of thing which nowadays is done all the time in Excel but can't easily be printed in one sheet without reducing the print size. But mine would have made good Ersatz wallpaper. "He's done another *Magna Carta*" is how they joked about my trademark analyses. Had I had a readier grasp of what was going on, I could have abbreviated a lot of these, and that was a major aspect of the humour to be found in them. Still, they got the job done, eventually.

Now at this time I had been leaving the learning of new languages a little bit on one side in order to concentrate on getting the numerical side of my brain up to speed, and as I did so I discovered that in fact numerical analysis could be very interesting. I found that setting numerical goals for work, monitoring the achieving of these goals in percentage terms, could be very motivating. And I thought about bringing that aspect into language work at some stage even though I was not actively learning of languages at the current time. Occasionally, once every few months, signs of life from Olga would start to appear, but they were not encouraging, but I continued to be motivated to succeed in my course of action by the idea that this was the best way to get to her, or get her out. People started talking about glasnost and perestroika, and what a wonderful man Mr Mikhail Gorbachev was. At this time I didn't believe it, but later I was convinced that indeed he did do a great deal for humanity, and told him as much when I met him and shook his hand many years later.

After beginning to earn money I was able to pay back the

loan made by my friend Stephen from college, and be gradually paying off the bank loan I had also which my father had guaranteed but wasn't expecting to pay, neither would I have allowed him to had he had the inclination, as I wanted to be stand on my own feet, and then I started to learn to drive. I was a little bothered about one thing though – when I left university and joined my firm, my starting salary was GBP 7,000. Now lenders were willing to lend three times a person's salary, which meant in my case GBP 21,000 as long as about 25% of the value of the property had been saved up previously. Effectively that meant that they wanted me to save a year's salary before they would lend the three-times salary.

Now saving a whole year's salary of course is not easy, it takes more than one year to do it I was very impatient to be independent financially. I knew how much property prices had been increasing, and indeed the cheapest property in Hemel Hempstead was a studio flat at about GBP35,000. At first I felt a little bit despairing about that state of affairs, and wondered whether I would ever become a homeowner. At work we used to discuss these things with each other, that is the other student accountants and me from time to time, and in the course of discussion we pretty much worked out that there was something not quite right about the situation with house prices. It simply couldn't be sustainable that really good university graduates working towards a professional role would not ever be able to become homeowners. If they couldn't do it, who could do it?

So something had to give. And of course in 1988 all of a sudden as if from nowhere, the house prices in the UK tumbled by about 25%, and a new term entered the

English language, that of 'negative equity'. Those of my university friends who had been able to get property immediately because of help from parents or because they had got married and had two salaries, were by the end of 1988 already in negative equity. After working for two years and paying to the bank for two years, if they wanted to sell back their property they would have been at a loss equivalent to a whole year's salary for one person for doing so.

Suddenly there emerged a completely different set of calculations – I actually had an advantage in never having bought property, and in the meantime we had all passed some exams and achieved experience, and we were paid maybe 50% more than on day one, and in the meantime the house prices had fallen by 25%, and when you put those things together that was already much more realistic to see how it wouldn't be long before any of us would be able to have their first foot on the property ladder. It was a motivation to save money, and I regularly made calculations and projections to see how far it would be, as having a home to put Olga in and be able to look after her was a pre-requisite to be able to bring her to the UK,as even if the Russians allowed her out one day, there was still the question of whether the UK would allow her in, and I believed that being able to demonstrate home-ownership and a strong financial independence from state benefits to the authorities would help on that side. This belief was based more on intuition than experience though, and had I known then what I know now, I would not have set so much store by it.

However, it is a long time, to wait two or three years for someone when you are young, and once two years had gone by I became weary of waiting and began to think that nothing would ever happen, and that I was maybe simply wasting my time and other opportunities to be happy. I was never 100% sure whether she really liked me anyway or was simply told to be with me, and that state of doubt didn't help matters. I gradually became more susceptible to the attractions of ladies other than Olga, and to see things I was virtually blind to for two years.

Once I passed my driving test my weeks usually looked like this – Monday nights and Tuesday nights – longer study of accountancy. Wednesday nights were Church Bible Study, and then watching Dallas which had been recorded during the Bible Study when I got home. On Thursdays I would drive up to Cambridge to learn some Arabic from someone who had been learning it at my college. Fridays were prayer meeting nights and Saturdays I basically studied accounting again to make up the 15 hour a week study quota. Sundays were always off and I went to the morning and evening services and sometimes spent the whole day with others from the Church. My parents were not enamoured with my Calvinism or the Church I went to, but it was always their way to let me make my own decisions, and they saw me at mealtimes through a large part of the week. Also all the time I was working I paid my share of the household bills and my own food and clothes. This started as soon as I started working for Hillier Hopkins.

After a year of this kind of lifestyle and two years after being kicked out of Russia, I happened to meet in London a girl I liked the look of, and I spoke to her in the underground train station at Marble Arch as I was on my way back from a course to Hemel Hempstead. What happened was, she was coming out of a tube train platform, going upstairs and the wind from an incoming train billowed up her skirt. She snatched it down, but not before I had seen an incredible pair of legs. Before I had time to think it over, I had gotten into conversation with her, asking whether she was related to Marilyn Munro, since she was re-enacting so well that scene from a famous film of hers. She responded in a certain accent which I recognised, and was able to use some phrases of Polish from my Slavonic Philology study days. I got to know her suggesting that I teach her English in exchange for her teaching me Polish. And we did that, but romance bloomed and we became boyfriend and girlfriend. But she was not an appropriate choice for a partner for me. The church, already unhappy that I had been with a non-believer in the case of Olga, were completely unhappy at my repetition of this same sin, and it wasn't long before I was excommunicated from the Church, but I was simply unable to resist the attraction she had for me at a physical level. I simply put up with the bad match of characters, because I had been without anyone for so long, and I simply couldn't stand it any more.

Probably most people get to sow their wild oats at University, but my strict principles had prevented me from doing so, however I remembered perfectly well the pleasure of sex, as I had lost my virginity and had a fairly serious girlfriend at only 16 years of age. And yet I was totally inexperienced at the age of 23, and ready to put up with all kinds of nonsense as long as the sex was good, and also give up the communion table of Alexandra Road Congregational Church, and at that point I lost also the majority of my friends, as they were Christians and were not willing to have anything to do with me if I was outside the Church.

They did surprisingly little to try to restore me, but they all had their own families and issues, and maybe even some of them took a secret delight at my fall and found it better that I was gone anyway, who knows? Certainly the meeting at which I was supposed to be excommunicated and which I was not supposed to be at but turned up anyway was far better attended than any other Friday night meeting I could remember, and not a single one of them planning to speak for me, they simply loved the scandal. You could see it on their faces. So I was privileged to receive the bell, book and candle treatment from Alexandra Road Congregational Church. In the end the person who got expelled from the Soviet Union because of the Church got expelled from the Church also.

One fine man of the Church, a deacon and a builder, even took a delight in pushing me down the steps of the church, such a valiant saint he was, and a defender of the true faith against prurient fornicators such as I. And he selflessly shared with me a goodly portion of his holy oral venom. But the Lord God could not bear for such an one so perfect as he to be without of the bliss of heaven, and so took him soon after this to be with Himself on high. In fact most of those involved in kicking me out of the fold of God in Hemel Hempstead have been, in the meantime, relieved of their earthly duties and taken to their everlasting reward in what some, doubting the wisdom of God, who alone knows whose are His own, might regard as a premature fashion.

One thing I never did was to try to redefine what I believe because of the fact that I couldn't live up to it. I simply said "I do believe this and this, but I am not living as a Christian because I am not strong enough – somehow my faith has not resulted in the right works, according to the New Testament that would define it as dead, but still it is what I believe and I am not going to persuade myself to be an evolutionist just so that I can go get laid in peace." Which is what I saw other fallen people doing time and time again. In the end it comes down to the fact that we are fallible. Pride goes before a fall, and I'd had a lot of spiritual pride. Probably I felt that I was a better Christian than many other Christians, but the Bible says that we should each consider others as better than ourselves. Well, since I was very poor at that I got a little lesson about myself and my own fallibility which meant that ever since it's been impossible for me to think of other Christians as anything other than better Christians than I am. Even those who delighted at my downfall and crisis of faith. I'm 100% convinced that they are far better than I am, and can only take comfort in knowing how these delightful souls will have been consoled and confirmed in their Christian walk by knowing that I was severely dealt with. It gave them someone they could legitimately speak negatively about and shun, and that's what passes for fellowship in some circles.

As far as I am concerned I have no real bitterness about this any more. We all make mistakes, we all need forgiveness. Putting someone else beyond forgiveness may well be the closest thing to the unforgivable sin that you can get, but I'd prefer to forgive those who did that to me because I also need plenty of forgiveness for the things I've done. Pride in the spiritual arena is an insidious and frightening thing, but like the cold virus you always have it in you, you just have times when it mutates and makes you really sick, and other times when it just gives you a runny nose for half an hour. If anyone thinks themselves uninfected by pride, then put it this way – I don't advise sitting in any drafts.

So I was rejected by the atheist communists and rejected by the believing Christians as well, and there were really moments when I felt my only friend on earth was my cat. These were not the days of the internet, where you can go online and find a discussion group with a dozen people going through the exact same thing as you, just having been chucked out of an enemy state for alleged espionage, also who got recently excommunicated from their Church and are currently struggling with getting to grips with the elements of accountancy. These days you can find at the click of a mouse virtual roomfuls of people who have been there, done that, and uploaded the T shirt template to their shop on cafepress.com, but not back then. I hadn't even held a mouse in my hand at that time, not counting living ones, of course. So I didn't have a great many options at that moment, and you can see how that would make me cling to my profession stronger than ever.

One manager I had, Fiona, taught me that if you have any trouble in your life, instead of moping about it and taking leave to dwell on it and just feel worse, go to work harder and fully apply yourself to the practice of accountancy, and it will see you through. I found that advice helpful in practice on many occasions in life afterwards also. Self-pity is no good, but drawing up a set of accounts manually and having it balance first time, even via a *magna carta*, that's good. That will make you happy. As happy as only an accountant can be. At school, Fiona had been just one year ahead of me, but having joined the profession at an earlier stage she was years ahead of me as an accountant and a great role model for professionalism, as were all the people working at Hillier Hopkins.

So still the accounting study continued, and I grew more familiar with accounting systems. I liked drive to stock takes and think also about systems of stock control. For the benefit of my US readers, this means inventory counts and inventory systems in your version of English. I also helped Izabella, my Polish girlfriend, in her study to become a nurse, and that got me started on reading Psychology textbooks. That was something which she had to study and I think she found it interesting, and I found that there were some very interesting things in those books also – that was where I read for the first time about Ebbinghaus and how he researched the human memory, using made up words which he presented to himself, mainly, in staged repetition instead of trying to learn them at once. He was the one who mapped out the things that the human memory would do very well all on its own, without anyone needing to screw up their face and concentrate, if only repeatedly presented with the learnables in a systematic way.

That's when I started mulling over that in terms of how it could impact language learning. Language learning was coming back on my agenda not so much because of the brief flirtation with the learning of Arabic, but because now I had a chance to get better at Polish, a language I had always enjoyed, and practice it with Izabella.

I found the old vocab book I had started for Polish long ago in Germany before I had gone to University, and started to work it forward with the combined perspective of knowing what Ebbinghaus found, knowing quite a bit about how to control work with the use of numbers, knowing about inventory management and starting to think of words as units of inventory (later the first name I gave to the Goldlist method was LIDS – Lexical Inventory Distillation System, but in time I thought Goldlist method was easier) and also the whole perspective of the study of an uncircumspect number of languages, living and dead, for my degree.

All these aspects were key ingredients to being able to hit on a really good system for learning languages, but if you looked at that book, you would only recognise it as a prototype of the Goldlist method as I use it now. There was some distillation in there, but I did not use the proper time spaces, and so in fact the system was not in essence the same, even though the shape of the system was basically there. And I used that in 1990 and 1991 to get to a basic fluency in Polish. I was in no hurry to perfect it as a system as I was mainly concerned with learning accountancy for the professional exams which are extremely demanding. It was simply a way to relax for me, as was the puzzle I set myself as to how to assess the best levels of distilling to aim for. I looked at all the factors that could effect whether while distilling one should aim at cutting out 3 or 4 words out of 25, or 5 to 6 words, or more, right up to distilling half per run through. I knew that Ebbinghaus had found that the average word was learned on the third staged repetition, which meant that 30% distillation was the "default", but I assumed that if the language was less familiar, or the times spent with the language in between formal vocabulary study, and whether the learner was a trained linguist or not, could make a difference.

Later on I came to realise that really these things don't

make much difference. The brain – the long term memory – is a natural born random sampler, and does its work unconsciously, and I was trying to micromanage and dictate to the brain a process when that process would really work much better if I allowed the brain to do what it does and then come along after some time and ask "what has it remembered, in fact" after 14 days or longer. All it really needed for me to get to that last part and have a working Goldlist method was really to remember things that David Morgan and others had already explained to me about how the memory works right back in school, but somehow I was obtuse enough to have spend another two years and really the Goldlist method became the real Goldlist method only in 1993. I had a family and simply had no time to indulge in learning sub-optimally, and so in the end I analysed until I got almost by trial and error to the system which enabled me to get the most real, long-term mileage from the least time actually spent doing languages, and which enabled meaningful, measurable portions of the task to be done in small bursts of work done in such little free time as I had.

At that stage the Goldlist I did on looseleaf pieces of A4 paper folded into A5, so that each was 100, and I did the next distillation also working to 100 but on a different coloured A4 sheet. I had a template made in Excel photocopied onto all these sheets and I kept them in A5 lever-arched files. But the system was clunky, and in due course I worked out that using a single book as I had in the prototype was actually a lot more handy, and that in a 40 line book you could use 25 on the top left page, then distill to about 18 on the top right, later on distil those to about 12 on the bottom right, and there would be plenty of room, and then room for 8 to be distilled to the bottom left under the Headlist, and only after that go on to a second book. That immediately saved the fiddly work of matching the different colour sheets to do the distillations. The only downside was more writing out of the numbers, but in the end I got used to it and it didn't matter or take long.

Let's just round up this section, though, as I have run on a bit. In 1990 I was well on the way to becoming a chartered accountant as I so wanted to be, I had a new girlfriend with whom the relationship was turbulent but very exciting for me, and then something happened which I had not believed would ever happen, even though David Morgan had told me eight years earlier that it would certainly one day happen, and before the end of the century. The problem is I had too much of how the people in charge in the Soviet Union liked to stage-manage and falsify things, and what matryoshkas their characters could be, and therefore I didn't believe it. I had been even part of a group lobbying parliament to support imprisoned believers in the Eastern Bloc, and had been to see MP Jim Lester in the House of Commons, and he himself told me that the signs were that the old Soviet Union was freeing up, believers were being released from prison, they no longer cared about enforcing communist ideologies on people, they wanted to become democracies in the western sense, but I must have been the last person in England actually to believe it.

Even when Vladimir Khailo, a noted dissident, (a leading unregistered church officer from the Ukraine and one of the people who became guinea pigs when the Communists decided that they would intern leading believers in psychiatric hospitals that were really prisons like the hospital I was in, and treated with psychiatric drugs to try to make them lose religious faith, which they did to him for nearly ten years) was allowed out on Sakharov's request and Sakharov himself was released from house arrest, and I took a holiday from Hillier Hopkins and traveled around the UK translating for Khailo - I still couldn't believe that this turnaround could have happened. Christians and Jews had been praying for the fall of Soviet Communism for so many years, and finally the prayers were answered, and I sat like Jonah under a gourd and told everyone it wouldn't last. I didn't even believe that God had answered my own prayers for the Fall of Communism, amongst those of so many others. I was afraid it was just too good to be true, and I wanted concrete proof. But Richard Hibbs, a good friend from University who went over to Berlin to check whether it was really true with his own eyes, as I think he was nearly as cynical as I was, came back with one piece of the Berlin wall for me, some real "concrete proof" if you like. Now so many of my friends would be free. And in the end they were. I started getting letters from friends from the GDR I'd met in Russia, but they weren't writing from Halle an der Saale, but from Munich, with stories of how they got out, the one thing they longed for and dreamed about for so many years. They were finally free.

Now maybe at last Olga would be free? Very possibly! But, of course, irony of ironies, I was no longer free.

This was not the end of the story with Olga, but I do not want to let this narrative stray too far from matters linguistic, and in order not to write too much of irrelevence to the current audience, she need play no more part in it for this version. The long and short of it was, she came to England, and she went home again.

6. "And the walls came tumbling down..."

The reality of totalitarian rule under communism, the events that took place in Eastern Europe in 1989-1991 and the subsequent period of reforms, the working towards being part of the EU and the gradual evening out of Europe are things which almost everyone who takes an interest in world events will be well aware. In my own case, what had started out as a love of languages driven by the need to understand, which eventually incorporated accountancy as the language of business by which I came to understand also how economies and businesses really worked, placed me in the maelstrom in a way that never would have happened if I had not been a linguist.

Had I not been a linguist I never would have gone to live a year in Russia, I never would have got on the wrong side of the authorities there, I never would have met people I deeply cared about on that side of the wall. So the experience of a linguist is not just that of poring over verbs in a course book. You have to have that part of it, of course, or you will never be a linguist, but once you are a linguist in the field it is going to bring you insights and ways of thinking and experiences that non-linguists are simply not privy to.

They say that travel broadens the mind, and maybe it does, but I can't see anything all that mind-broadening in the way many people travel, namely in taxis that all look the same with the taxi driver whom they try to communicate in English, to an airport where each one looks the same and the procedure becomes as well known as matins to a medieval monk, and everyone speaks the new Latin which is English. Then getting of the plane in another identical airport and taking another taxi to another international hotel which always looks the same and everyone speaks English. There is nothing challenging about that. It is not the sort of travel as the one the earlier generations had in mind when they say it broadens the mind, and that sort of travel is less and less easy to obtain.

Language learning on the other hand puts you inside the experience of what it is to be a Russian. You watch a film with them or hear a song listening to the same words, finding the same things funny, understanding gradually all the nuances. And so you become a little bit Russian by knowing Russian, a little bit German by knowing German, and a little bit more human by becoming a little bit more than just the nationality whose passport you carry.

I was not born Russian, or Polish, or German, or French – it's impossible for a person to have that many nationalities. But what the polyglot can achieve, which for me is the single most rewarding and exciting part of being a polyglot, is to experience the moment when people of his chosen language group come to forget that he or she is not one of their own and start to trust him or her and treat him or her as "nash chelovek" ("one of us") as the Russians put it. This is not possible with only beginner level knowledge. Beginner level knowledge shows courtesy and gains a special goodwill on the part of the people you go to, but it doesn't make you "nash chelovek".

The person who achieves functional fluency and starts to think in the language and is capable of reacting like a member of that country because of also a degree of cultural flexibility, he becomes a member of that linguistic nation. I coined a term for the "linguistic nation" which means the cultural mass of people comfortable using a common language, and that is "Linguation". So if I speak about the English Linguation, I mean the body of people around the world who can function together well around the English language, people who know English well enough that their human interaction is unimpeded on a personal level, regardless of where they pay their taxes or where the piece of toilet paper they call a passport allows them to go. For me, the idea of linguationality is much more important than nationality. You can have one, maybe two, exceptionally three nationalities, but you can be in ten linguationalities, and you don't have to ask the by-your-leave of any so-called "official" behind a desk in order to join it – it is entirely up to you, and the work you do on language and culture! And you know when you are in the Linguation – it's when the walls break down.

It's when people acknowledge that they are able to speak with you and understand you because you took the trouble to learn their language, and treat you as one of them because of it. You'll know it, because it's like a wall came tumbling down. There are no more serious walls of misunderstanding, and you can deal with people face to face and do your business with them, and they theirs with you. When you're in the English-speaking world you're in the English Linguation. The German speaking world, including anyone anywhere in the world comfortable with German is in the German Linguation. You may never get a German passport, but the fact is that passports are handed out by the accident of birth and not by deserving, whereas with no document at all you become by learning that language part of the Linguation, and nobody can stop you doing it or ask you to fill in an idiotic form. You don't need to pass a stupid exam in it either, because if you really speak a language well enough to be in the

Linguation of it, it's self-evident and nothing more could be added by a paper certificate.

And you become a member of the Linguation in a way you cannot become if we are talking about the Nation. You become a little bit German by thinking in German, at least Linguation-wise (you may never get a passport or any other piece of paper for that but it doesn't change the reality) but without being in anyway less of what you were before. That's why they used to say that to have five languages is like being five people. Of course you do not really have that effect, because there isn't time in a person's life to do what could be done by five people, but certainly it increases your ability to think in international situations and see other people's point of view, in other words, it broadens the mind in a way travel alone cannot really do. It enables you to have insights and uses that even five people, taken together, may fail to arrive at.

This is one of the reasons why, when they was a wall, an Iron Curtain, across Europe, the communist rulers in the East made sure that English was taught in school only in a limited way. In Poland under communism there were more Russian teachers and English and German were taught only to a few students, by teachers who had never had much in-country experience of English, as there were no Communist countries in the English Linguation, and they generally were reluctant to allow people to travel. They wanted to isolate their people from knowing English in order to isolate them from British and American political thought. So language teachers were not encouraged – they were not well paid and the only concession they had was that when they were given state housing (and everyone's housing was state housing in Russia) they could get a flat one room bigger than a normal family their size, as the extra room was supposed to be a study for marking and preparing lessons. Some encouragement to make that your career, when a dustbin clearer would be taking home more actual pay!

When the walls came down, people in East Europe were anxious to learn English, French, German and other Western languages. They wanted to travel to us, but were not immediately able to come and work, but they were willing to pay all they could for language lessons, as they knew that knowledge of English or German would make the difference between winning a management post in one of the incoming western companies, and not winning one. People who spoke western languages typically earned at least double the money of those who did not, but who otherwise were equally qualified.

How different to the UK, where (and they never tell you this in school, so listen up) employers who are offering jobs with foreign language use in some sectors actually pay less, not more, as they know that linguists are out there and really want to work with their languages. They regard the fact that they are offering work the linguists find interesting as part of the incentive, an element of the pay. That's an inevitable result of the law of supply and demand at work, and nothing to be surprised about. But people are taken by surprise as they are not told by their languages teachers, "oh, by the way, if you learn what I'm teaching, you'll actually earn less in the market", but on the contrary are led to believe that the languages will increase their market value. After all, it should, shouldn't it?

In Poland in the nineties, the study of languages certainly did and today if you don't know English you can't expect to get very far, or will find it harder to get far, and in fact there are fewer and fewer people whom this applies to.

But in 1990 and 1991 the Polish people wanted to learn not only the Western languages but everything they could from Western people, and there was an article by Andrzej Kinast, one of the early Anglo-Polish accountants to go over to Poland and he became head of Grant Thornton there until 2007. I read the article and was encouraged by it to want to go over to Poland, although not to Grant Thornton, whose poor manners to me several years earlier were not forgotten, but to another international Firm, especially as I could go over with my girlfriend, by this time fiancée, who was from Warsaw. However , I was under training contract at the local firm Hillier Hopkins in Hemel Hempstead, and the deal I made was that after the three years of training required by the Institute of Chartered Accountants, I would stay an additional year in order to pay back the investment made. In fact, knowing the fact that I had been slow at the start, I happily would have given them two years to pay back, although I longed to be out there as part of the events going on in East Europe.

But the Iron Curtain and the Berlin wall were not the only walls that were tumbling down in the turn of that decade – in the UK we had a recession - by no means as large as the current recession, but for our profession an historic one as for the first time ever it was hitting accountancy practices and there were no jobs in accounting firms, and people were being made redundant. Hillier Hopkins also found that its clients were reducing and delaying costs. Not having audits if the audits were voluntary, delaying consulting advice they would have been taking if times were easier, some companies were going under and the client list was reducing. And so the walls that had surrounded our profession, making it seemingly immune to any trouble in the economy, also had seemed to crumble.

And so it was that at the end of 1990, Michael Kent, Hillier Hopkins' staff partner, asked me to come and see him in his office. His message was simple."When you started with us, I wondered what we had let ourselves in for. For a Cambridge graduate you seemed extraordinarily slow and unable to grasp what was going on around you, and what we expected from you. At that time I half expected we would be having to say goodbye at the end of the year, but you passed the Graduate Conversion course and so we kept you on and lost the people who failed it" (this being the deal we all had signed up to – you expected to be sacked if you failed GCC, all the Firms were the same and there wasn't anything unusually strict going on here) "… and then, gradually, you seemed to wake your ideas up, and these days you've turned into a really promising accountant." I thanked him.

He explained about how because of the current climate he had looked at the budget and discovered he needed to lose one of us. "When you first came to apply for a job here, and I asked you were you saw your future in 10 years, you said that you wanted to work in Europe, using your languages. Now I have to make someone redundant, and you are no longer first on my list of people I would want to lose. In fact, I think all the team we have now among the finalists are very good accountants. I would prefer to keep you in the Firm, but if I lose someone else and then you tell me after the gentleman's agreement year is up that you want to go to Europe, then I'll be one person down and will have to recruit someone from scratch, which would be a big cost, and a pity to have lost that other good person for nothing. So tell me honestly, do you still have this dream of working in Europe?"

Well, I was not about to lie to him, so I told him that I still had that dream, and now more than ever now that the East was liberating. So he thanked me for my honesty (which was more than he'd had from certain other student accountants in the past who used the Firm and then moved on suddenly after saying how loyal they were going to be) and said that in this case he would release me from my obligation of the gentleman's agreement year, and put all reasonable resources at my disposal so that I could win a job in the New Europe. He said "Don't think about it until the New Year, don't worry about it over Christmas, just have a nice Christmas, and in the New Year take all the time you need. You can have all the time off you need for interviews, you can write your applications on paid time, use the printers, photocopiers, anything you need." Had this conversation taken place five years later, he'd have been enjoining me to use the computers, but at this stage they were not online and nobody had seen the world-wide web.

I met a slightly different world-wide webb, Richard Webb of BDO, a pillar in our profession, and a person who inspired me and many of my peers and taught us so much, offered me a job helping set up BDO (at that time the number ten network in the world) in Poland from scratch.
Remembering how decent BDO had been in the University recruitment round, unlike certain other Firms I already did mention, I was well-disposed to them, and preferred their

offer over two others I obtained in the three weeks I spent on the search. Incidentally, only having languages plus accountancy made me a commodity in that tough market moment. If I'd had only the one or the other, it would not have been so easy.

Anyway, off to BDO I went, in April 1990. There were some Polish professionals of a similar age and myself, and we set up a Warsaw firm starting with a one room office in the pre-renovated Hotel Polonia and then in the Universal Building and finally we found a lovely building in Ujazdowski Park in Warsaw. We also set up offices gradually in Katowice, Poznan and Wroclaw, and had about 80 people at the end of 6 years hard work. In the middle of this time my first wife had enough of her home country and wanted to go back to London "I thought I'd married an Englishman, but you've turned into a Pole. You love Poland and I don't want to be in Poland, I want to be in London." So off she went, with her mother, to our London property which I had purchased, as well as another house in Cippenham in Berkshire. I stayed behind sharing her parents' home with her father, an affable and likeable gentleman, and we turned into a couple of bachelors for few years.

By this time I had got into the habit of using the Goldlist method on and off, and had shown it to some people as invariably I was asked how I learned my languages. But in the form it was then it probably looked too complex for most people, and also I wasn't sure that it would help them – I knew I had found the system that helped me, but when they looked at it and said, OK, you do it that way, but I'm not talented at languages, you're method probably won't work for me, I didn't know then what makes it work is something in memory which is common to all of us and that it would indeed work for all sorts of people as long as they understood what it was about, namely about surrendering the learning process to an algorithm, and didn't keep trying to force feed their memories like a pate-destined goose, which is what people intuitively think they should be doing. The Goldlist method is counterintuitive, and so it should be, but at that time I could not not explain why it was that it worked even though it was so counter-intuitive, and so I had no takers, and so there was one user of the Goldlist method from 1993 to 2006, and that was me, and I didn't do it all the time, just on and off, and I perfected my Polish with it as well (over 7,000 words in addition to those I knew from before) as beginner level Czech to 500 words, Danish to about 3,000 words, Romanian to 2,000 words, beginner's Hungarian to about 500 words and Spanish to 5,000 words. I didn't do more than that because I was busy either working or studying other things also. I started to be online in 1997, immediately became an aficionado of usenet group discussions, the verbal parrying and the virtual community. There I honed my writing and from that basis developed the few internet skills that I have.

In about the year 2000 I changed from a loose leaf way of doing the Goldlist method, with each distillation on different coloured photocopied sheets, to the simpler way of using an exercise book whose every double page is taken to be four zones, the way I do now and the way it is shown on all the videos. I found this greatly improved the facility of use of the system, and also that's when I changed the name of it from LIDS (Lexical Inventory Distillation System) to the Goldlist method. That's because it seemed to me that I was panning for gold when I was distilling the words – the "gold" in question being the evasive words that my particular long-term memory was reluctant to sample, or got confused. It seemed to me that by going through, with the necessary breaks of two weeks which I had been practising since 1993, I could arrive in the end with a list only a tiny fraction the size of the original list, but which would contain the essence of the "difficulty" of the original list, and that by the time I got there, I really would know these words anyway, at least as well as I would have if using conventional methods anyway.

In that time (in fact in 1998) I also met Elena, and as my first marriage was dead anyway since 1995 from the distance between Poland and London and anyway it had never been happy, and as it is between believers and non-believers, we pulled in different directions. But Elena is a Christian, of Belarusian Baptist stock, and I soon realised I had found the person I really wanted to be for the rest of my life, and so I went back to the UK in 2000 to divorce Izabella, and then Elena and I went to Moscow in 2001 where I was CFO of a TV station (by this time all my old record in Soviet Russia was meaningless and I even got to shake hands with Gorbachev in the course of my duties). Nobody brought up any of my 1985-86 debacle in Russia at any time when I was there, I had no issues with co-operating with the authorities whatsoever, and I seemed very popular with my Russian colleagues who seemed genuinely upset when we decided to go.

Meeting the man who changed it all...

Arguing about philosophy and religion on the internet helped me get my faith back after being pretty much in the refrigerator drawer for seven years, and this time, in Elena I had married a believer. Yes, God is against divorce, but it is not the unforgivable sin, and God has great mercy to people who screw up time and again as long as they basically acknowledge that they did screw up and need new mercy. Sometimes you can get yourself into such a situation that without even more sinful behaviour you'll never get out of it. The thing is to get it over and done with, repent, and face the music. Those who won't forgive those who divorce, especially those who won't forgive the other partner and carry on being bitter after the divorce, they are actually closer to losing their own access to forgiveness. Jesus told his disciples how you can't not forgive others and still expect God's forgiveness for yourself. We need God's forgiveness more than anything, and His strength to avoid doing the things that need the forgiveness more than is necessary when we use what He has given.

In fact God does give you more than you might think. Not only are His mercies new every morning, as the Psalm

510

says, but also the way in which he has equipped us means that many things simply work without us needing to be in conscious control, or work best when we are not trying to be in control. One of these things is our breathing, another is our long term memory, (which is why the gold list system is all about not trying to force it to remember on cue, but to present it with interesting material and two weeks later to go back systematically and see what it did learn, without using repetitions to try and drive it into our heads in the course of a day. Even the Lord Jesus Christ says "use not vain repetition, as the heathen do".

But staged presentation is not vain repetition, it is a review after a period of time in order to separate the items we learned automatically from the sample our brain took subconsciously, (a separation of wheat and chaff, of gold and gravel, if you will) because that's how God made these brains of ours (or how they evolved, if you believe that we evolved. If you want to be an evolutionist then my suggestion is that you consider that man's memory may have become honed in the quest to hunt that other animal that is reputed to have a fine memory, namely the elephant, and that elephant and man went on one of those memory "arms races" that Dawkins talks about in his book "The Greatest Show on Earth".

We used our memories, elephants and men, to stalk and evade one another. We chased them as mammoths up into Europe, we chased them from Africa into Asia, both kinds speciating in the process, and everywhere they went, we went too. They were really our favourite prey – plenty of food from one kill, plus hides, building materials, all sorts. In order to make sure that we could get the building materials without actually killing them, the elephants decided to go to special places when they needed to die, giving the mysterious "elephants' graveyards". But we ended up gaining, from the attenuation of the memory function that the two kinds forced on each other, the gift of speech, whereas their speech has remained rudimentary. Scientists like Andrea Turkalo are right now working on the Elephant dictionary, and that is likely to be the first non-human language to achieve a dictionary that is readable by humans.

Personally I don't believe a word of it, but one thing about evolution is that it fits anything that you can see, (as indeed so does Creationism if you don't get hung up on certain assumptions in some people's readings of Creationism) and so when you see by observation that the long-term memory is separate to the short-term memory and the short-term memory is a conscious function that in humans, and as far as we know only humans, since we are really nowhere near as far in understanding elephants, we try to control in the process of learning, then it is also easy to find evolutionary explanations for why this short-term conscious memory appeared and the role it had in early man's hunting expeditions seeking out the elephant and mammoth, as their own memory function developed in their seeking ways to evade us. Also the hunting expeditions had to be two weeks long, because that's the period in which the moon is over half full, enabling the hunting at night, when man had his clearest advantage over his elephantine prey. They could not find their way easily home once the moon was dark so easily at night, they needed to be certainly home by then. That's also why the human menstrual cycle is four weeks, by the way. The women had to be fertile when the men were home. And 7 days before and after the period's beginning is the time when the woman cannot be fertilised and it was safe for the men to leave them behind, because even if another tribe came in that period and mated with their women, they would not be with child by those other humans.

So the short-term memory is two weeks for exactly the same reason as why the fertile and infertile periods are both 2 weeks. They all follow the hunting cycle of the elephant and mammoth, and this in turn the cycle of the moon. That's if you believe in evolution, otherwise, you can take it as I do that God gave us these facilities because He wanted us to have an analogy to the Christian walk, which is by faith, and not works. Sure we do do things, but we trust God to add His blessing and his strength, rather than try to do things in our own strength. The Goldlist method, and the reason it is successful, is either because it encapsulates and analogises some truth of the Gospel, or because it taps into something that evolved in early man. One or another – you choose! Either way the Goldlist method works, and either way, it's free and will empower you and enable you to do more without a teacher than you possibly could if you were shackled to one for any time. Whether you're a believer in God as creator or a staunch atheist evolutionist, you can work out why you think it works, but neither group needs to be put off using it just because the other group can have its differing view on how it works. That's pretty much true for many things that are going on on this planet and universe.

Anyway, in the end we decided to go back to Poland from Moscow, since I had been invited back quite heartily and I joined a firm which was made up of people I'd worked with in BDO, and we joined the Horwath International network. I stayed there from 2003 until 2009, when I joined the Baker

Tilly (number eight in the world) network to be involved in the Polish as well as Czech firm of that network.

That brings us pretty much up to date, as I don't need to tell you for this account much of what happened once the Goldlist system was invented, even though it also contains plenty of interesting things – some of which I will never tell as they involve the clients, and the clients of an accountant must always be able to be sure that this accountant will never breach his sacred duty of confidentiality – but there is one final chapter that I need to add, which tells of how thanks to YouTube the Goldlist system became not just a one-man system, but has been seen and tried by thousands of people and hundreds have written to me to thank me and to state that it has also worked well for them. Needless to say of the whole twenty years since the year 1990 I could write twice as much as I did on all the other chapters and no doubt someday I will, but in order not to add one 't' to many into Claude's collection of polyglot literature, I shall wind up that part of the history and just conclude with what YouTube did for the Goldlist method. Since it's YouTube that brought together pretty much the people featured in this whole volume, I'd like to give the final chapter in my piece to outlining how YouTube helped the Goldlist turn from a one-man project into something that is now widely known among linguists and something having a real chance to benefit humanity.

7. YouTube carries the message

I don't think that YouTube needs a great deal of introduction to the readers of this book. After all, Claude made his appeal to people to contribute to this book via his own YouTube channel, and it's likely that everyone who contributed here as well as the majority of people downloading the book or buying their copy in print if it goes to print will have seen YouTube and have a pretty good idea of what it is, how it works and what an unparalleled resource it is both for people wishing to learn and also willing to teach languages.

Probably most of you who are reading will have been involved with YouTube, watching videos, hopefully registering as well so that you can comment on videos, and many of you hopefully also have active channels with your own content up. If you do not, I can only encourage you to try it, as it is an amazing hobby, and just about anything else can be included and bound up in it – any subject matter, image, music, literature, voice, you name it. Film covers it all.

YouTube language teachers fall as far as I can tell into two broad categories; the pure hobbyist who is sharing without much, if any, thought of profit, and those who place material for language learning on their channels but these are basically a way to lead traffic to other sites where they sell, and try to make either a living or a decent supplement to their living from language teaching.

Now I happen to be in the first category, but let me make it clear that I am not saying that or doing that in order to belittle the people who do seek to make a living from language teaching. Thankfully, so far I have managed to get by without needing to ask for donations and you cannot donate to me even if you want to, as there are no buttons or anything. If someone feels they have to, they can give something to charity, but I don't even want to know about it. It's not because I want to be smug about the fact that I make enough as an accountant – I'm always happy to make more as an accountant and if you want to recommend me to anyone doing business in East Europe for audit, tax or business advice, or their bookkeeping, then that would be worth far more to me than a donation!

The reason really is that people I've described above, people like Margarita Georgovna and Marina Buck, also schoolteachers who were paid by the county or but did for me so much more than the minimum they could have done and earned the same. University people also. It's really just passing on the benefits I received. And if the Goldlist method helps you, then I expect the same from you – to pass it on with attribution of its authorship, but without profit. And if the Huliganov Russian lessons help you, then I would like you to pass them on freely also, if possible reciprocating and adding to the value chain by doing your own lessons on your own subject or language also for free. In a world where governments are doing their utmost to dumb us down, wouldn't it be fantastic if the internet becomes a place which is everybody's Open University? Where people can find whatever they need for free, presented in hopefully an entertaining way?

That's what I'd urge every reader of this book to take part in. Encourage the YouTube and other Internet content providers, especially the free ones but not only, and do join in with providing content on what you can. It doesn't have to be perfect – if you look at the channels of people who are in this book as the main YT polyglots you'll see technical errors all over the place in their films, but if they were perfectionists, they probably would not be either content providers in the first place or even linguists for that matter, as a fear of making mistakes is something that shipwrecks many a budding linguist, and those who continue are those who can laugh off their own mistakes and try to get the right the next time, or the time after that, or the time after that, etc, ad infinitum. So we need you to join in the fun.

If you really cannot make your own films, then a useful contribution is always to give thumbs up, subs or comments rather than just watch passively and leave the filmmaker with only a "number of views" statistic to deduct whether his or her work was valued or not, and to join in groups and fora made in order to enable learners to help each other along.

In my own case, as I stated above, I myself had used the Goldlist system in something close to today's version of it since about 1993, but although I had explained it one on one to some people, there were not many takers, and in consequence the penny did not drop with me that in fact this could only be due to people misunderstanding the Goldlist method being about letting the process take over and not forcing the memory. They were doing something that looked like a Goldlist book, but not observing the key points about writing it in a relaxed way and then not going back over it for two weeks or more. They were also not observing the proper breaks because they didn't **feel** tired, not realising that the long-term memory is the unconscious memory, and the unconscious mind feels nothing. You cannot tell when it is tired and the long-term memory is not sampling at the usual level. By the time you do feel tired, it means that you already pressed for too long and the short-term memory cut in. The work done that way cannot be effective and so a Goldlist book based on wrong understanding of the key aspects of the method won't do much for you. It will be no better than any of the other short-term memory techniques. That's why some of the videos I've made about it are quite long – it's so people get a chance to cotton on to what the essence of this method is, and why it's different to the received wisdom in language learning.

And many of those who understood what I was saying, probably just didn't believe it as it is counterintuitive and runs directly against everything they are taught in school about how to learn languages. People didn't believe I was giving them a method that would work for them, and so I would occasionally get asked how I learn, would spend an hour or sometimes more explaining the system, and the person who had the one-on-one session receiving this information would go away thinking "that's how a linguistic genius can learn a language, when it obviously won't work for me", whereas in fact if I learned languages the way that person does, I certainly wouldn't look like a linguistic genius in anybody's eyes, and this method works for people because it addresses the way we are, the way our dual-state memory actually functions.

Anyhow, with the arrival of Goldlist method onto YouTube, things went like this: I had been travelling to lots of different places on business as an auditor and not taking photos and soon afterwards discovered I had very little to remember these interesting business trips by, and so I bought a digital camera in 2004, a Fuji Finepix. I started avidly taking photos of the interesting places I went on conferences and business, and regretted not getting it earlier as I would have had a record of the Barcelona and Berlin conferences I was at in 2003. The first time I used it was in a visit to Prague in May 2004, and to Milan shortly after, but took very few photos at first and I didn't even know it took video and never bothered to read the instructions and indeed on the tiny memory card I had not much video would appear anyway and with the technology I had even tiny films seemed to have huge amounts of kilobytes, and if I took just a couple of minutes then that was the memory full, instead of a few hundred photos, so at first all my video was tiny clips with not much by way of post production done on them. I noticed that there was a growing site called YouTube that people on discussion groups and usenet had linked to a few times, and I decided to put them on there just to see if anything came of it. So in February 2006 I registered my account and started to put up these first tiny steps in being a videographer. They are in fact very poor but I keep them there as a reminder of how I started. And I got a bigger memory card that could do longer video and also I started playing about with Windows Movie Maker to join footage together, trim it, add effects, titles and all the other bits of post production.

I called my YT channel "usenetposts", as my old website was called www.usenetposts.com - the idea of that was to harvest a lot of writing I had done in the past on Usenet – (These things are going to be collected onto www.Huliganov.TV now), and 3 months after launching it, I decided what I really needed was a webcam in order to do the sort of videos that some others on YT were doing. I looked at people like Bowiechick, ZenArcher, Brookers, and others who did "talking head" style stuff, and I wanted to branch into that, so when my parents asked what I wanted for my birthday, I got a webcam that year. And the very same day, the Russian character from school and University days appeared as Viktor Dmitrievitch Huliganov on my channel, the first of a number of personas which I decided to do having really been influenced by Bowiechick and Brookers and their growing collections of personas. I did some pieces of him and a bunch of other characters doing poems and songs with zany introductions, but then, after about 2 months of this, I decided to do a series as Victor just on the Cyrillic alphabet. The response to this was stronger than anything I had done up to this time on YT, in fact it was stronger than I'd had on just about anything. I was used to being happy if I wrote a post and 50 people only read it, or doing a video and maybe 10 or 20 would be shown as seeing it, but this was running into the hundreds fairly quickly, which made me want to do more.

I had set out to do just a ten lesson series on the alphabet only, but the responses and comments clearly showed a hunger for a Russian course that would go beyond a simple presentation of the alphabet, and I decided to do it as a three part course: RL101 would be the ten lessons of the alphabet. Each one had a joke and a song, and the jokes and songs were not necessarily topical or even in Russian. By RL 102, which is the first part of the grammar course featuring verbs and adverbs and pronouns and prepositions, but not numerals, expressions of time or other numbers, adjectives and nouns – they would come in RL 103. In fact because of the amount of work it took to make these lessons after about 10 or so of the RL 102 lessons I started to lose momentum, and it needs right now to be kickstarted to get to the end of RL 102 and then into RL 103, which is likely to be easier to do.

People showed their appreciation of these lessons and started calling Huliganov "Professor", and many actually thought that he was a real person and registered shock when they came across other films in which I was speaking with a normal British accent. At the same time, people started to ask me questions about how to go about learning languages, and so I decided that, having already established some authority as a language teacher by making this popular series, to show the Goldlist method using YouTube as the vehicle.

And so in May 2007, just shy of one year since the first appearance of Viktor Dmitrievitch Huliganov, I have him expounding the Goldlist method in a two part video on YouTube and this pair has been viewed since then on average by 3000 people per year. Since then, 250 new people per month learn about the Goldlist method, and I started to receive from all over the world private emails and public comments now going into the hundreds from people who confirm what is actually psychologically only logical and which I should have expected all along – that the method will work for all sorts of people. I saw people who had dearly wanted to learn languages and who had failed with the conventional methods in the classroom, wasting both their time and their money only to have the false notion reinforced that "they had no talent for languages" finally getting empowered to teach languages to themselves with this method, once they got over the initial reluctance to do something counterintuitive.

But not only people who had failed to be linguists were appreciating the method. For example, your current editor, Claude, an accomplished linguist and polyglot already, was one person who was kind enough to go on record in a video saying that although he was initially skeptical, he decided to try it and found that indeed the method works better than he thought. This teaches the linguist extremely valuable things about how the language learning process really works and that certain types of effort not only do not add anything, but can actually detract from our ability to learn and memorise vocabulary.

One day I then was informed by a viewer that the polyglots on www.how-to-learn-any-language.com had devoted a very active thread to discussing whether there was anything in this here Goldlist method that people had started talking about. There was no short of skepticism there either, but soon in the long thread the overwhelming voices were positive – which meant that I had received the accolade not only of having supplied a method which could give a fresh chance to the failed linguist and turn him or her into a successful linguist, which I already knew I had from the hundreds of letters, but even I had been able to place into the hands of some of the most seasoned polyglots on the net, each of whom already were successful as linguists and had their own preferred and cherished methods, an additional tool that they were quick to appreciate and add to their more advanced armouries of learning tools. Also the general discussion about the method and thinking about how best to present and explain it has helped me to think about it a little more and dot some "i"s and cross some "t"s in it. The book of the Goldlist method will be a comprehensive manual for how to use it, why it works and some advances variations and techniques that you can use for some of the tougher language tasks with it.

So if it were not for YouTube, not only would a book like this probably not have appeared, but also the Goldlist method would have probably remained the reluctant secret of one linguist, whereas now it has helped thousands along the way of their desired route to be a linguist or polyglot.

As I have shown in my story, being a linguist is not necessarily an easy route to take in life. The linguist is like someone who takes the red pill because he wants to understand humanity on a different plane. Becoming a linguist is driven by the desire for more understanding and involves very deeply the very process of human understanding. Language itself is the vehicle for any kind of human thought and understanding – is there any other? – and when we increase our linguistic knowledge by learning other languages well enough to think in them and take part in the experience of the group born into them, we increase our capacity for human understanding more than is possible by any other process.

Prior to learning someone else's language, everyone outside your own language group seems foreign and strange to you, and yet these are humans as valid as you, and you share the planet with them. The linguist can enjoy a higher plane of understanding of what it means to be a human being resident on planet Earth, and not merely a member of his or her own limited language group, with its particular set of cultural perspectives. The gaining of this understanding is in itself exciting, intoxicating, addictive, rewarding, and also sometimes the pursuit of this can be exceptionally troublesome and painful, as I have shown in these paragraphs from my own story.

But life wasn't designed to be easy, nothing of use or beauty was ever achieved without pain, or at least hard work so grasp the nettle. Open yourself to the human panorama that you can view by becoming a polyglot. If you are tempted to learn, then give it the time it needs, use the tools in this book, take my advice about the

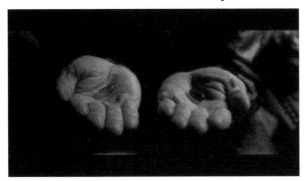

"Becoming a linguist is about the pursuit of understanding. The linguist can enjoy a higher plane of understanding what it means to be a human being, and not just a member of his or her language group"

Goldlist which is entirely free for you and will save you time and money, and enjoy the ride.

To become a polyglot you need to make less effort than some people intuitively think, but you do need to put the hours in, and find ways to enjoy the process. If this book has inspired you to start on the road of learning languages, or return to it if you were on it once but gave up, then don't delay. If you put it off you may never do it, and the intellectual vistas and perspectives as well as the human relationships and additional life opportunities that you will certainly gain if you do are a very rich reward.

Made in the USA
Lexington, KY
29 September 2014